D1194878

CONTEMPORARY DIGITAL ARCHITECTURE DESIGN & TECHNIQUES

LINKS

Contemporary Digital Architecture:
Design and Techniques

Author: Jacobo Krauel
Graphic design & production: Cuboctaedro
Collaborator: Oriol Vallès, graphic designer
Text: Contributed by the architects, edited by William George and Jay Noden
Cover photograph © Judson Terry, IwamotoScott Architecture

© Carles Broto i Comerma
Jonqueres, 10, 1-5,
Barcelona 08003, Spain
Tel.: +34-93-301-21-99
Fax: +34-93-301-00-21
info@linksbooks.net
www.linksbooks.net

Printed in China

CONTEMPORARY DIGITAL
ARCHITECTURE DESIGN & TECHNIQUES

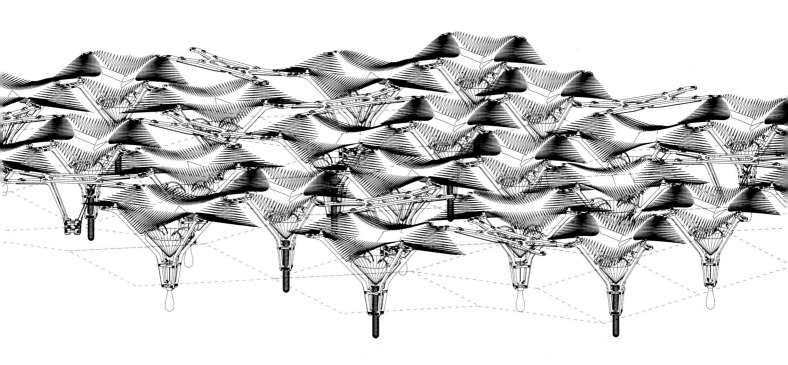

LINKS

9 Introduction

10 Fabrication

Contents

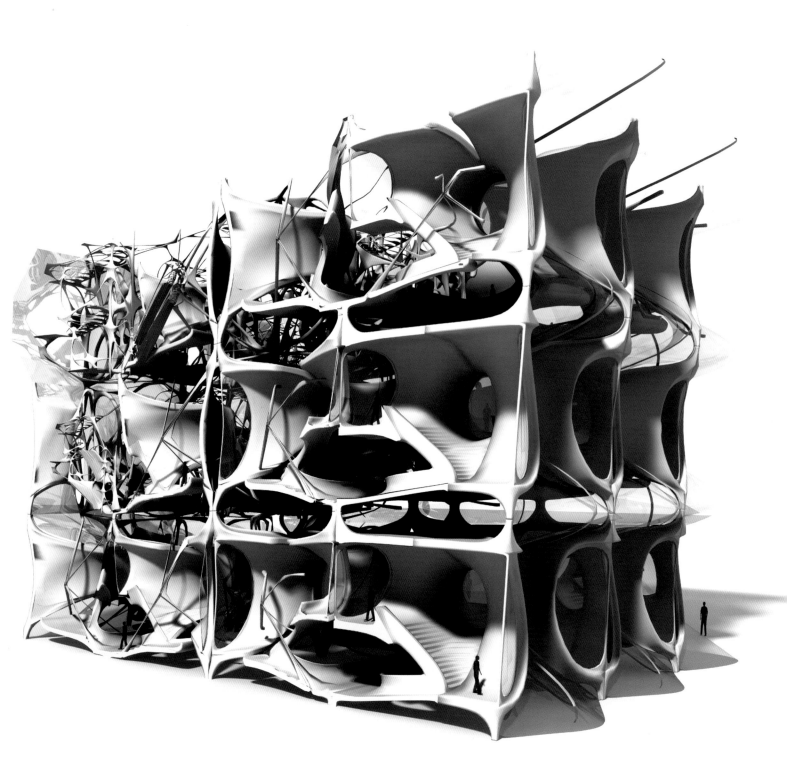

Introduction

The book presents the latest developments in the field of architecture as it has been reshaped by the use of digital technologies. Digital architecture is shaped by a broad range of events and technologies that go beyond the use of architectural software. These include the proliferation and great availability of CNC technologies, the possibility of designing parametrically with the use of many different programs, the use of algorithms and simulations of natural and biological processes as morphogenetic strategies, the development of hardware and software for interactive applications as well as the exploration of digital imaging and other techniques developed in fields remote from architecture.

The works selected for the book come from young architects who have found in digital media their natural working environment. Both built and un-built works have been selected. While selecting built works the focus was on small-scale projects, making evident that the technology of digital fabrication is available today to any designer (or even student) and is not limited to big budgets and great engineering firms. The not-built (or unbuildable) experimental projects on the other hand are daring proposals that may involve city-wide areas and express the imaginative and creative potential of a young generation of architects.

The book has been separated into four parts. The first, Fabrication, presents the most innovative uses of digital fabrication techniques for both architecture and interior design. The focus is on small-scale projects, often constructed by the architects themselves.

The second part, Scripting, involves the use of computer programming in architectural design. The architects presented here do not limit themselves in the use of the ready-made forms of commercial software but explore the possibilities of creating forms through algorithmic processes.

The third part, Responding, presents some daring works in the field of interactivity as related to the other themes of the book. Finally, the fourth part, poetics, presents works that go be-yond the technical possibilities offered by digital technologies and explore the expressive potential of digital media.

It should become clear by looking at the projects that most of them could belong at least to two different parts of the book. The areas of algorithmic design, digital fabrication, interactivity and digital media are all closely related and many of the projects transverse the entire field presented in this book.

The introductions to each part present a detailed overview of the subjects in both a critical and technical sense. The book seeks to present a clear picture of the developments in digital architecture accessible to both insiders and newcomers. As digital technologies evolve and intermingle, it becomes clear that we cannot expect digital architecture to become a stabilized body of techniques and formal rules. Digital architecture is still, and will probably continue to be, a field of experimentation and exploration.

Fabrication

The architecture of an era is always dependent on the techniques of representation and fabrication employed by architects and constructors. As it has been noted by William Mitchell *"architects draw what they can build and build what they can draw"*. Baroque architecture, for example, was dependant on the developments of perspective and projective geometry both for drawing and for stonecutting. But while the geometric techniques of the Baroque era were developed partly by architects for their own use, at other periods technologies developed in other fields have been introduced into architecture and construction and their assimilation has been more difficult. Steel and glass, although developed technically from the 19th century, became an integral part of the architectural idiom much later and after much reluctance and theoretical debate.

A similar situation has arisen with the development of digital technologies for construction. At first most architects used computers only as drawing tools that had no impact on the form or the construction of their buildings but only offered an optimization of the drawing process. The turn towards complexity in architecture initiated by the postmodern theories of Robert Venturi and given a twist by deconstructionism made architects explore digital technologies out of sheer practical necessity.

One of the first buildings where digital technologies were used for its construction was the Sydney Opera House by Jørn Utzon. The complex seashell-like forms of the building could not be calculated and constructed by traditional means. A project that became a landmark in the history of digital construction technologies was Frank Gehry's Fish sculpture for the Villa Olympica complex in Barcelona. As was his usual practice, Gehry had designed the sculpture by working directly with paper models. While in earlier projects the office team took measures from such models and created conventional plans for the development of the project, in that case the complexity of the design and the limited time available to develop and construct the project before the Olympics made such processes impossible. It was then that Gehry's team started investigating the possibilities of digital technologies and eventually found CATIA, a software used by the aeronautic industry. As it turned out, ship and airplane building engineers had already developed a completely digital workflow that made little, if any, use of traditional drawings (plans, sections etc) and relied on 3-dimensional digital models and CNC machines for prototyping. Following this example it is today possible, at least in theory, to design and construct a building following a seamless digital workflow that allows the construction of forms of a high degree of complexity at relatively small cost.

The Guggenheim Museum in Bilbao by Frank Gehry. Gehry's office was one of the first to use the technologies of digital fabrication and assemblage on a large scale.

The first step of this workflow is the design of the building as a 3-dimesional digital model instead of a set of plans and elevations. A 3D model that can be effectively used in a digital workflow is not the same as one that is used for visualization purposes (the creation of photo-realistic renders). Rendering is usually done with the use of *surface models*, models where solid objects and spaces are defined by their enclosing surfaces. Unambiguous geometrical definition is of secondary importance and complex 3-dimensional curved surfaces can be defined with some degree of approximation without jeopardizing the success of the results. A complete digital workflow however, requires the geometry of the design to be clearly and unambiguously defined. NURBS surfaces and *solid modeling* are the preferred methods of modeling in that case. Defining the dimensions and properties of elements parametrically is another step towards a complete digital workflow. The ability to create parametric variations of a design will allow testing and optimizing to be done more effectively: "A *family of parametric variations all stem from the same characteristic shape but slightly vary in dimension or shape from one to another. They are instances of the same design. The essential shape and constituent elements of the design are clearly set within certain specified constraints, but the exact dimensions and shapes of individual elements vary from shape to shape.*" In such a model relations between parameters are defined and a hierarchy of dependencies is created.

A well-defined three-dimensional model of building elements can be easily passed to a CNC (computer numerical controlled) machine for direct fabrication. Such a machine will require little control and it can create copies of the same object or different instances of the object with the same ease. This ability of CNC machines makes mass-production of identical elements unnecessary in economic terms. Instead of mass-production, mass-customization can be applied and each copy of the element can be allowed to vary from the others. CNC machines exist in many different forms but they can be grouped in three major categories:

Cutting: CNC fabrication of two-dimensional elements is the most commonly used technique. Flat panels of almost any material can be cut to shapes of any complexity with a variety

Top: the installation m.any was created from two-dimensional elements. The use of a great number of different parts makes labeling necessary for the correct assemblage.

Bottom: the complex form of the Bone Wall elements required a 5-axis milling machine for their creation.

of cutting technologies. Laser, water-jet and plasma-arc cutting are the most common. Each technique is more appropriate for certain materials and has its own limitations in terms of panel thickness and of the thickness of the cutting line.

Subtractive fabrication: Subtractive fabrication involves the removal of parts of the volume of a material in order to create the designed form. The removal can be done with chemical, electrical or (most commonly) mechanical means. The degree of freedom of the milling tool (the number of axes around which it can move) determines the complexity of shapes that the machine can create. Four or five axis movement creates complicated paths of movement for the tool and the operation of such machines can be done by skilled professionals only.

Additive fabrication: This process is known by many different names (rapid prototyping, 3D printing, layered fabrication, solid freeform modeling) that may correspond to slightly different technologies that work on the same basic principle. In that case the material is added on a layer-by layer basis. The thickness of each layer can be as small as 0.1 mm which allows a lot of detail to be reproduced. Complex forms with perforations and cavities can be easily created. Each machine operates using a specific material and the only limitation on the forms it can create is in the overall size of the object.

With the application of mass-customization for the creation of complex forms, the design can consist of a very big number of similar but not identical elements that must be assembled in a specific way. In such cases appropriate labeling of the parts at the moment of fabrication can be critical. For large-scale projects (as for example the Guggenheim Museum in Bilbao) the positioning of elements in their exact location can be done more effectively using GPS coordinates instead of traditional measuring techniques.

As it becomes clear when one revises the process of digital fabrication, the current separation of roles among architects, engineers and constructors and the dominant mode of documentation through drawings are not effective tools and may even become unproductive or problematic: "*The ability to digitally generate and analyze the design information, and then use it directly to manufacture and construct buildings, fundamentally redefines the relationships between conception and production – it provides for an informational continuum from design to construction. New synergies in architecture, engineering and construction start to emerge because of the use of digital technologies across the boundaries of various professions. As communication among various parties increasingly involves the direct digital exchange of information, the legacy of the 20th century in the form of drawing sets, shop drawings and specifications, will be inevitably relegated to the dustbin of history.*"

Urban A&O
Bone Wall

Within the site of pattern making, what is the relationship between surface and depth? The Bone Wall explores this contemporary question.

Preoccupations about the seemingly limitless effects of a building's skin as a material artifact in current architectural practice have relegated this surface as a primary domain of creative interest and oftentimes singular focus of the architect. It has become an increasingly thin site of performance. As a result, this emphasis on surface has arrested our understanding of space at the building envelope, and pattern, for all intents and purposes, remains an extrinsic and two-dimensional application.

As a counterargument to this trend, the Bone Wall aims to demonstrate through geometry, structure, materiality and spatial configuration that pattern is in fact multi-dimensional, intrinsic, programmatic and capable of occupying complex spatial geometries and substantially deep space. For example, a CATIA "part file" is an example of the base cell component and its generative parametric modeling constraints from which all cells depart, according to the CATIA "product file", the overall wall armature.

The ambition of this experiment was to explore continuity of surface and modulation of light within the wall, in addition to providing programmatic elements including storage and seating. The design of the Bone Wall began with parametric modeling of a base "cell", or rather, ½-cell, which was then inverted and rotated to combine into a complete cellular unit. The base cell has six triangular "horns", 3 up and 3 down, a total of 18 corners, or «control points». Through iterative manipulations of these control points along the wall's organizing horizontal splines as configured in CATIA, the body of the wall and its cellular web-like structure stretches and undulates. Any changes made to the geometry of the splines regenerate the shape of each cell, demonstrating both non-linear and reciprocal relationships between software and designer that is intrinsic to parametric, or parameter-based, modeling.

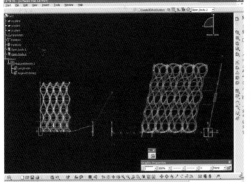
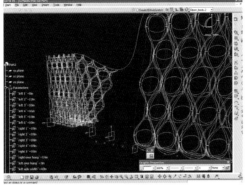
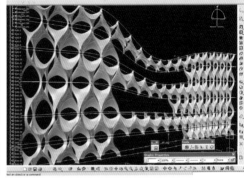

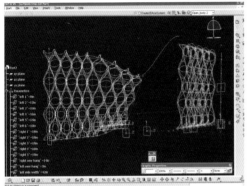
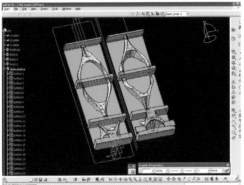
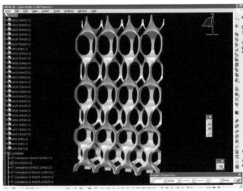

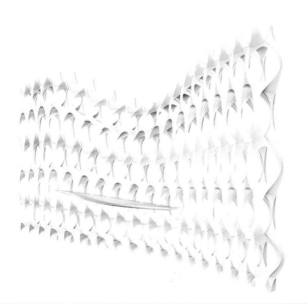

Using CATIA's "product-file" structure and "part-file" (the cells) in-context modeling, geometric dependencies were established whereby modifications to the form of the wall would propagate down CATIA's hierarchical tree, updating affected cell geometries along the way. A total of 72 cells combine to comprise the wall, or 2,592 control points, all parametrically linked: all points "know" the relative location of all others at any time in the design process.

Five cells are arranged on a 4' × 8' × 4" sheet of 15-lb high-density foam. Each cell is divided into three parts in Rhinoceros, to be exported as an IGES file for CNC-milling. The cells were fabricated on a 5-axis CNC milling machine in high density foam. Upon close inspection the router's tool path can be seen on the surface of the Bone Wall. It is not entirely smooth to the touch. The milling machine was set on a 1/32" step-over, resulting in a topographic plan-like finish. The cells were then joined together with adhesive by hand and the final wall was painted following assembly.

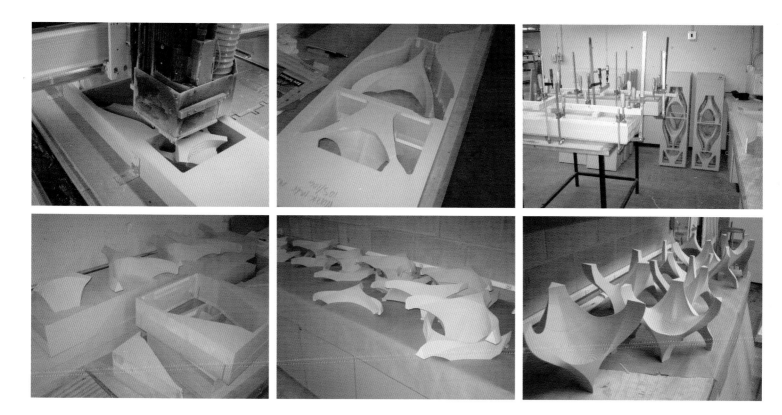

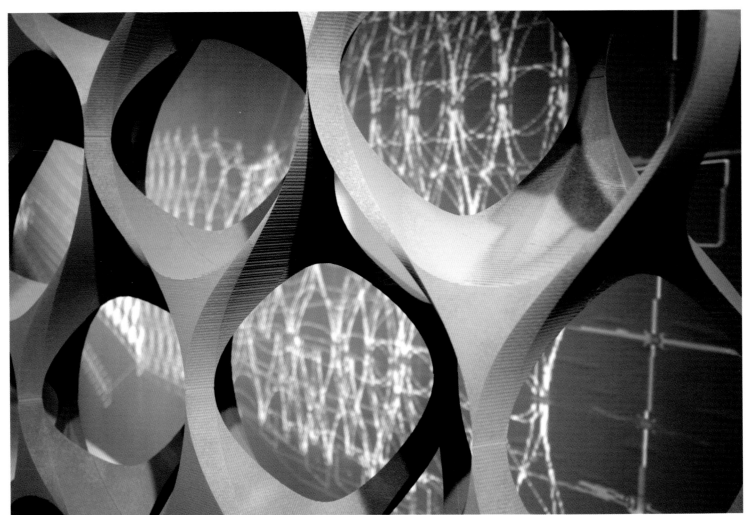

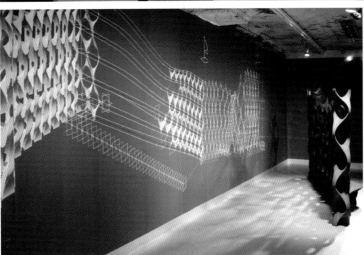

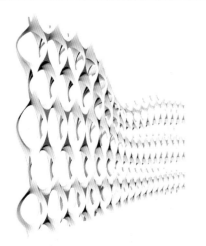

The Bone Wall in its use of parametric modelling serves as an experiment aimed toward the advancement of contemporary architectural practice. Parametric modelling environments shape new cognitive environments within which design procedure is conceived. The Bone Wall also demonstrates a new opportunity for designers to participate more directly in processes of fabrication. In our contemporary architectural context, a resuscitated debate over the role of ornament is unfolding; the Bone Wall strives to demonstrate ornament's intrinsic necessity over extrinsic contingency.

Urban A&O
Metropolis Booth

This project merges contemporary digital practice with an ambitious ecological imperative, demonstrating that the two are powerfully commensurate. The Metropolis booth for ICFF, 2007 is a living showcase of form, function, and sustainability. The aim of this project is to render evident emergent, ecologically progressive materials and methods in a unique and imaginative display, through a wide array of technological advances.

The light-weight monolithic skeletal structure of the Metropolis booth is framed in an eggcrate assembly of interlocking recycled/recyclable white plastic fins. Unlike recent projects that employ similar CNC technology and interlocking grids, in this proposal, no two cells are the same. Cell size and shape are dependant on location and function. A new 100% recycled white polyethylene sheet material (UHMWPE) is replacing PVC in green buildings, and has been used here. Cut by waterjet (no chemicals involved) a series of thin and flexible curving fins have been created that when assembled, produce the rigid single-body chassis of the Metropolis booth.

The Metropolis booth exterior's "living carpet" of brilliantly colored vegetation invites visitors to enter under a massive arc of flowering plants and wild grasses into a comfortable conversation zone lined with Metropolis magazines and related materials. The space accommodates several people seated in groups of two or three along an undulating bench padded in bright white felt. The cellular floor pattern is topped with an Ecoresin™ walking surface by 3form®. Overhead, pockets holding hundreds of Metropolis magazines are within reach. The "Next Generation® Design Competition" projects are projected in a display space located just over the back of the bench. The Metropolis magazine "wave" interior culminates in a giant LED lamp, a flowering bulb form that will illuminate the entire space. A twenty-foot wide back-lit Metropolis logo announces the front reception desk. Concealed storage space is provided just behind it. At the end of the last day of ICFF, the plants will be removed from their beds and given away to the public. The structure will once again be recycled.

Urban A&O
Cairo Tower

The Cairo Tower is a 5 m (16 ft) tall 3D SLS stereolithography rapid prototype print based on the 2D pattern known as the Cairo Pattern. The 2D pattern was lifted and framed to form crystalline geometries of differing scales that were then stacked vertically to form the structural frame of the tower. The frame was then thickened to form a series of unique instantiated struts and joints where no two conditions are exactly alike. Parametric modeling tools in CATIA were used to create the form which was then tested for stability in SAP software. Minor revisions were then made to the tower prior to printing.

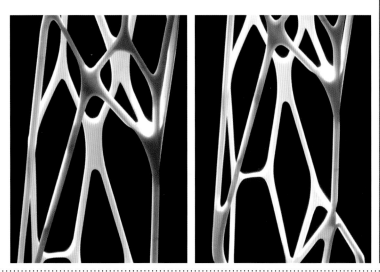

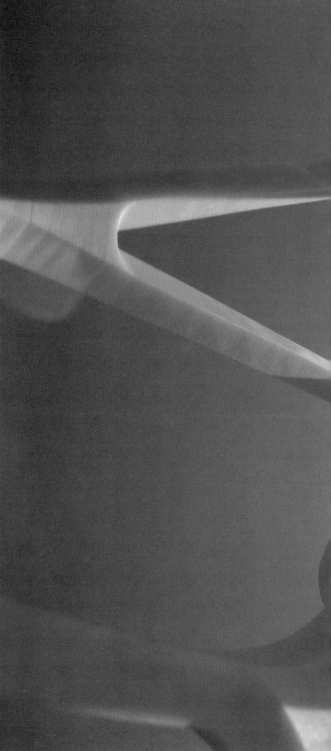

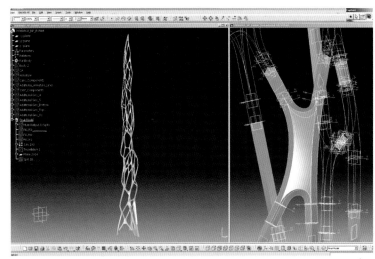

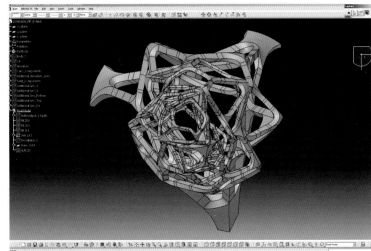
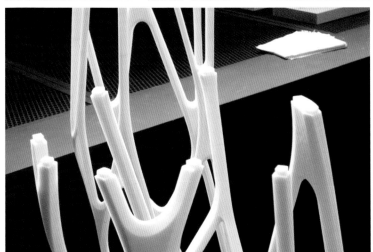
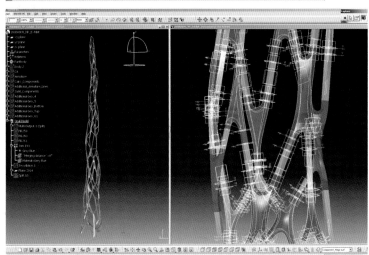
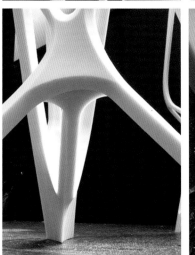

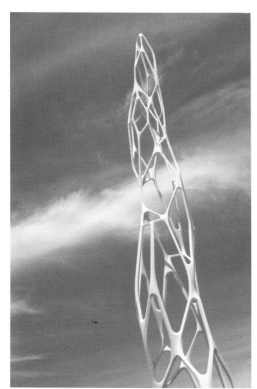

Alan Dempsey & Alvin Huang
[C]space

[C]space is the winning entry in the AA DRL10 Pavilion competition, which was held to celebrate the tenth anniversary of the AA Design Research Lab in conjunction with an exhibition and publication of a book that comprehensively documents the work of the course.

The competition was open to all 354 graduates and the winning entry was designed and developed by Alan Dempsey and Alvin Huang. It was selected by the jury for the proposals radical use of material, it's expression of form as a continuous transformation of furniture to floor, walls and roof structure; and it's constructability within a tight schedule and budget. The design was proposed to be entirely constructed from Fibre-C, a thin fibre reinforced cement panel that is normally used as a cladding solution.

The striking presence of the pavilion invites inspection from a distance and upon closer interaction reveals its ambiguity through the merging of sinuous curves, structural performance, and programmatic functions into a single continuous form. As you move around, the surface varies from opaque to transparent, producing a stunning threedimensional moiré. The surface encloses while also providing a route through for passing pedestrians blurring the distinction between inside and outside.

The jointing system in the pavilion uses a simple interlocking cross joint which is tightened by a set of locking neoprene gaskets. Close consultation with the Fibre-C technical department in Austria and extensive material testing were required to develop the design. Over a period of 6 weeks 16 iterations of the design model were analyzed before a structural solution was found. In parallel to the digital modelling, numerous rapid prototypes, scale models and full scale physical mockups were built to develop the design of individual elements and test the tolerance and fit of entire assemblies.

Location: Bedford Square, London, UK, 2008
Client: Architectural Association, Design Research Lab
Structural engineers: Adams Kara Taylor

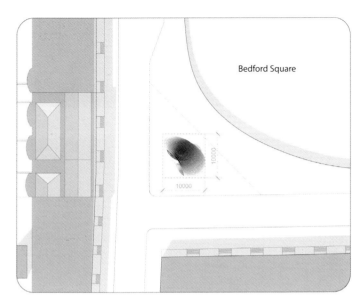

Site plan

Plan

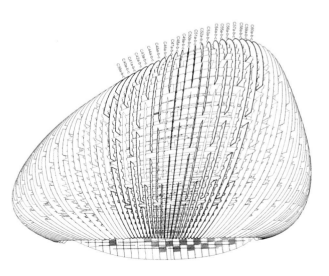

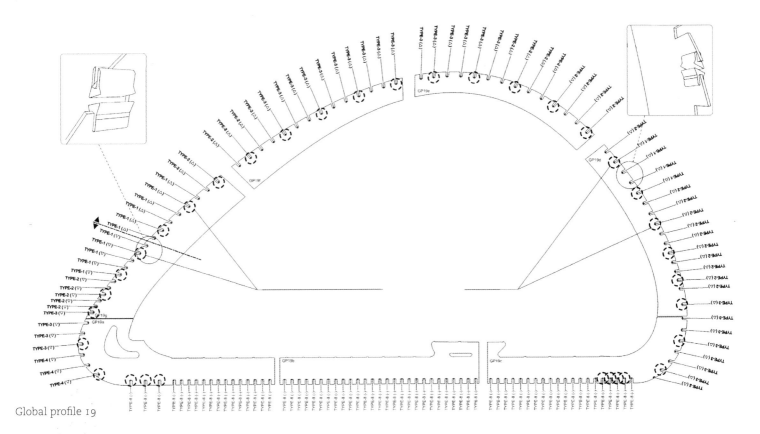

Global profile 19

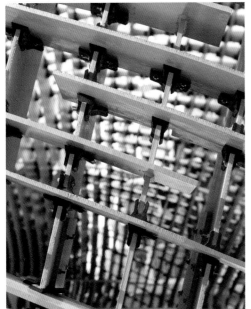

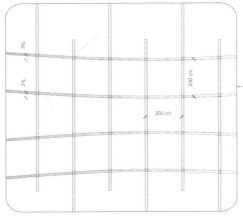

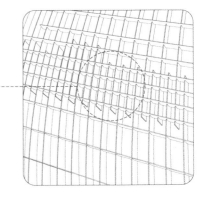

Each profile is joined to the next with at least three cross members set at 200 mm apart. The notches are located so that the profiles must be slightly flexed to lock in to each consecutive cross profile thus creating a tight joint.

The final pavilion was constructed from 850 individually unique profiles that are nested on standard 13mm flat sheets and CNC water cut. Once delivered to site the entire pavilion was assembled over a period of 3 weeks by a dedicated team of DRL staff and students with assistance from Rieder. Over 70 drawing sheets were produced by the design team that described in detail step by step assembly sequence and accurately located each piece within the overall structure.

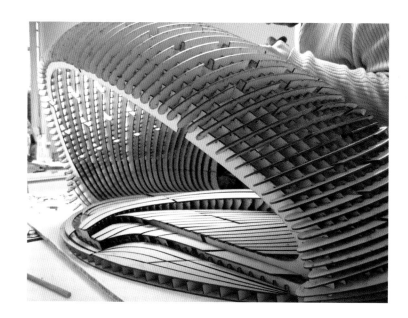

Gasket assembly

A. Pre-glue gaskets to notches on concrete global profiles prior to assembly.

B. Slot concrete cross-profile into glued gasket assembly from above.

C. Insert punched gaskets on to cross profile notches from below

D. Fasten bolts to fix second set of gaskets to cross profile.

1. Un-punched gasket
2. Concrete global profile
3. 50 mm notch
4. Glued gasket
5. Concrete cross-profile
6. Pre-drilled 8 mm holes
7. Punched gaskets
8. M6 bolts and washers

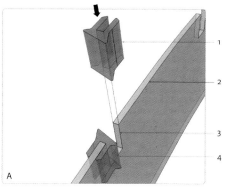

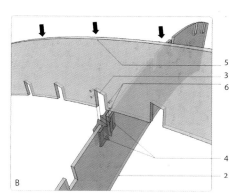

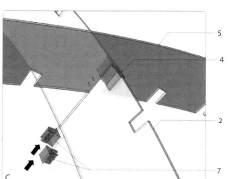

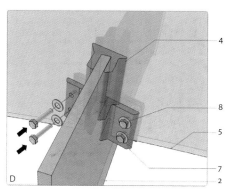

Mike McKay
PERFORMA_08

This work seeks to create multi-performative material systems utilizing optimization, aggregation and efficiency. Simple units and semi-finished materials were physically tested in order to extract potential performative characteristics and limits. These limits were negotiated through rigorous digital and physical techniques in order to produce strategies of fabrication.

The formal systems have inherent structural capacities as well as an ability to adapt to changing conditions. Although the system is adaptable, the form must be self-structural and fabricated using material that can weather. Because of the system pliability, variation can occur within a seemingly homogenous system.

The PERFORMA_08 system is comprised of identical aluminum units that are aggregated by utilizing the characteristics of the unit shape. Because of the shape characteristics, the system can achieve a pliability that allows for a dynamic and highly adaptive formal system.

PERFORMA is an advanced graduate seminar taught at the University of Kentucky College of Design.

Professor: Mike McKay
Design team: Chris Harris, Spencer Dohrman, Martin Franks, Eric Lahm, James Rich
Fabrication team: Madelynn Ringo, Jon McAllister, Trevor Kidd, Donovan Justice, Geoffrey Sorrell, Margaret Barrett, Brad Ostendorf, Terry Driggs, Laura Mattingly, Jonathan Erwin, Matt Nett, Dan Everhart, Gina Kuharevicz
Photographs: Mike McKay unless noted.

John McAllister

John McAllister

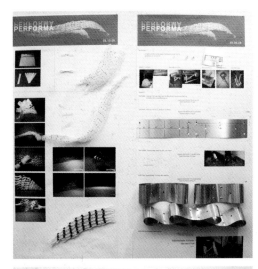

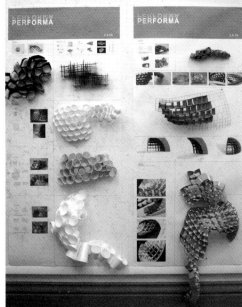

Off-the-shelf rolls of aluminum roofing flashing were unrolled and cut into identical strips. Brass tent grommets were used for the connections. Tools were custom made in order to assemble the units.

Eric Lahm

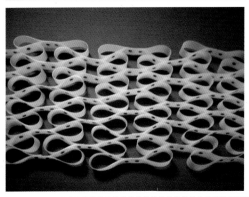
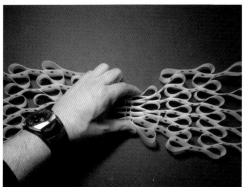
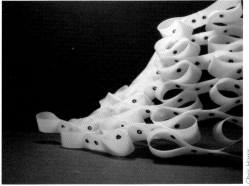

Chris Harris

Atelier Manferdini
West Coast Pavilion

"Emerging Talents, Emerging Technologies" is an exhibition of some of the most progressive architectural work in the world today, placing a particular emphasis on new design and fabrication technologies. Atelier Manferdini was invited to curate the West Coast USA session of the exhibition and design one of the six pavilions for the courtyard of the Millennium Museum in Beijing. The pavilion is a sandwich of undulating layers, which diverge and coalesce around and through its volume. The surface of the skin combined with the diamond shaped structure behaves like 3-dimensional lacework, creating a dynamic screening and filtering effect.

Design architect: Atelier Manferdini
Local architect: Xu Wei-Guo
Client: Architectural Beijing Biennale 2006
Biennale curators: Neil Leach; Xu Wei-Guo
Photographs: Courtesy of Atelier Manferdini

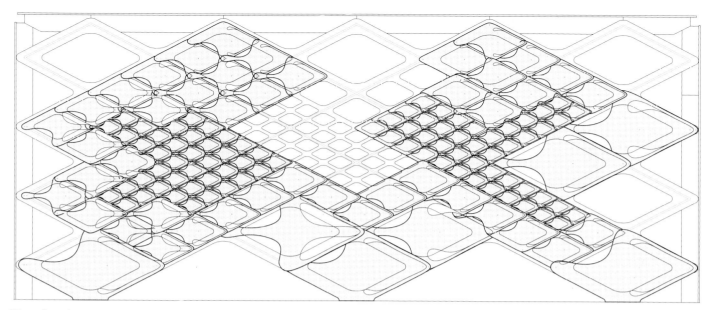

West elevation

Outside skin

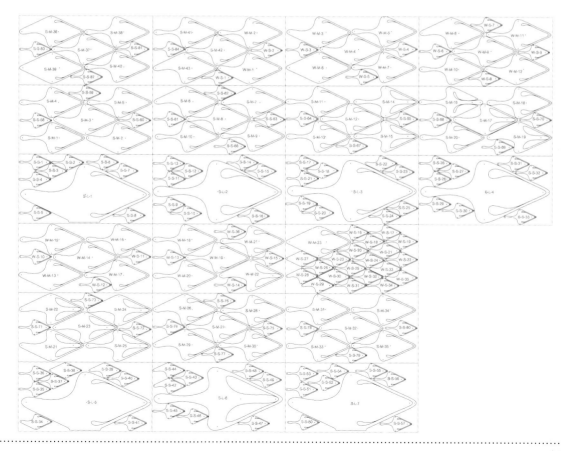

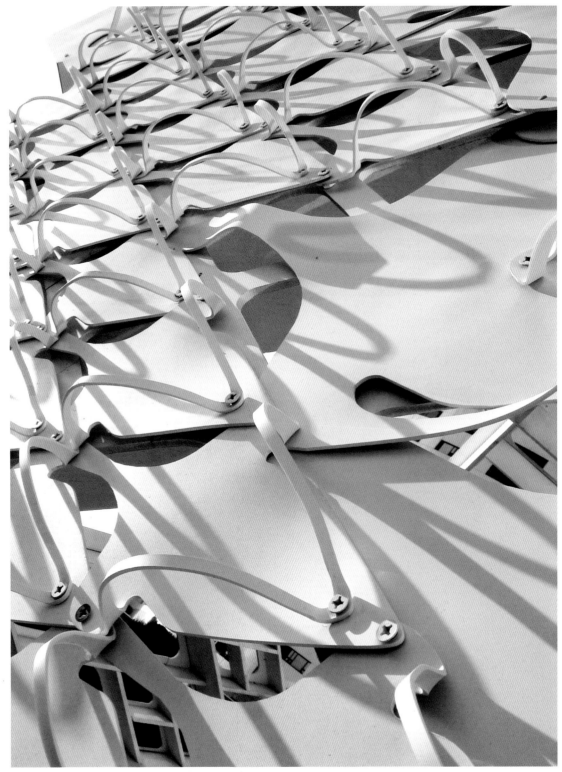

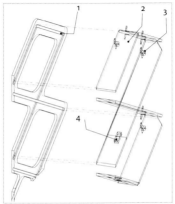

Exploded beams

1. Milled channel groove on inside of flange for web to notch into.
2. Cut plywood web.
3. L plates connecting web and flanges.
4. Tie plates connecting web members

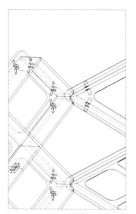

Web & flange connections

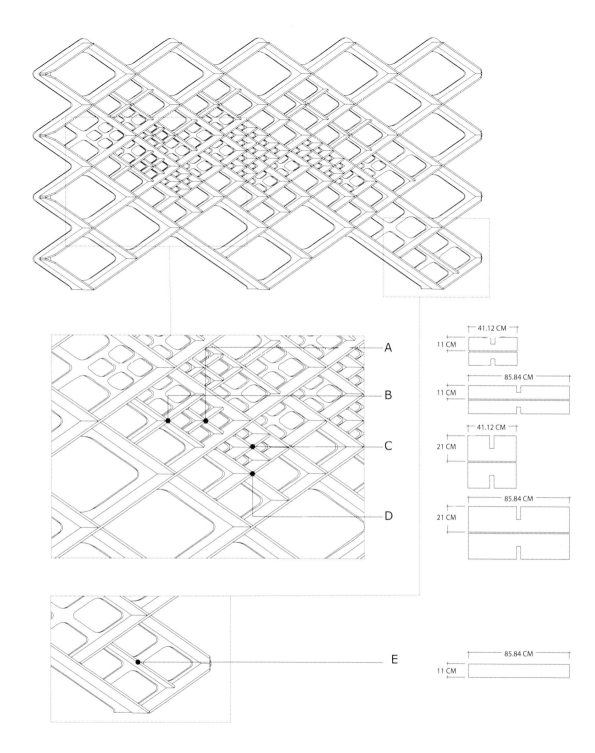

A

B

C

D

E

41.12 CM
11 CM

85.84 CM
11 CM

41.12 CM
21 CM

85.84 CM
21 CM

85.84 CM
11 CM

Elena Manferdini
Merletti

Elena Manferdini's installation explores the intricacies of lacemaking at a scale far beyond the intimate size and connotation that this term conjures up in our minds: minute, decorative, demure, "woman's work." Painstaking and intricate, lace is made by the knotting and intertwining of multiple threads to construct a complex surface. Merletti, the Italian term for antique Venetian lace, carries along with it meanings that reach far beyond the nuances of the term lace in English. Merli are the crenellations that frame the top of defensive buildings. The dynamic dance of lacemaking is boldly brought to the scale of the SCI-Arc gallery in Manferdini's suspended canopy.

Her work, which weaves itself along catenary supporting wires, engages the observer at the impossibly small scale of lace suspended within the space of the gallery. One is drawn into the installation while in the gallery space with the work billowing above, where the emphasis is on each element or knot; but the work best reveals itself in its space between the two- and the three-dimensional from the view from above, where the viewer is able to appreciate the entire interwoven, lace-like structure. Manferdini's installation is exceptional in its innate protest to the assumption that the machine-made is without the deep resonance of the handmade. Rather, she pushes the use of advanced computer-numerically controlled laser cutters to produce the filigree cuts in the individual elements that make up the lace-like installation. In a similar spirit, but in the opposite direction, Manferdini's sumptuous garments use small cuts in a homogeneous fabric to produce a filigree structure that both accentuates the form of the body sheathed in this intricate surface, while producing an attenuated and animated surface interface between the body and the environment.

Design: Elena Manferdini
Engineering: Stephen Lewis (Buro Happold)
Matthew Melnyk (Buro Happold)
Tom Reiner (Buro Happold)
Fabio Zangoli
Lighting: Heather Libonati, Lenna Minion
Renderings: Steven Ma
Production team: Amir Aboganhem, James Barge, Nick Benner, Sofia Castillo, Loke Chan, Jerry Chang, Guille Chiu, Christy Coleman, Alex Cornelius, Joseph Curran, Eileen Dikdan, Jiwon Eom, Daniel Gelormini, Teahyoun Gu, Monica Gutierrez, Michael Harrison, Linawati Hasmy, Jonathan Henry, Yu Ping Hsieh, Laura Karnath, Dorina Kastarti, Yu Nong Khew, Dimitri Kim, Edward Kim, Melissa Kim, Martial Marquet, Monica McKay, Matt Menendez, Chang Min-Cheng, Jeff Morrical, Adam Murray, Sciotto Francesco Myles, Dayana Solis-Carvajal, Mrinal Suri, Reine Wong, Wu Di Lyla
Photographs: Joshua White, Courtesy of Atelier Manferdini
Text: Alicia Imperiale

Joshua White

Courtesy of Atelier Manferdini

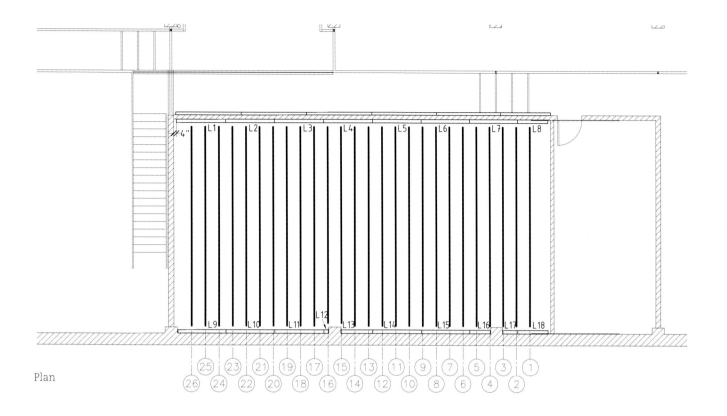

Plan

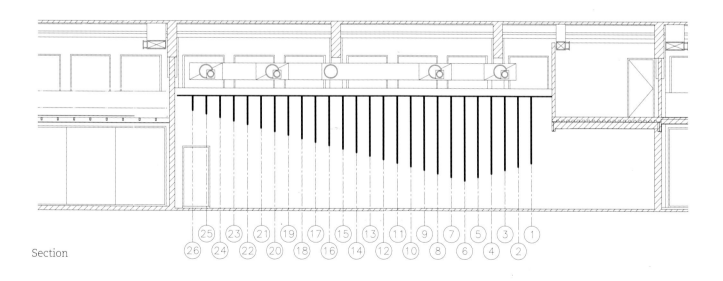

Section

Emergent / Tom Wiscombe
MoMA/ P.S.1 Urban Beach

The P.S.1 Urban Beach, realized in 2003 in the PS1 Contemporary Art Center courtyard, was based on two distinct but interrelated systems: the Cellular Roof and the Leisure Landscape. The landscape integrates various programmatic elements such as long lap pools, furniture for sitting and lounging, and promenade catwalks at different heights. Also, at key points, the landscape begins to adapt into structural supports for the roof. All of these behaviors are integrated into a coherent gradient of use, spilling out rhizomatically into the courtyard, parsing the space into microclimates and passageways. The design for the Cellular Roof was based on creating a long-span structure through the use of a non-hierarchical structural patterning of distinct but interlaced units, or cells. The location and geometry of each cell was determined by local shading requirements, by its required shear and moment reactions, and also by the behavior of neighbor cells. The interconnected cells operated in alliance, enabling large, clear spans and forming a structural ecology. A crenellated second skin wraps these elements into a singular multiplicity, a unified shade structure. At night, however, this provisional body transforms back into an atmospheric light-emitting swarm characterized by its cellularity.

One of the driving goals of this project was to integrate issues of fabrication and erection into the design process. As a temporary event roof which had to be designed, manufactured, and installed in just two months, the project team was forced to jump directly from conceptual design to shop drawings--a feat which was made possible by digital fabrication techniques. The key was to avoid designing a fixed shape and concentrate on creating a controlled geometrical logic which could adapt easily to changes in structural stresses, scope, program, and other conditions.

Design team: Tom Wiscombe, Lucas Kulnig, Mona Marbach, Mona Bayr, Patrick Ehrhardt
Construction team: Burr Dodd, Dionicio Valdez, Kai Hellat, Matthias Peter, Greg Williams, Greg Ramirez, Michael Sims, Neiel Norheim, Ed Stevens, Pearl Son, Dennis Milam, Lindsay Radcliff, Kat Arboleda
Structural: DeSimone SF/ NY, Derrick Roorda, S.E
Metal fabrication: Amsterdam Metalworks
Client: The Museum of Modern Art
Location: New York, USA, 2003

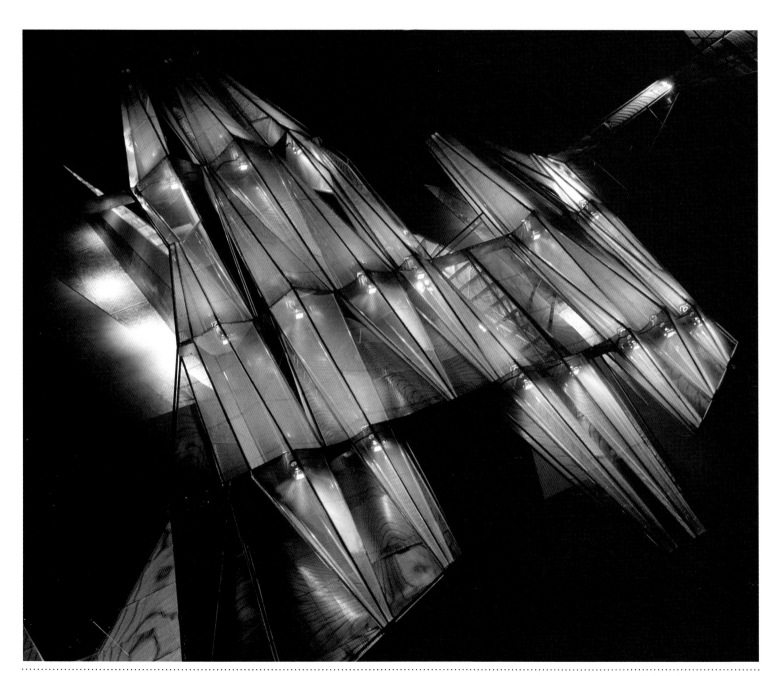

The expanded aluminum skin cladding was generated using minimal surface geometry, primarily conoidal and parabolic surfaces. These surfaces were generated by lofting straight line segments with parabolas or rotated line segments, creating a slight warpage to each panel. This warpage and the associated vaulting stiffened the panels to avoid sagging. The warpage was taken up in the meshwork of the material itself, and therefore the panels could still be unfolded flat and water-jet cut for economical manufacture.

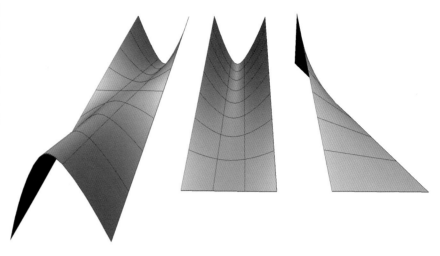

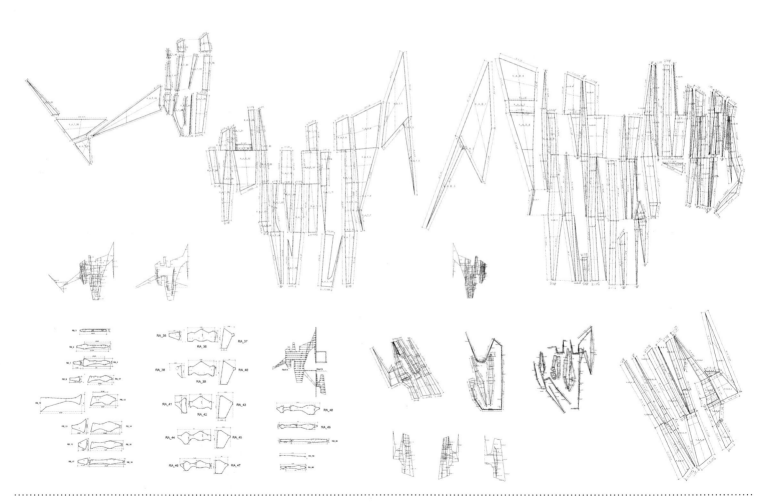

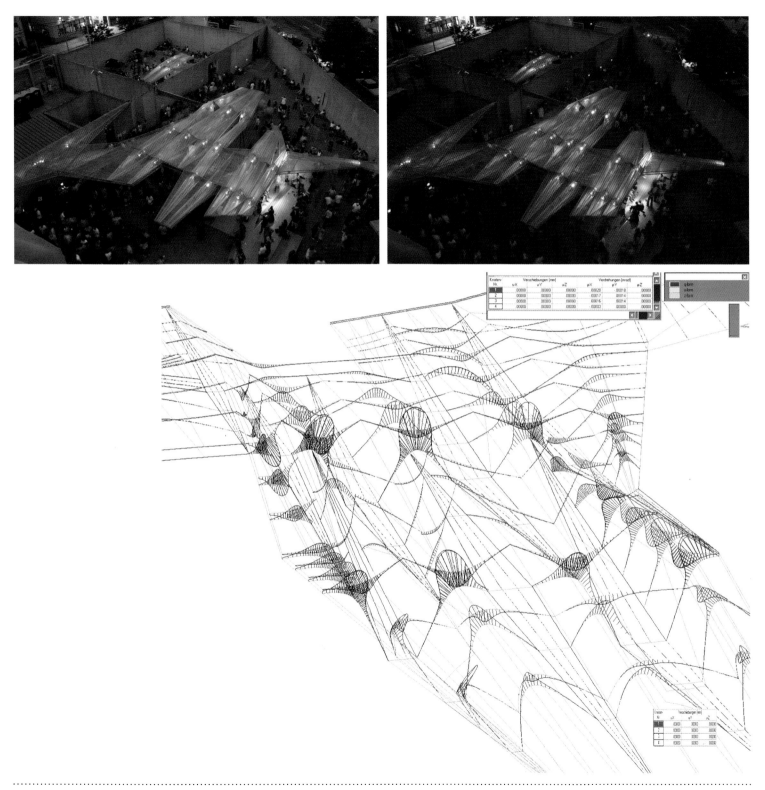

Nader Tehrani
A Change of State

This installation is the result of a one year research process with a core team of students as part of the Thomas W. Ventulett III Distinguished Chair in Architectural Design at the Georgia Institute of Technology. The pedagogy of the course focused on a series of formal exercises seeking to establish an innovative relationship between geometry, material performance, and methods of assembly. Specifically, the task of the fabrication project was to analyze and develop a three dimensional installation whose method of fabrication was limited to two dimensional material sources such as sheet metal, aircraft ply, or polycarbonate sheets. From the perspective of technique, the most important aspect of this project was the identification that two dimensional surfaces gain access to the third by way of the ruled surface.

Of the various contingencies that helped form the installation, the structural imperative played the most salient role. If traditional categorizations have identified such variations as form-active (arch), vector-active (truss) and surface active (shell) structural typologies, the idea of this project was to develop a technique that could seamlessly navigate between these variations through the invention of a transformable geometrical code, something without precedent. The aim of this geometric code is to operate at a topological level, accommodating difference within a continuous and unmediated logic. The logic of the geometric unit, then, was based on the introduction and elimination of vertices-- in combination with surface rotation—in order to create transformations in the structure without succumbing to the limitations of conventional typologies and the requisite ancillary mediating details for joints and connections.

Professor: Nader Tehrani
Instructor: Tristan Al-Hadid
Project lead: Brandon Clifford
Project team: Richard Aeck, Jonathan Baker, Daniel Baron, Vishwadeep Deo, Brandi Flanagan, Steven Georgalis, Jason Mabry, Mohamed Mohsen, Lorraine Ong, Vinay Shiposkar
Location: Atlanta Georgia, USA
Photographs: Nader Tehrani

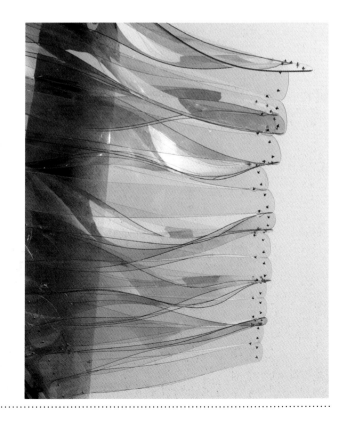

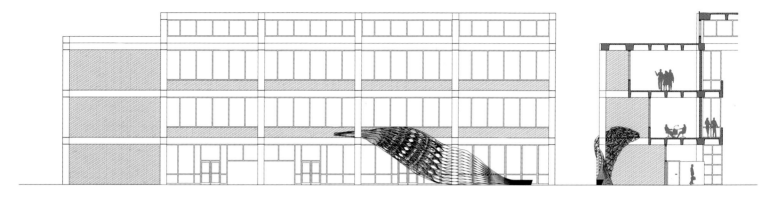

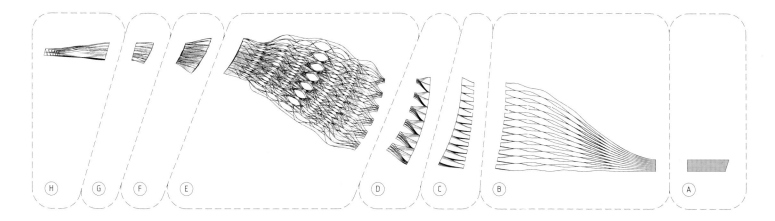

After many tests and a dialogue with various material suppliers, polycarbonate sheets were donated by Bayer Films as the basis for the final installation. This material demonstrated the pliability to rotate and function effectively for the projected ruled surfaces. It also has the benefit of exhibiting a strange stealth ambiguity as viewed in different light, between day and night but the silence of its transparency was perhaps most significant because of the way in which it underscored the presence of geometry, while erasing its material presence.

Starting from the east, at its base, the structure is organized according to the stacked logic of masonry construction. Dense like masonry, the stacked polycarbonate works in compression, while its transparency forms a deep grey mass as the layers amass creating a long bench. Next, as the plates delaminate, they rotate to form stacked box beams, vaulted on top of each other, akin to a form-active logic wrapping around one of the columns of the south porch. Next, as the structure lifts off the ground, the box beams transition yet again, exfoliating into different vectors to produce the compressive and tensile members of a truss. Maybe the most enigmatic of the various phase changes, this segment seduces intellectually in the way it spatializes the surface, while offering a beguiling visual phenomenon that eludes any rational understanding of it simple vector active geometry. Spanning about 9 m (30 ft), the unwound plates of polycarbonate reassemble to box beams to create a base for landing the spanning truss on the second floor beam of the south porch. Finally, the geometry of the plates undergo one last phase change to create a folded plate cantilever at the west end of the installation, bringing the installation to a terminus by way of a surface active condition that gains its rigidity through the geometry of the surface.

Though the installation is site specific, the evolving geometric and structural transformations suggest a broader and more flexible encounter with other possible permutations. Thus, the installation was developed as a system that can be confronted with a range of scenarios, and thus adaptable. The system is broken down into discrete twisted panels, each of which can be connected to neighboring units by way of rivets. In turn, each panel is designed with a family of details that provide for tolerances that accommodate for the variability of rotations, material flexibility and the desired effect of continuity. In this installation, the detail is the prerequisite to the form, and the precise connections, rotations, and joints provide for the configurative base from which the transforming figures of the various structural conditions emerge.

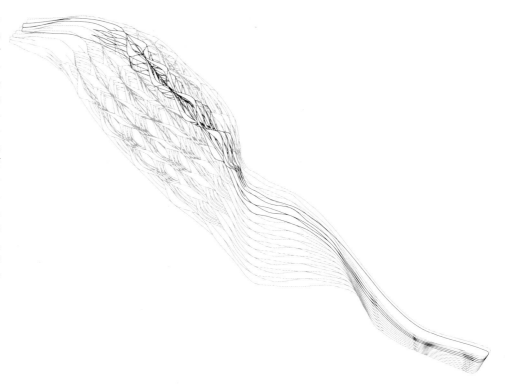

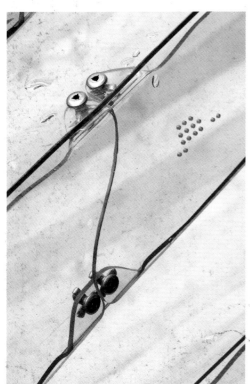

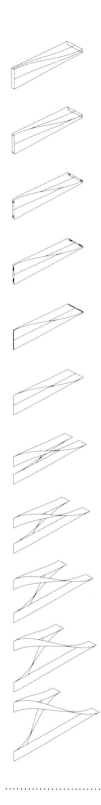

Nader Tehrani
Immaterial/Ultramaterial

Using digital craft, the project focuses on the interface between problems of geometry and aggregation—aggregation referring to traditions of construction that involve the assembly of discrete units. When confronting problems of geometry and standardization, different strategies have emerged throughout history for the resolution of edges, corners, and junctions. Some strategies are related to making allowances and tolerances for construction, while others are directed toward defining a particular linguistic attitude. Either position defines a relative idea about architectural resolution. Both Mies van der Rohe's didactic corners and Frank Gehry's open-ended formal experimentation are invested in relative ideas about architectural resolution – the different forms succeed on their own terms. Drawing from these two divergent traditions, this proposal attempts to mediate between broader geometric problems and the manner of assembling units of construction.

The installation is conceived as a wood membrane whose geometry can accommodate -indeed radicalize- a variety of conditions in a seamless and continuous surface: defining the ceiling, sagging over the information desk, and wrapping the column, among other potential conditions. The wood membrane is fabricated out of smaller units of construction that create its particular geometry by introducing slits, and in turn enabling compound curves. Facilitated by CAD-CAM manufacturing processes, the individual units of construction are customized while developing a consistent language of connections. These units are thus conceived systematically, with the possibility of calibrating different amounts of light, air, and sound through varied incisions in the wood membrane. Here, tectonic and form are reciprocal: the overall form demands the precise relationships of the thin-ply units, while the thin-ply units determine the overall shape.

Project advisor: Nader Tehrani, Assistant Professor
Project collaborators: Kristen Giannattasio, Heather Walls
Installation assistants: Hyuek Rhee, Mario D'Artista
Photographs: Dan Bibb

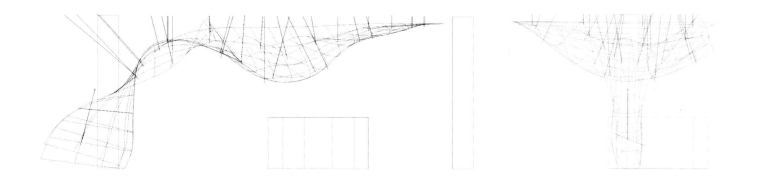

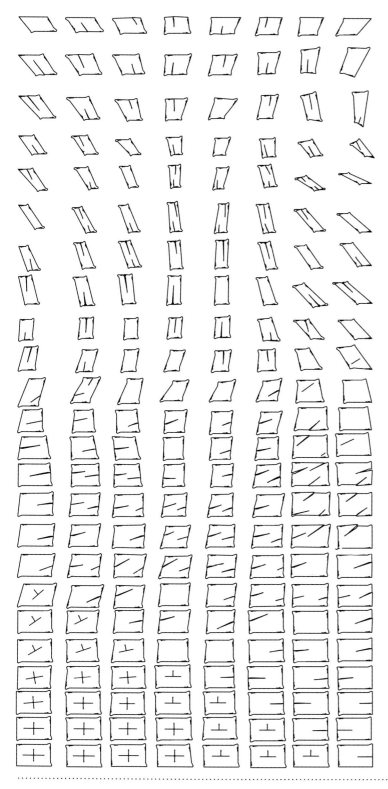

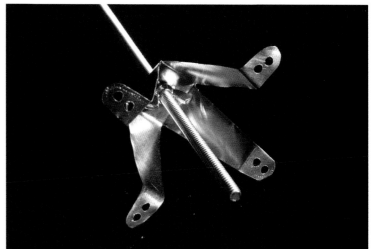

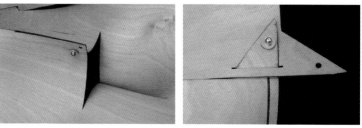

Tobias Klein & Roberto Bottazzi
Topotable

As part of the Department of Architecture at the Royal College of Art in London. Architecture Design Studio 1 (ADS1) – taught by Roberto Bottazzi and Tobias Klein – has been working on an innovative project that has been constructed in the occasion of the Graduation Show between June 21 and July 4 2008.

The proposal was to test the possibilities of digitally-based architecture in the context of exhibition spaces by interface using CAD/CAM methods. The organization of the exhibition design often advocates generic spaces–often labelled "White Cubes" – against which to display works of art. This is at odd swith the complexity of digital-based design which requires immersive conditions and flexibility that necessitate a re-thinking of the relation between the displayed object and its exhibition environment.

The project aims at challenging the traditional sectional pro-file that characterizes table designs. Freed from the function-al necessity to be strictly flat and neutral in relation to the objects displayed, the top surface is altered to engage in a deeper and more dynamic way with objects and viewers. By "inflating" the horizontal line coinciding with the top plain, two undulating, continuous landscapes – the top and bottom profile of the table – provide a range of spatial conditions for models to be positioned.

This apparently simple move transforms the tables from a neutral surface into a volume; a body whose presence affects both the surrounding space and the objects exhibited. Like a curatorial strategy, the models need to establish their own relation with the "peaks" and "falls" of the table.

The project focuses on the gap between the demand for ge-neric exhibition spaces and exuberant and complex geom-etries made available by digital tools. The final piece is an interface design that makes use of the potentials to manipu-late and implement complex surfaces through computers, to establish a closer interaction between the body of the viewer and the material displayed. The best students' works of the 2007-8 academic year were displayed on the piece.

Design: Tobias Klein, Roberto Bottazzi, students of ADS1/2008/09 of the Royal College of Art

Sponsored by: Cordek, department of architecture at Royal College of Art

Thanks: Prof. Nigel Coates, Alastair Seaton, Trevor Larkin, Michelle Sheperd

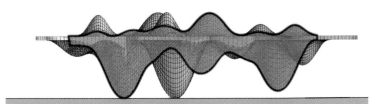

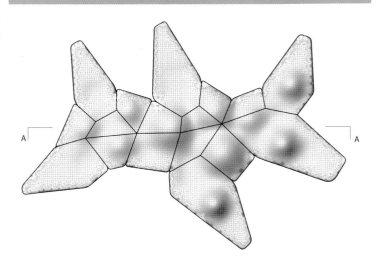

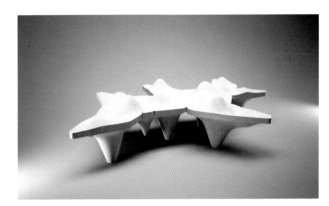

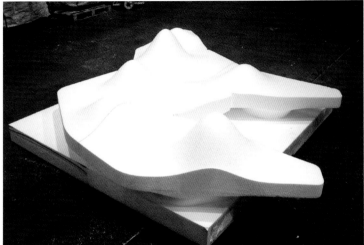

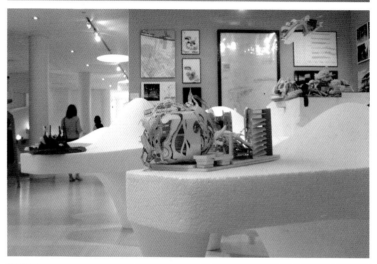

Thom Faulders + Studio M
Airspace Tokyo

The project creates an exterior building skin for a new four story multi-family dwelling unit with professional photography studios in Tokyo, Japan. Located in the Kitamagome Otaku district, the site was previously occupied by the owner's family with a residence uniquely wrapped by a layer of dense vegetation. Since the entire site was razed to accommodate construction for the new larger development, the design invents an architectural system that performs with similar attributes to the demolished green strip and creates a new atmospheric space of protection.

Conceived as a thin interstitial environment, the articulated densities of the porous and open-celled meshwork are layered in response to the inner workings of the building's program. AirSpace is a zone where the artificial blends with nature: sunlight is refracted along its metallic surfaces; rainwater is channeled away from exterior walkways via capillary action; and interior views are shielded behind its variegated and foliage-like cover.

The screen façade provides privacy from the street to occupants living in the open-plan private residences, and buffers the weather from exterior walkways and terraces. Architecturally, the screen façade unifies the separated Living Unit blocks on the top floors with the commercial spaces and landscaped areas below.

Separated by a 20 cm air gap, the double layer screen is derived from a compressed combination of unique patterns generated with parametric software, and is constructed using a composite metal panel material used for billboard backing and infrastructural protective coverings (such as on raised Tokyo freeways for sound isolation). To allow the cellular mesh to visually float, a matrix of thin stainless steel rods is threaded from top to bottom, to which the panels are affixed.

Screen façade design: Thom Faulders, Proces2, San Francisco
Building design: Studio M/Hajime Masubuchi, Tokyo
Photographs: Faulders Studio

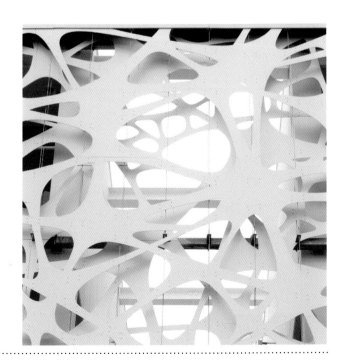

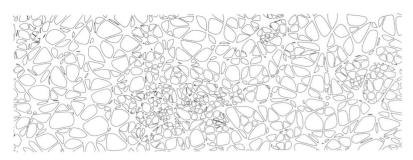

North façade - inside

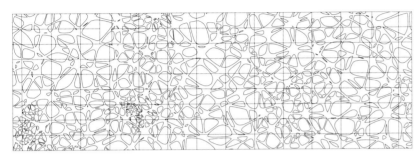

North façade - outside

South façade - inside

South façade - outside

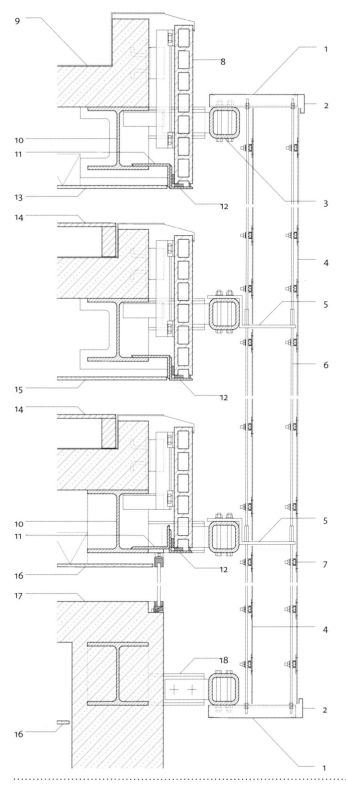

1. 75/40/5 mm steel U-section, galvanized
2. 0.8 steel sheeting, polyurethane-coated
3. 100/100/12 mm steel O-section, galvanized
4. 3 mm Álpolyic
5. 44/9 mm steel flat, galvanized
6. Diam. 6 stainless-steel rod
7. aluminum bracket
8. cocrete panel
9. roof construction: 3 mm roof sealing layer, reinforced concrete in permanent ribbed, sheet-metal shuttering
10. 100/100/8/12 mm steel I-beam
11. 120/75/7 mm steel angle
12. 75/75/6 mm steel angle, galvanized
13. 9.5 mm calcium board, painted, 100 mm thermal insulation
14. floor construction: 15 mm uline boarding on 45/95 mm battens, 3 mm sealing layer, reinforced concrete in permanent ribbed, sheet-metal shuttering
15. 9.5 mm calcium board, painted
16. 9.5 mm plaster board, painted
17. Floor construction: reinforced concrete in permanent ribbed, sheet-metal shuttering
18. 100/100/6/8 mm steel H-section, galvanized

AION, Aleksandra Jaeschke & Andrea Di Stefano
Continuous Laminae, Laminated Timber Screens

The aim of this research was to develop a sustainable and biodegradable construction system made from laminated timber that is capable of modulating defined environmental conditions by utilizing the specific characteristics of timber. It seeks to demonstrate the potential of timber when assembled intelligently, considering material properties on a micro-scale from a biomimetic approach and at a macro-scale with respect to manufacturing and assembly logics. The task is to develop a self-supporting material system made of laminated wood that is capable of bearing wind loads that can cope with abrasion and utilize changes in relative humidity, while simultaneously modulating air flow, light intensities and potential interaction with aggregates such as sand accumulation in coastal locations. In order to combine these performance requirements in one sustainable and biodegradable system two strategies were adopted: [i] continuous use of one material (laminated wood with no joints), [ii] use of curved geometries (assuring structural and material integrity while allowing for control of environmental dynamics through local differentiations).

Underlying this project is a desire to give an everyday material a new life: to go beyond the conventional framework of use through an investigation of its micro-scale material properties and its macro-scale behaviour and context-modulation capacity. The work unfolds as a resonance between the intrinsic properties of wooden veneer and the extrinsic organizational and performative desires introduced in the course of the research process.

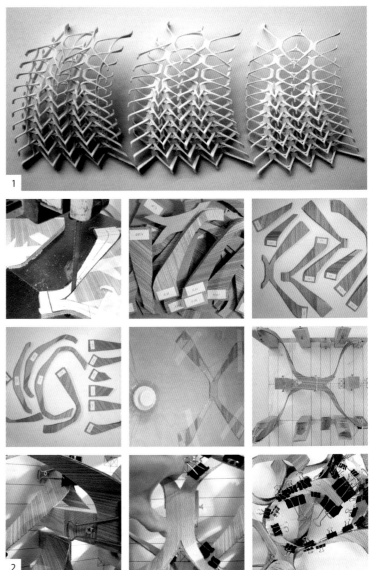

1. Local system differentiations, rapid prototype models
2. Continuous lamination, process development
3. Full-scale timber prototype, fragment

3

At the basis of this research is the anisotropy of wood, with its specific fibre-directionality and related response-range to environmental stimuli tested against the specific requirements of the context. Initially the basic elements were finite length strips made from layers of laminated veneer; rotating layers against one another allowed an investigation of different fibre-layouts. In existing approaches to making laminated structures, individual components are laminated in pre-designed moulds and then joined using plates or other connection systems. Most of the time only single curvature can be achieved; for double curvature, pre-bent components must be cut to final shape or else the system will store energy. In this research, however, shifting the layers of veneer made a continuous lamination process possible, able to produce a large assembly without construction gaps.

A correlated manufacturing strategy was developed, incorporating: i) replacement of the moulds with a plate support system allowing the laminated components to find the most suitable form during the fabrication process; ii) introduction of a double curvature during the process of fabrication through rotation of the end points at support plates; iii) exploration of a continuous sequence of fabrication (continuous lamination) in which primary laminated components are joined through successive laminations. Thus, while the overall assembly consists of finite lengths of veneer strip, the continuous laminae arrangement does not require a division into elements. The overall assembly becomes a single element, in which each local dimensional change produced by environmental stimuli affects the system at large.

Changing the fibre orientation between the veneer layers, so as to adapt it to the changing geometry of the sub-locations and the required curvature of the overall system, helps to induce the particular material behaviour required for the process of lamination. Allowing the individual components to self-organize during the process of fabrication helps to achieve the most natural form relative to strategically defined and placed constraints. Achieving flexibility across individual paths and accommodating local deformations helps to absorb stresses caused by shrinkage and swelling due to changes in temperature and humidity.

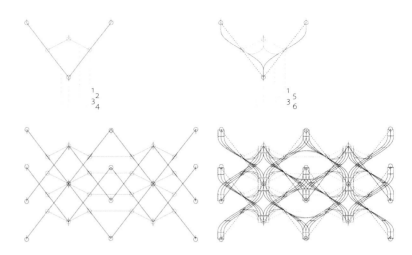

Basic Set-up

1. Secondary constraint point
2. Secondary component direction
3. Primary constraint point
4. Primary component direction
5. Secondary component path
6. Primary component path

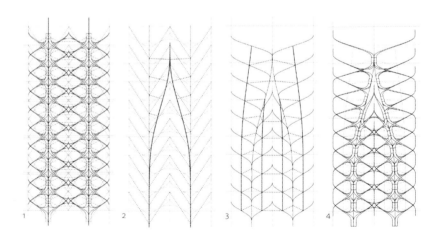

Differentiations

1. Equal density regional set-up
2. Displacement of primary component guide rail
3. Mapping of secondary components guide rails
4. Differentiated density regional set-up

Differentiated Set-up

1. Secondary component path
2. Primary component path
3. Forming support plates

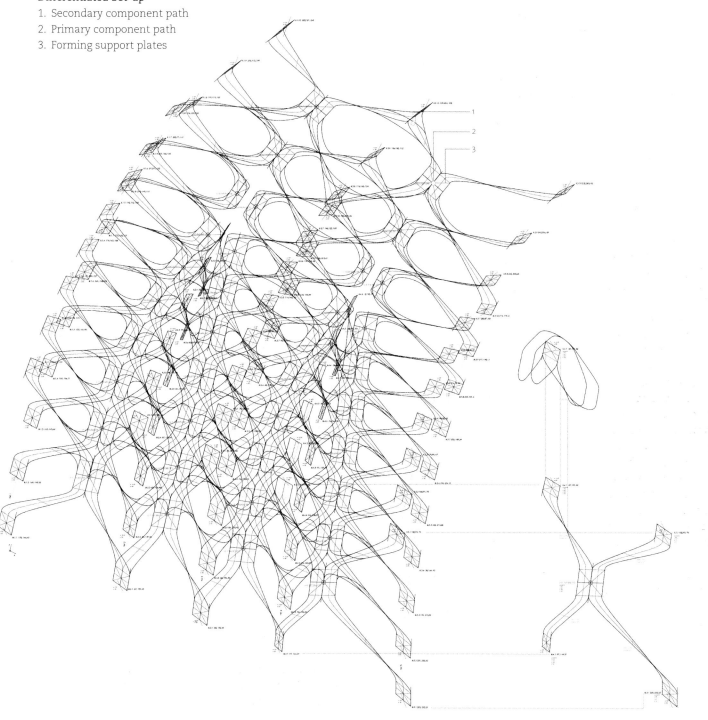

Pleats Please, Issey Miyake

The Pleats Please space in Berlin is the first in a series of retail spaces for the Japanese fashion designer Issey Miyake. The space is in the Galeries Lafayette building by Jean Nouvel. The design intends to give to the space a unique environment that reflects Miyake's personality and approach to fashion design while retaining direct focus on the clothes.

All of the design components relied heavily on the use of CNC (Computer Numerically Controlled) machines. Being fabricated in Chicago then shipped and assembled in Berlin, the ease of shipping and assembly created a challenge for this project. The primary design consists of a wall made of two overlapping pieces. This wall creates both a fitting room and a storage area.

Two materials, aluminum and polycarbonate, are used within the space. Half-inch 50 × 100 × 0.5 aluminum plates are cut using waterjet techniques. The aluminum serves as the structure supporting the wall polycarbonate panels, the racking system and table structure. Polycarbonate is used to create the organic surface and table top. The surface is modeled on the computer, unfolded using 3D software, then fabricated using router CNC machines. The polycarbonate panels are assembled using zip ties. The lightweight polycarbonate material and zip tie fastening creates a system that is both easy to transport and quick to assemble.

Location: Galleries Lafayette, Berlin, Germany
Client: Issey Miyake
Photographs: Christian Richters

In 2005, this project received the AIA (American Institute of Architects) Chicago Chapter: Interior Architecture and Divine Detail Design Excellence Awards.

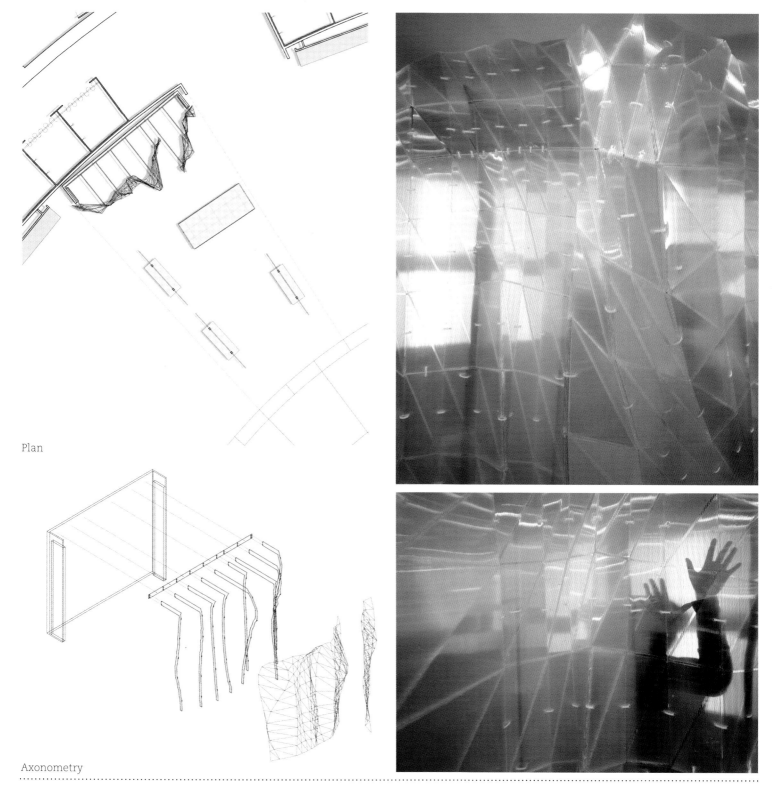

Plan

Axonometry

Ammar Eloueini is the recipients of the VIA 2006-2007 Grant for the CoReFab #71 chair design. VIA, a Paris, France based non-profit organization, yearly awards a limited number of unrestricted grants for the purpose of developing and manufacturing prototypes to fruition.

CoReFab #71 is a chair design created from computer digital animation and realized through 3D print technology. VIA has awarded the fabrication of three CoReFab#71 chair designs, which will be debuted at the Paris Salon du Meuble and Milan Salone Internazionale Del Mobile in 2007.

CoReFab#71 is a chair within an infinite series of possibilities. This chair is the result of a computer designed form which is layered with varying patterns, animated then slowed down moment by moment or frame by frame—such as a frame in a movie or a photographic still. This frame or moment of computer-animated form is then manufactured through 3D print technology.

3D printing, which is primarily used for creating design industry models, is engaged here to create a full-scale piece of furniture.

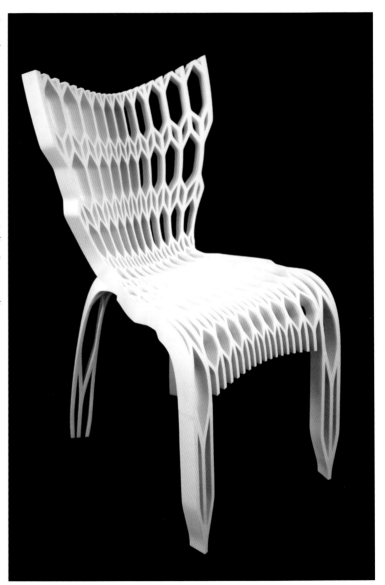

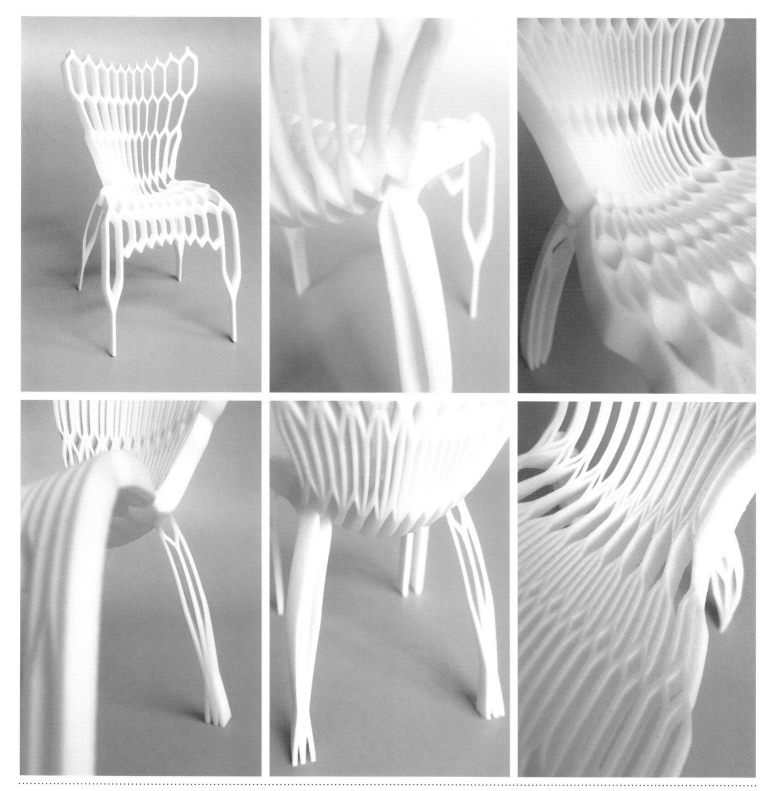

Florencia Pita
Pulse: Tendril Formations

The site-specific installation Pulse: Tendril Formations emphasizes the manipulation of color and material as a double mechanism for the production of spatial affect. The Gallery is transformed into an entirely pink landscape with winding walls, or structural tendrils, made of 300 CNC lasercut Sheets of thin plastic, with contoured benches coiling out of the meandering walkways. With pink floors and walls, the exhibition offers an environment and spatial effect of total immersion in color, atmosphere and material. The structural tendrils, formulated through mathematical computation, allow the building material to be the structure itself, without any supporting structure. The structure's complexity, achieved through multiplicity, is created by the proliferation of layers of single curvature. The extrusion of two-dimensional materials into a three-dimensional pattern and flow accentuates ornamentation through structure and volume without infrastructure. Inspired by the late 19th Century nature photograph of German Artist Karl Blossfeldt and by the complex fabric structures of contemporary fashion innovator Junya Watanabe, the installation investigates notions of color and form as performative elements that embed spaces with mood and atmosphere.

Fabrication team: Daren Chen, John Klein IV, Zarmine Nigohossian, Clair Souki, Joe Tarr, Chris Eskew, Jin Tack
Location: SCI-Arc Gallery, California, USA, 2006
Photographs: Joshua White

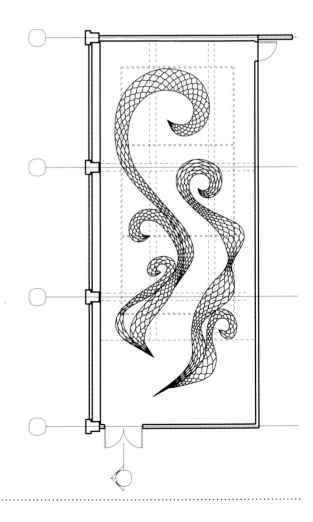

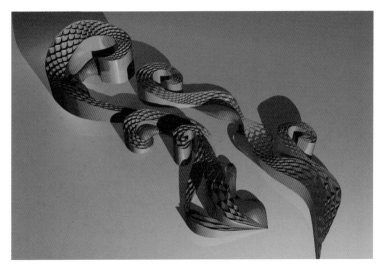

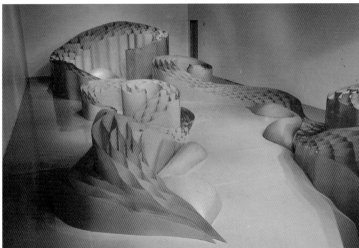

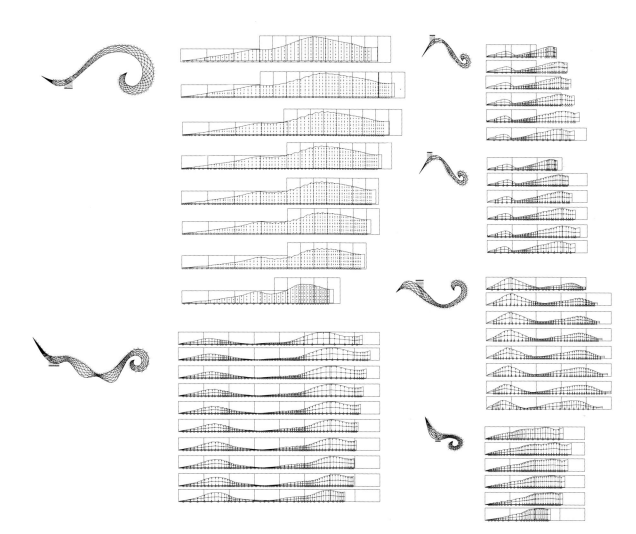

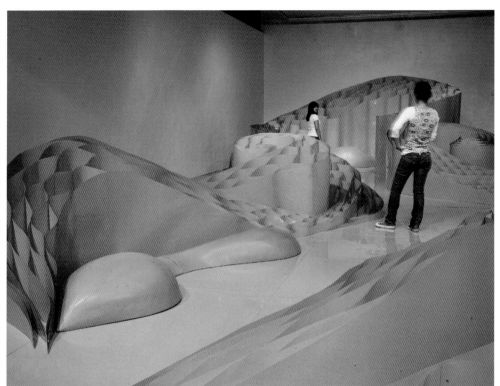

IwamotoScott Architecture
Voussoir Cloud

Voussoir Cloud explores the structural paradigm of pure compression coupled with an ultra-light material system. The project is the result of a collaboration of IwamotoScott and the engineering firm, Buro Happold. The design fills the gallery with a system of vaults to be experienced both from within and from above. The edges of the vaults are delimited by the entry soffit and the two long gallery walls. Spatially, they migrate to form greater density at these edges. Structurally, the vaults rely on each other and the three walls to retain their pure compressive form. The fourteen segmented pieces also resolve to make a series of five columns that support the interior and back edge.

Buro Happold used both computational hanging chain models to refine and adjust the profile lines, initially modeled in Rhino, and form finding programs to determine the purely compressive vault shapes. In this case, however, the structural and material strategies are intentionally confused. Each vault is comprised of a Delaunay tessellation that both capitalizes on and confounds the structural logics – greater cell density of smaller more connective modules, or petals, gang together at the column bases and at the vault edges to form strengthened ribs, while the upper vault shell loosens and gains porosity. At the same time, the petals – the reconstituted "voussoirs", typically defined as the wedge shaped masonry blocks that make up an arch – are reconsidered here using paper thin material.

The three dimensional petals are formed by folding thin wood laminate along curved seams. The curve produces an inflected and dished form that relies on the internal surface tension of the wood and folded geometry of the flanges to hold its shape.

Design: IwamotoScott Architecture, Lisa Iwamoto/Craig Scott
Team: Stephanie Lin, Manuel Diaz, John Kim
Scripting: Chris Chalmers, John Kim
Scripting consultant: Andrew Kudless
Engineers: Buro Happold Engineers; Ron Elad, Stephen Lewis, Matthew Melnyk, Tom Reiner
Photographs: Judson Terry, IwamotoScott Architecture

In the design, the petals are defined with less offset, and are therefore flatter towards the base and edges where they gain density and connect to purely triangulated cells, and with greater offset, and more curvature at the top to create the dimpled effect on the interior. The Rhinoscript instantiated each of the 2,300 petals according to these criteria. Once the three dimensional petal geometries were digitally modeled, a second batch process was developed to unfold each petal for laser cutting. Finally, the petals are reconstituted by folding along the curved score lines, and simply zip tied together.

In the end, Voussoir Cloud attempts to defamiliarize both structure and material to create conflicted readings of normative architectural typologies. It is a light, porous surface made of compressive elements that creates atmosphere with these luminous wood pieces, and uses this to gain sensorial effects.

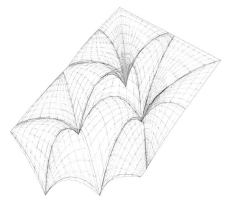

1. ISAr initial vs. form-found geometry

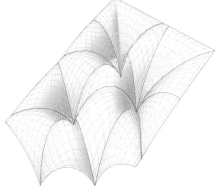

2. Form-found surface

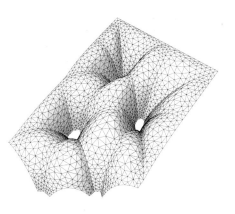

3. Tessellation of form-found surface

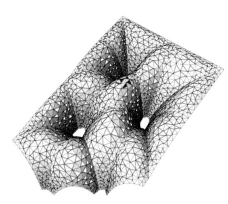

4. Porosity diagram

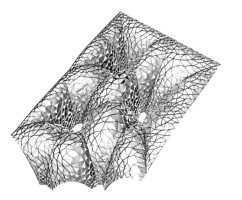

5. Module generation

© Judson Terry

1. The form of Voussoir Cloud was found through an iterative digital design process. First a 3D digital surface model was created approximating the desired structural form. From this surface the engineers created a network of quadrilateral bar elements- a digital hanging chain.

2. The chains were then used the structural analysis program ROBOT to form-find the geometry of the vaults. The vaults were allowed to deform under a uniform self-weight just like a hanging chain. The displacement between the initial and the form-found geometry was up to 12", and the form-finding process reduced the bending and deflections in the structure by 90%.

3. Using this form-found geometry, the surface was re-created and then applied the tessellation and petals. As a final check a finite element analysis of the tessellated structure was done to test its performance and ensure that the load values and the load path were as predicted.

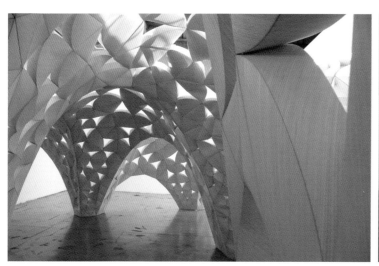

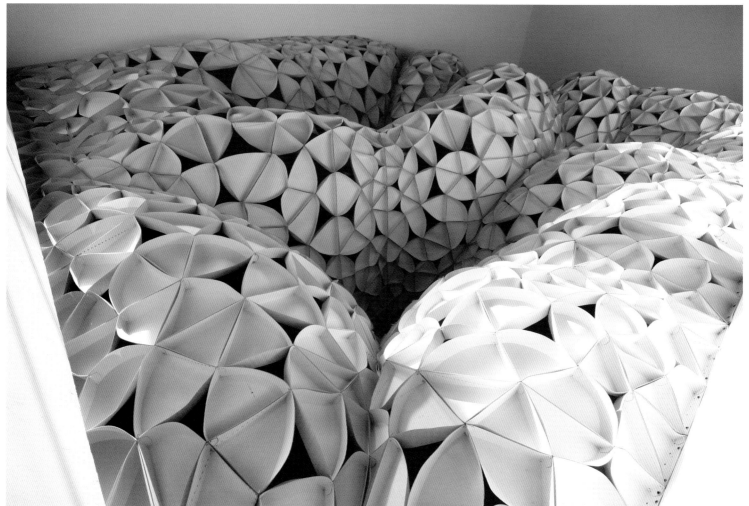

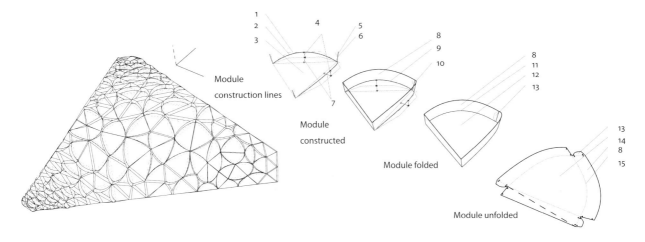

Module

construction lines

Module
constructed

Module folded

Module unfolded

1. Polyline segments give tangent requirements
2. Curve fulfulling tangent and offset conditions
3. Base geometry
4. Displacement normal to face
5. Face normal
6. Averaged normal of multiple vertices on convex surface
7. Displacement offset in plane
8. Flange
9. Curve fulfulling tangent and offset conditions
10. Averaged normal of multiple vertices on convex surface (flange edge)
11. Fold
12. Folded face
13. Flap
14. Unfolded face
15. Score

THEVERYMANY
Echinoids

How many people do actually believe in "failures"? Marc Fornes does. He has often argued in lectures and talks about the importance of "operative failures". In philosophy, empiricism is a theory of knowledge which asserts that knowledge arises from experience. One of many ways to gain experience is through test and trials and within the recent jump in scale of the digital craft and the "Do it yourself" paradigm, experience requires failures.

Despite often being displayed in art galleries THEVERYMANY's "constructs" are partly installation and partly prototypes, though not so much prototypes to see if the system is actually going to fail but rather when can failures be expected or even better anticipated.

"The lion sat", a localized part of Echinoids v1.0 slowly saddled; it didn't break but suffered from "fatigue". The Echinoids system is based on "calculated risk"; calculated risk is different from denying risk or maximizing efforts to avoid failures. Here the aggregate is designed through a variation of densities - balancing strength and weakness - fully closed macro-systems as stable larger parts and low density members at transitional areas - a curated aggregate system allowing within its own geometric nature possible partial re-configuration - "explosion" as a safe exit strategy - allowing second lives for a piece.

Design: THEVERYMANY / MARC FORNES, Skylar Tibbits with Mathew Staudt

Explicit encoded protocols: Rhinoscript / Marc Fornes

Assembly: Troy Zezula, Christine Rogiaman, Carrie Mcknelly, Elliot White, Brand Graves, Simon Kristav, Majda Muhic, Claire Davenport, Brian Doyle, Matthew DeLuca, Otilia Pupezeanu, Courtney Song, Melissa Funkey

Support: Anyline - production and prototyping PRATT University - laser cutting

Location: Bridge Gallery, New York, USA, 2009

THEVERYMANY
Aperiodic Vertebrae v2.0

Aperiodic Vertebrae is an installation by THEVERYMANY presented for the first time in Berlin in January 2008 and then in a reworked version in Frankfurt, in April of the same year.

Based on earlier experimentation the first installation is an assembly of nearly 500 flat panels (11 types) all milled within 6 sheets 2.5 x 1.2 m (8 x 4 ft) of corrugated plastic (4 colors: black, silver grey, white and translucent) and also nearly 500 assembly details (all unique), all laser cut out of 7 sheets of transparent acrylic. Despite measuring 4 m (13 ft) long (after being scaled-down nearly by half for simple reason of space available within the gallery), all the panels and assembly details can be nested in just one suitcase.

The subdivision algorithm that creates the installation is based on a recursive protocol which involves first drawing a primitive tetrahedron (within a choice of four primitives) which then gets subdivided. The process is repeated many times within itself to generate self-similarity.

One issue encountered during the first installation was that in each generation of subdivisions small rounding errors were made that tended to accumulate. These errors became apparent in the montage process.

The problem was addressed successfully in the second version of the installation (consisting this time of 360 polyethylene panels with 320 nodes) which was assembled by only two people in 24 hours using two laptops.

Design: THEVERYMANY / MARC FORNES with Skylar Tibbits, Jared Laucks
Explicit encoded protocol: Rhinoscripting / Marc Fornes
Sponsors: Quadrant EPP USA, Inc. - material
Continental Signs - CNC cutting
Dick Dunlop - laser cutting
Location: NODE08, Frankfurt, Germany, April 2008

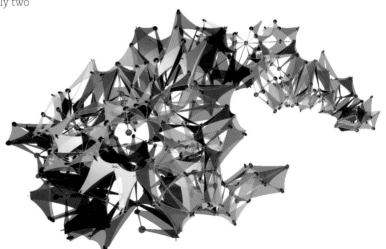

THEVERYMANY
n|Edg

"n|Edg" assembly is written within a continuous series of investigations on different scales:

The general description: development of protocols of surface relaxation - in order for the surface to generate optimum fitting curvature in response to fixed hanging or support points (floor, ceiling, walls) as curvature - despite generating apparent complexity - also provides natural structural stiffness.

Surface description (or sampling): re-understanding the resultant surface as a series of points - whose densities are relative to the degree of the curvature – the more curvature the more points and eventually parts.

Surface reconstruction (or tessellation): previous work focused on describing complex surfaces with flat components – after working for different "high end" architectural and design practices - the only way to keep pushing non standard environments is to introduce the economy of parts as part of the equation – therefore early tests were first looking at ways to triangulate complex surfaces – and therefore strategize on panels cut within flat sheets of material – which very quickly evolved toward what is now the trendy "arrays of quads" components paradigm. "n|Edg" is now investigating the reconstruction of a surface with polygonal parts going from three edges to (n) number of edges.

Informed customization: each part is similar though not identical – so its change of size and proportion allows it to describe different radii of curvature – but also local re-reading of orientation drives the length and width of the branches – the flatter, the wider in order to provide a more surface-like coverage.

Design: THEVERYMANY / MARC FORNES, Skylar Tibbits with Mathew Staudt, Jared Laucks

Many thanks: Eric Deboos, Laurent Lucas, Marie Bassano

Assembly: Anne Vialle, Simon Feydieu, Lou Lucat, Tamara Maes, Sophie Roset, Charlotte Marrel, Benedetto Bufalino

Location: Galerie Roger Tator, Lyon, France, 2009

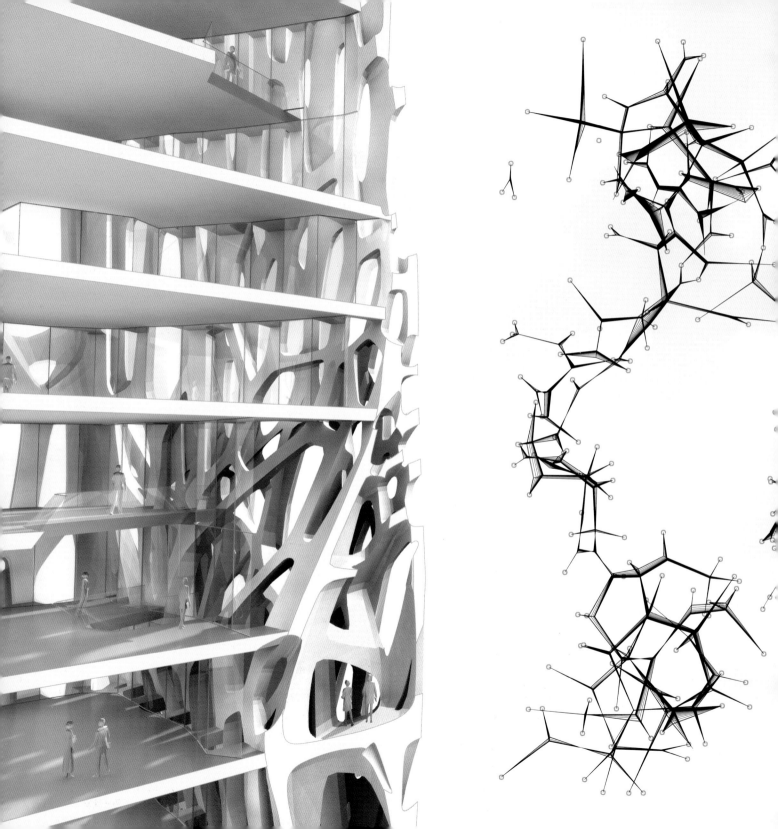

Scripting

"A digital computer is, essentially, the same as a huge army of clerks, equipped with rule books, pencil and paper, all stupid and entirely without initiative, but able to follow exactly millions of precisely defined operations… In asking how the computer might be applied to architectural design, we must therefore, ask ourselves what problems we know of in design that could be solved by such an army of clerks… At the moment, there are very few such problems."

Christopher Alexander,
"The Question of Computers in Design", 1967

As we can see from the quote above the question of the use of computers in architecture is not that new; it is actually about 50 years old. However, it is only recently that the possibilities opened by the use of computers have become apparent. For a long time the skepticism of Christopher Alexander was typical for most architects. It has been felt by many that the computer will mechanize the process of design leaving little place for intuition and personal talent, things that are always considered basic ingredients of good architecture. Computers were of course used by many architects, but only for the preparation of the usual construction drawings (plans, elevations, sections) where they could enhance productivity in an office while having very little (if any) influence on the final product of the design procedure.

In order for the computer to be used as a problem-solving instrument in the design process Christopher Alexander's question about the use of mindless clerks had to be answered. It was by looking at nature and the modeling of natural processes in the sciences that an answer became possible. Nature is very fond of huge armies of stupid clerks; ants are a great example. Each ant by itself is not very bright and not capable of many things. A huge number of ants are capable of constructing nests of great complexity. They do this without some master-ant directing them, the complex order of their creation emerges from the simple actions that each ant is able to perform.

This approach demands the complete re-interpretation of the computer's role in design. Instead of using the computer as a representational tool for the modeling of external form one has to use it as a generative tool, forming an internal logic which can be developed to produce an entire range of possibilities. This means that the design will be described parametrically and processed with the use of algorithms.

A parametric design describes a field of possibilities instead of a fixed object. Certain magnitudes and characteristics of the design can be described parametrically instead of being given explicit values. Different parameters can be linked with equations so that chains of dependencies and hierarchies among the parts of the design can be created. This technique allows the easy exploration of possibilities and variations in a given design. It is of great use in engineering as a way to find optimal solutions to various problems.

The Parametric Stalactites project offers a clear demonstration of parametric design. Controlling the length and density of the "stalactites" allwos the model design to be adapted to different store layouts and needs.

An algorithm is usually defined as *"a detailed and unambiguous sequence of instructions that describe how a computation is to proceed and can be implemented as a program"*. In general terms an algorithm can be thought of as a sequence of discrete sequential operations with a given goal. A cooking recipe could be thus thought of as an algorithm. Seeing thinks that way we understand that algorithms are not after all so unfamiliar in architecture. Architects like Peter Eisenman have used such procedures in their designs and one can go further into the past and see the theories of Durand or Palladio as algorithmic descriptions of the design process. These architects described the design process as an algorithmic manipulation of geometrical solids and architectural elements while the contemporary approach is to create an algorithmic manipulation of an internal structure composed of parametrically defined elements. This approach is open-ended and can create a broad range of different and at times unexpected results. While an algorithm consists of a finite number of steps it is possible that the process described will be infinite or that it will create results that can not be expected or visualized before the process has run.

Contemporary architects who experiment in this field use various morphogenetic algorithms, algorithms that have been design to simulate the emergence of complex patterns and forms in nature by using relatively simple initial arguments. A common form of such algorithms is **Cellular Automata**. A cellular automaton consists of a one-, two- or three-dimensional grid where each field can exist in a number of finite states. A simple form is to consider each cell as being either on or off (black or white, dead or alive). Time passes in discrete steps and a set of rules determines how each cell is influenced by its neighbors in each time step. Two-dimensional cellular automata with very simple rules are known to produce forms of great complexity and order.

Self-organization is a similar type of simulation of natural processes. Self-organization can be created through the use of autonomous **agents**. An autonomous agent is a unit that interacts with its environment and possibly with other agents according to its own set of rules, without taking commands from a leader and without knowing an overall

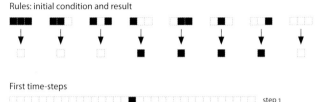

Rules: initial condition and result

First time-steps

step 1
step 2
step 3
step 4
step 5

A simple one-dimensional cellular automaton where the behaviour of each cell is determined only by its two closest neighbors.

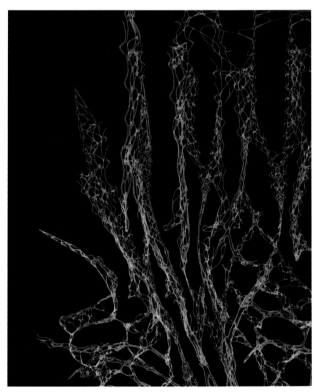

Swarm Matter by Kokkugia is a research project exploring agent-based emergent morphologies.

plan. Very simple algorithms that describe the behavior of ants as autonomous agents have been created and they can create results of surprising complexity. Other algorithms have been used to describe the flying of flocks of birds and other natural processes where a great number of similar individuals are involved.

A more complicated form of algorithm popular among the architects who explore the use of emergent morphologies is the **Genetic Algorithm**. A genetic algorithm is an algorithm written as a simulation of the process of evolution that can be used as a way to find solutions to many different types of problems. The use of genetic algorithms requires that the properties of a design that are to be evolved should be written as a number sequence in the form of a DNA chain. Various instances of the design are created by giving specific values to the parameters and these instances are allowed to interbreed and mix their DNA. Rules must be given for the process of mixing the DNAs and then for the selection of the "fittest" offspring who are going to interbreed again. The whole process can be allowed to run for a great number of generations in a short time. John Frazer, one of the first proponents of evolutionary architecture has described the process as follows: *"Architectural concepts are expressed as generative rules so that their evolution may be accelerated and tested. The rules are described in a genetic language which produces a code-script of instructions for the form generation. Computer models are used to simulate the development of prototypical forms which are then evaluated on the basis of their performance in a simulated environment. Very large numbers of evolutionary steps can be generated in a short space of time, and the emergent forms are often unexpected."*

As the description of the genetic algorithms makes clear, the use of a "huge army of stupid clerks" does not in any way imply the absence of a designer who needs to think seriously and take important decisions. While the rules for mixing DNA chains can be thought as fairly mechanical, the coding of a design problem to a set of parameters that can create such a chain is an act of design in itself, while the determination of criteria for "fitness" is the most important step that will guide the whole process. The use of algorithms can be thus thought of mostly as a way to articulate a design prob-

lem. Only after a successful articulation of the problem in the form of clear rules will it be possible to use the power of the computer to open up a field of solutions and then only through our own criteria will we be able to navigate this field and select the appropriate results.

Tang & Yang have used a genetic algorithm to expolre the possiblities of mutation of the Geno-Matrix façade.

Kokkugia
Fibrous Tower

This series of studies into fibrous tower skeletons explores the generation of ornamental, structural and spatial order through an agent based algorithmic design methodology.

The fibrous concrete shell of the tower synthetically incorporates and negotiates between a set of structural, spatial, environmental and ornamental imperatives. This project compresses the structural and tectonic hierarchies of contemporary tower design into a single shell whose articulation self-organizes in response to an often conflicting set of criteria.

The shell is at once performative and ornamental. It operates as a non-linear structure with load being distributed through a network of paths, relying on collectively organized intensities rather than on a hierarchy of discrete elements. The load-bearing shell and thin floorplate enables the plan to remain column free. At points of intensity the shell thickens to create a networked series of inhabitable spaces for circulation, refuge and vertical gardens, which weave from the exterior to the distributed atrium.

Several iterations of the tower have been developed. The initial study located the fibrous network within the thickness of a comparatively simple shell geometry enabling the use of conventional techniques to construct a highly differentiated tower. Subsequent iterations have tested the spatial possibilities of woven interior structure and atriums, which delaminate from the exterior shell.

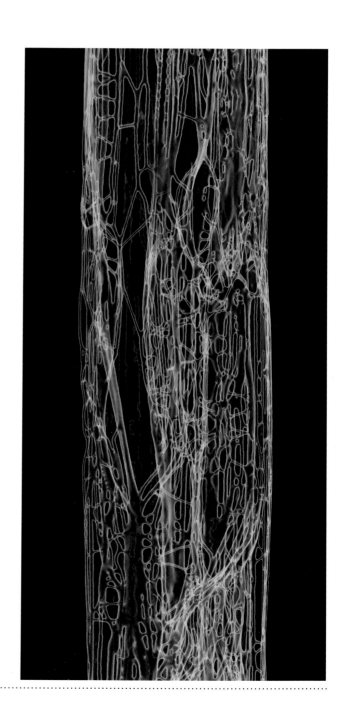

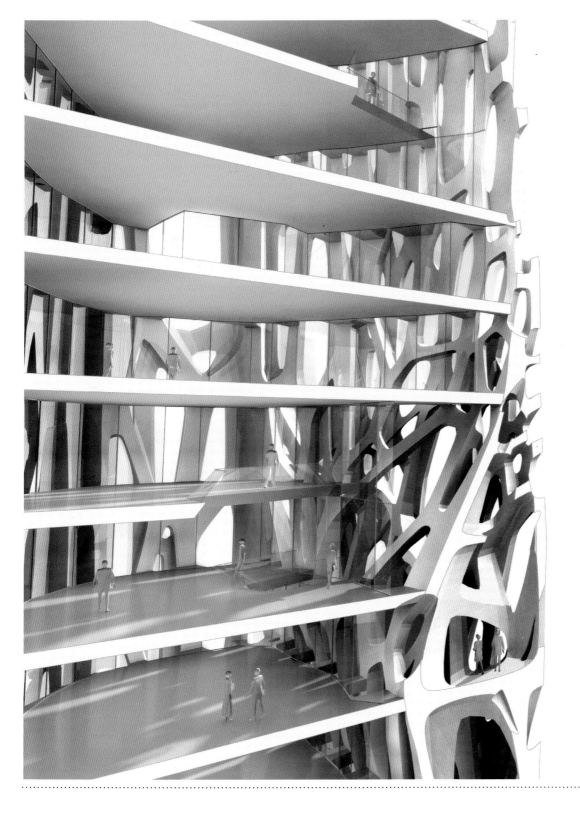

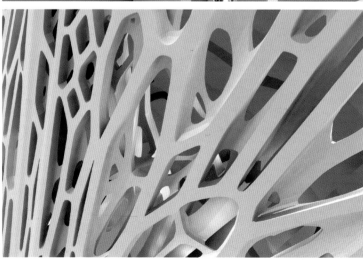

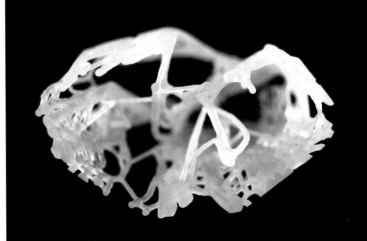

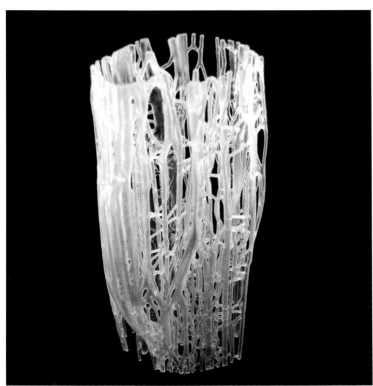

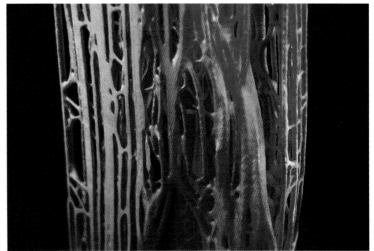

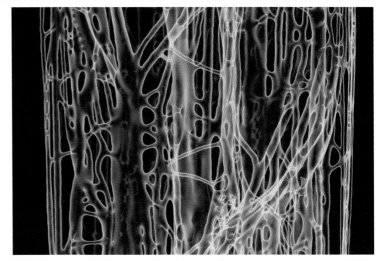

left page: Renderings of the initial study.
this page: Models of subsequent iterations.

Kokkugia
Swarm Matter

Swarm Matter is an ongoing research project exploring the generation of ornamental geometries through the agent based formation of emergent hierarchies and non-linear patterns.

This research project questions the contemporary understanding of component logic as elements that are subservient to a topological ordering device such as surface. Instead this exploration looks at the ability of macro order to emerge from the non-linear interaction of components at a local level. This non-linear methodology emerged from Kokkugia's ongoing research into systems of swarm intelligence and multi-agent algorithmic design.

This agent or collective intelligence embedded within the components avoids the need for an a priori distinction between various tectonic elements and enables a dissolution of normative architectonic hierarchies. This is an investigation into creating a constantly shifting relationship between line, component and surface. While there are no hierarchies encoded into the Swarm Matter project, local and shifting hierarchies arise as an emergent property of the system.

The project is concerned both with the emergence of figure from the complex order of fields as well as the dissolution of the figure into abstraction. At a local level a component has no base state, but instead it adapts to its conditions, consequently while local moments of periodicity may occur, a definitive reading of the component is resisted through it's continual negotiated transformations. Similarly symmetries while not being inherent within the system, emerge from specific interactions of components.

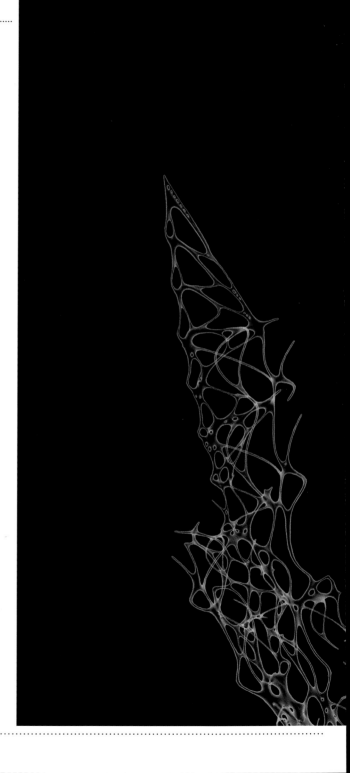

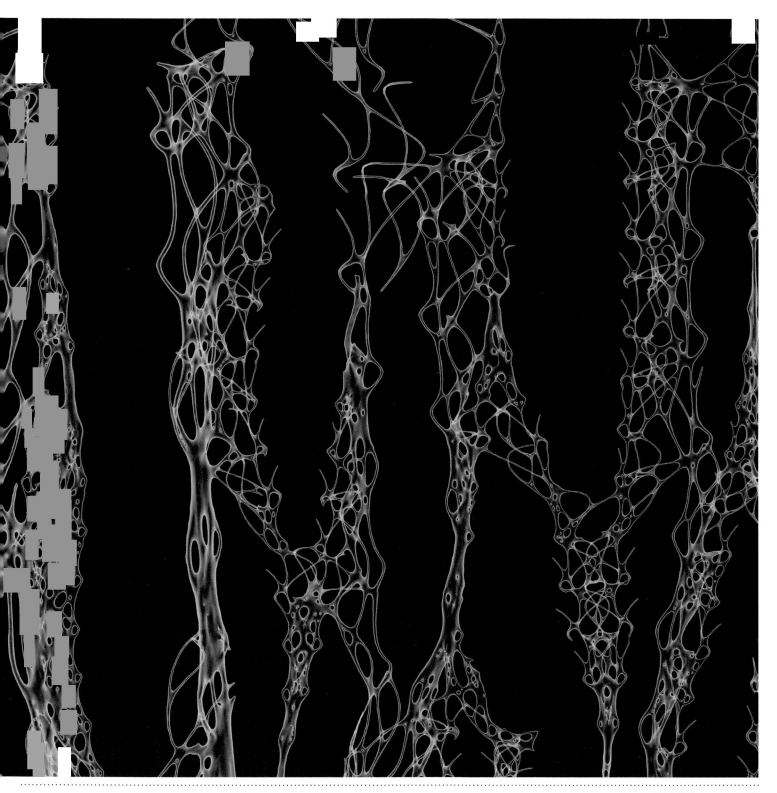

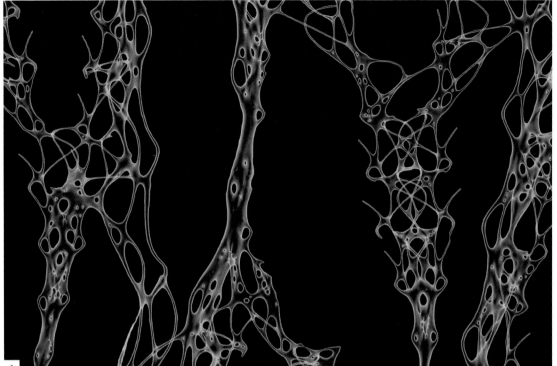

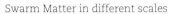

Swarm Matter in different scales
1. Detail.
2. Micro.
3. Micro.
4. Field.

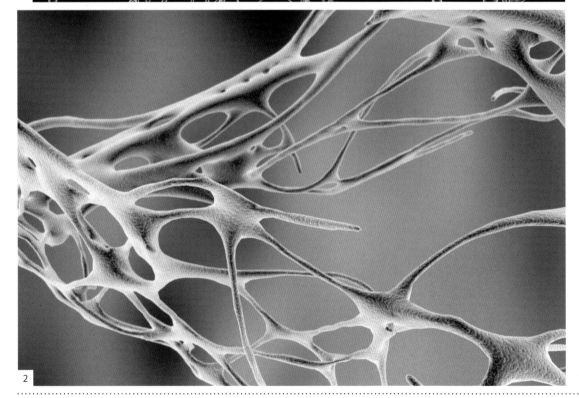

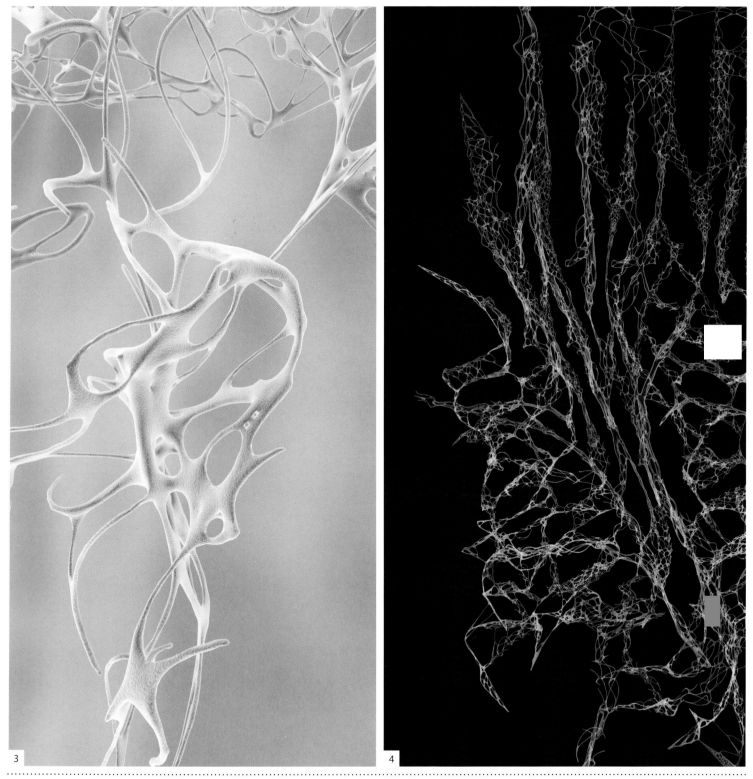

3

4

Kokkugia
Taipei Performing Arts Center

This project attempts to dissolve the normative conditions of spatial enclosure to create a performance venue and public space of spectacle. The proposal engages generative techniques drawn from the geological and cultural context to generate a vibrant space of performance and social interaction. The flows of the 19th century watercourse of Keelung River provided the impetus for a process that erodes a monolithic base in the generation of a public space carved between the auditoriums. This incision creates a gradient of enclosure and public access weaving together public plaza and theater foyers.

The recursive subdivision that operates to erode this base fractally dissolves the monolithic block of program, creating a resonance with the nature and scale of the adjacent night market. This fractal technique is again employed in the auditoriums in the generation of emergent forms of ornamentation and articulation. Simultaneously responding to acoustic requirements while aspiring to generate the richness of texture and detail of historically ornate theaters and opera houses.

The roof and spatial lattice are generated through a network of semi-autonomous agents, seeding design intent at a micro scale. The emergent properties of this Swarm Intelligence system generate an active networked topology in which agents self-organize in reforming their topology, enabling a gradient interaction between explicit design and emergent processes. A starting network geometry of the roof is explicitly modeled which then self-organizes within various degrees of freedom, enabling parts of the roof to maintain their original geometry, while other parts radically reform both topology and geometry. This process generates a material behavior through the negotiation of the internal motivation of the agents and the force within the network connections.

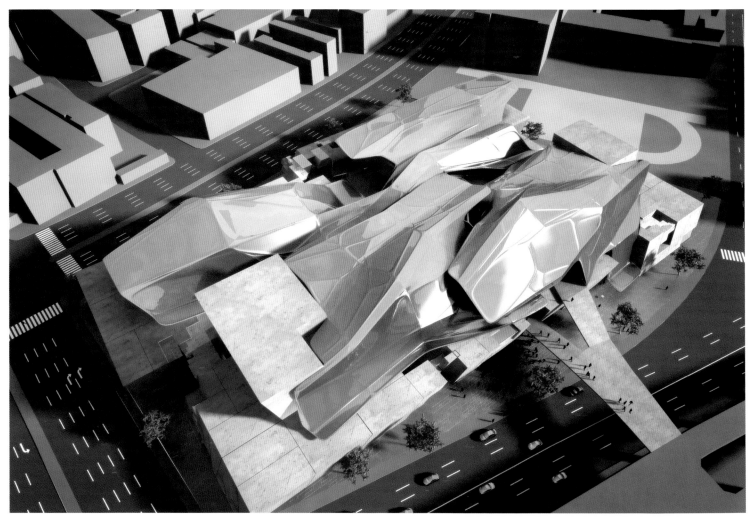

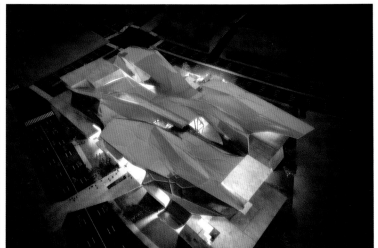

The areas of the roof enclosing the auditoriums maintain their explicit starting geometry while the area surrounding the main circulation spine has a more complex set of requirements and reforms to negotiate these. The agents are programmed with a set of spatial imperatives while the material nature of the network creates a tendency toward equilibrium topologies that operate with a degree of structural efficiency. The network structure of the system generates both space filling lattices and continuous surfaces where the network connections are articulated as a web of veins.

Tobias Bonwetsch, Sebastian Gmelin, Bergit Hillner, Bart Mermans, Jan Przerwa, Arno Schlueter, Rafael Schmidt

m.any

The m.any project was set up as a case study aimed at a fully integrated digital workflow from conceptual design to production rather than for a defined design output. The starting point was the definition of the desired spatial topology. For the case study, a three-dimensional spatial structure as found in natural cellular and crystalline structures was chosen for several reasons: Conceptually, these structures impose a new understanding of space: The generated space is not defined by fixed boundaries (wall, floor, ceiling) but by its dynamic relation to neighboring "sites", which allows a distinct three-dimensional disposition of space. These sites are created by growth processes, which are influenced by inner and outer parameters such as physical forces (inner parameter) or the situational context of the proposed building site of the structure (outer parameter). The manifestation of space is therefore process-driven rather than design based. These structures defined by numerous dependencies can only be evolved in a dynamic system. In order to design and realize such a system a digital workflow from design to production is necessary. The structure, its elements and their dependencies are too complex to be shaped, drawn or manufactured by hand. Inspired by analogies of nature the generative process is based on a dynamic system, mimicking the natural abilities of e.g. foams to find stable approximations of global states based on local acting rules. Based on the concept of cellular automata the generative system is composed of single cells, with each cell having an identical set of simple rules and its development depending on its neighboring relations. Spheres represent the cells which are the individual void spaces of the design. A three-dimensional Voronoi diagram of the spheres' center points in space defines the structural grid, which is then transformed into physical reality.

Philip Schaerer

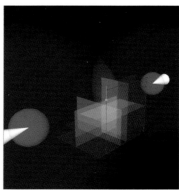

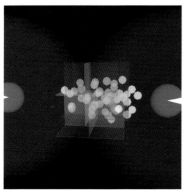

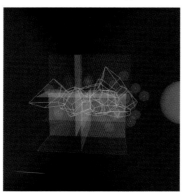

A program written in the Java programming language generates the geometry of the structure by incorporating selected parameters. The designer can control the form finding process by changing and adjusting the values. A three-dimensional wire frame model visualizes the result. The generation process is based on the principle of cellular automata. The cells follow few simple rules to coordinate their growth. The development of a singular cell depends on the condition of the adjacent cell. The spheres shown in the interface represent the cellular hollow bodies of the structure. They are enclosed by tangential planes whose intersecting edges form the physical edges of the construction system.

The designer determines the maximum volume of the construction as well as the number of cells and defines a particular value for the minimal and maximal length of the structure. With the help of force vectors it is possible to control the distribution of density within the whole structure. The program allows the organization of the cells according to the predefined coefficients. If, for example, the maximum length of one tangential edge is exceeded, the affected cell will divide. This process will continue until the system stabilizes. After reaching the desired form, the geometric data are translated into a generic data description, a XML-file, and can be passed on to other software.

The geometry is imported into the commercial CAD-Software "Rhinoceros". A specially programmed parser interprets the data of the model and creates the physical elements to be produced. The polygonal cell elements are offsets of the cell edges, customized by selecting inner and outer radii as well as edge curvature.

The scripts automatically create and arrange the necessary cutting plans for the machines. Each polygonal element, a so called "frame", is rotated into an even plane, necessary milling offsets for the machine paths are automatically calculated and added. A second procedure builds up the geometry for the frame connectors. It also generates the cutting plans needed for the production of the several hundred individual frame connectors, each one shaped in an individual angle derived by the geometry of the overall structure.

For the production of the frames the "Surfcam" milling software was used. In this program the two dimensional cutting lines of the construction plans are transformed into three-dimensional milling paths by adding the thickness of the 0.6 mm thick, coated MDF. Taking into account that the CNC-mill has an imprecision of 0.5 mm to 1.5 mm, more specific information is given to the CNC-mill through an interface, e.g. type of cut, spindle speed and milling tool. With this data the program generates a machine compatible code, the so called "G-code" which can be directly processed.

In addition to the milling process all parts are automatically numbered in a specially designed numbering pattern. Only this numbering makes the correct erection of the structure possible, otherwise the 1200 final parts could not have been physically "reassembled".

For the production of the frame connectors more precise results were needed, therefore the CNC-laser with an imprecision of only 0.2 mm was used. The MDF material gets "burned" away by the focused laser beam. This way the cutting edges are hardened in order to increase the stability and solidity of the frame connectors made out of only 5 mm MDF.

Within three months, the postgraduate students of Computer Aided Design (CAAD) at ETH Zurich, Switzerland, realized m.any as their master thesis. The realized prototype should be regarded as a proof of concept, showing the potential of using current information technologies in architectural design and construction and displaying a seamless digital workflow from design to realization.

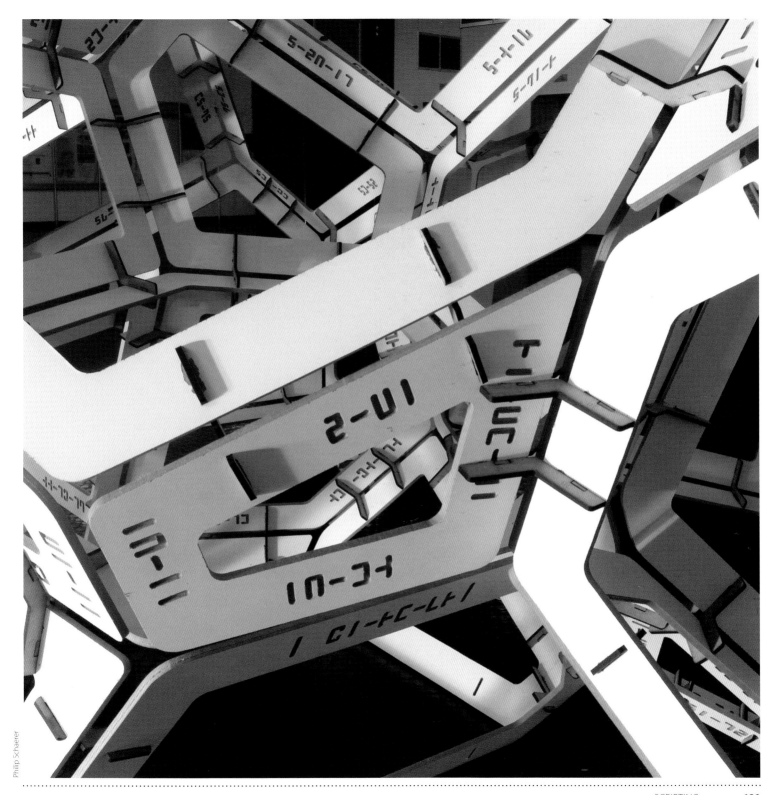

Jerry Tate Architects
Dubai Waterfront Hotel

This proposal for a high-rise hotel tower in Dubai re-conceives the arrangement and construction of a skyscraper through the understanding and reworking of structures and systems in nature. The forms of individual modules were derived from studies of insect exoskeletons and wing structures. Mimicking the complexity of a natural ecosystem there are no abrupt transitions between discrete spaces. Instead a smooth transformation between module variants produces a multifarious range of "alternative" or unique spaces, able to accommodate the wide range of functions in a hotel.

The digital design process is an amalgamated series of separate systems, some of which can be viewed as "generative" in terms of bottom-up production of spaces and "operative" in terms of organizational effect. Although the project is an investigation into a combination of mimicked natural systems in the digital environment, it is not a self-organizing proposal. Rather the scheme demonstrates a prototypical method to steer natural systems to human requirements, similar to the development and integration of early agriculture into naturally occurring eco-systems.

The "generative" elements in the project are those that produce the inhabitable spaces within the scheme. Essentially the proposal is constructed from modules and, in fact, there are three distinct types each associated with a distinct program activity. These were all developed in the digital environment through a combination of MEL-script and sub-division modeling. The basis for this development was the generative algorithm of natural forms and especially, in this case, those associated with the morphogenesis of insect exoskeletons. It should theoretically be impossible to distinguish the three module types within the proposal as there is a smooth transition between the three base module conditions. This was developed using a series of exploratory diagrams and MEL-scripting so that all transitional states between the three modules remain tectonically navigable spaces and connected throughout the three dimensional base-grid.

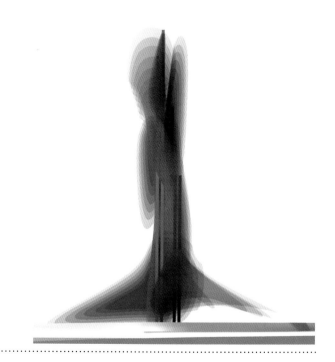

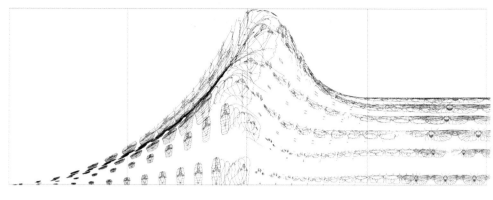

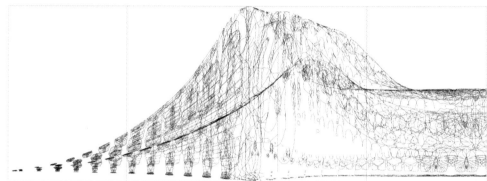

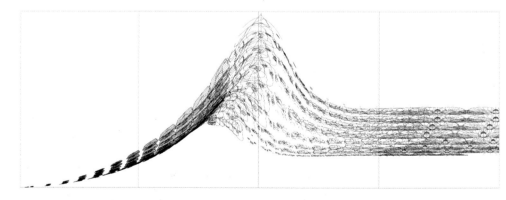

The "operative" parts of the proposal are those which are used to steer the "generative" systems. In this case a three-dimensional dynamic fluid-field was created which contained program attractors at pre-determined coordinates across the scheme. This dynamic field was linked to the transitional states of the generated modules, thereby determining the concentration and scale of programmatic spaces across the scheme. As the operative and generative proposals were linked it was possible to produce a series of iterative schemes in order to develop and explore specific spatial relationships, for example testing integration of the building with a certain site strategy and ground condition, or introducing a passive ventilation strategy to control the internal environment.

This study was more concerned with the development of design techniques within the digital environment than manufacturing and production techniques. However as part of the investigation a series of rapid prototyped models were printed using an SLS machine so that the physicality of the modeled spaces could be understood. This also provided a physical record of the iterative changes within the systems as they were developed.

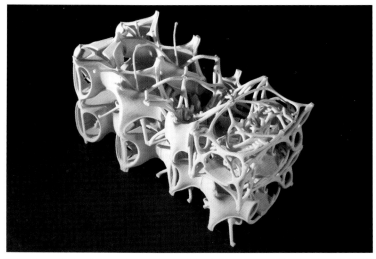

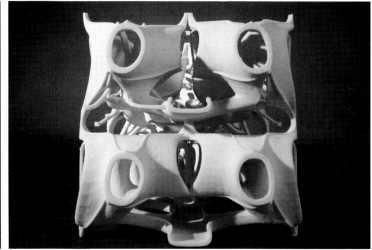

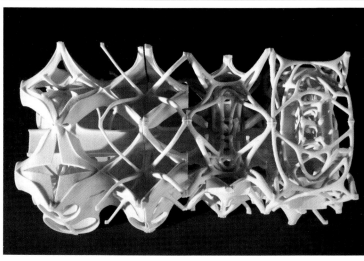

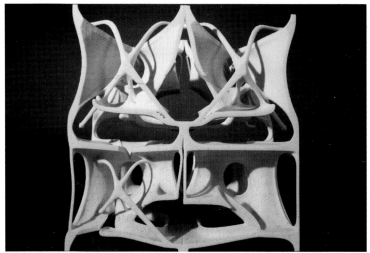

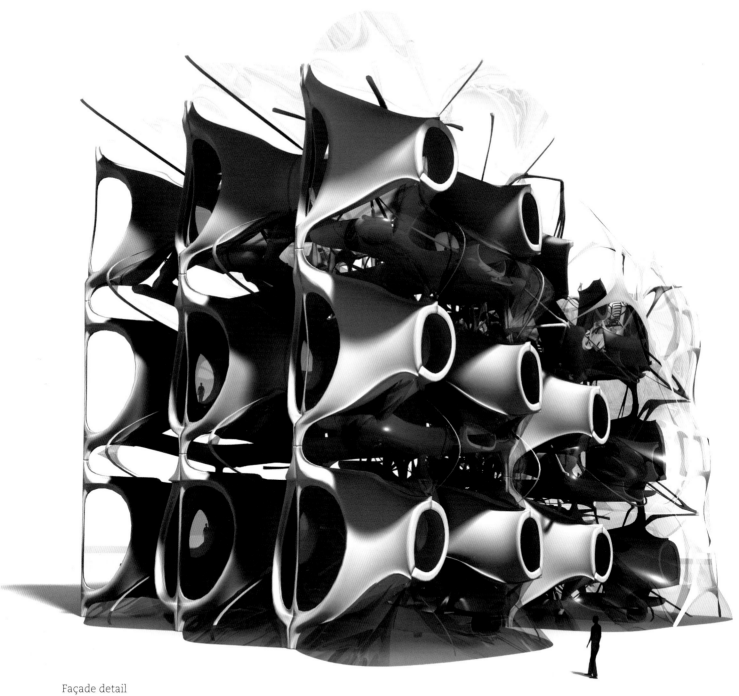

Façade detail

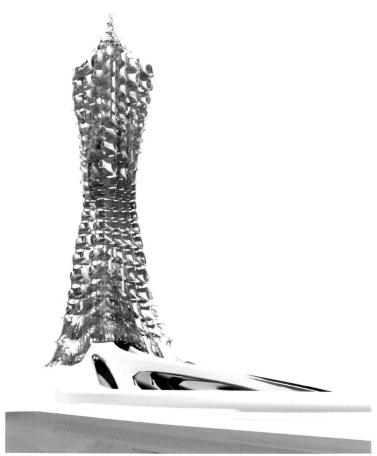

Landside elevation

Waterfront elevation

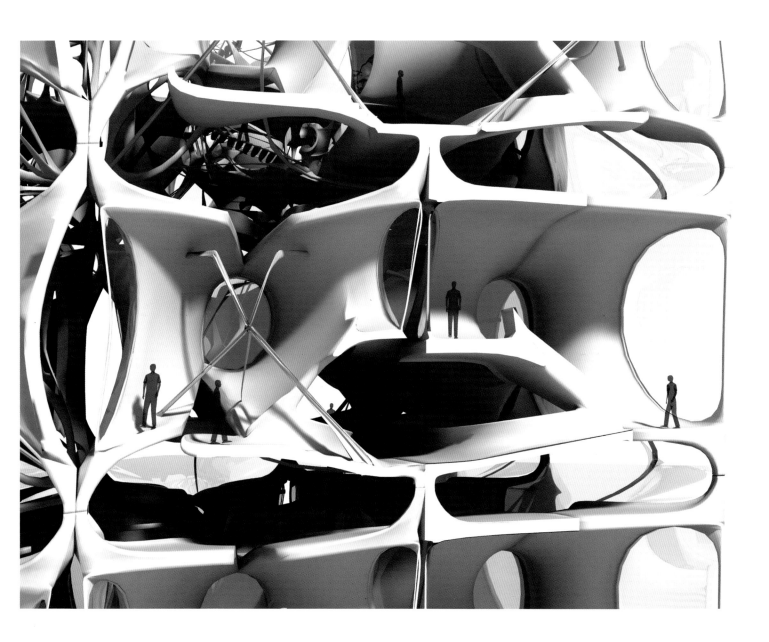

Section detail

Sorrento Bathing Platform

This is a modern re-interpretation of Victorian bathing; a platform inspired by programmatic studies of bathing areas in Sorrento, Italy. The forms of the platform were derived from studies of aquatic shells and skeletons combined with a fluid dynamic system to mimic water in a computer environment. The smooth transition from shops and restaurants, to individual paddling pools and areas for swimming, produce spaces of surprise and delight in the interstitial conditions.

The scheme contains both "generative" and "operative" systems which combine to produce the overall spatial configuration of the proposal.

The "generative" systems of the proposed bathing deck are composed of three basic modules which fit together in a linear fashion. These each support an extreme of a programmatic activity which is contained in a form produced through a combination of MEL-scripting and sub-division modelling. The scripting elements of this process were achieved through the integration of natural generative algorithms, in this case those associated with natural shells and carapace forms. Once modelled in their basic state the three individual modules were developed into a single transitional system so that they became indistinguishable parts of a smooth spectrum of different spatial possibilities. Careful development of this "blending" process allowed all these different tectonic configurations to be inhabitable spaces which support a wide and varied range of different programmatic activities.

The "operative" systems of the proposed bathing deck were produced through the manipulation of a dynamic fluid-field. Two "attractors" representing different programmes were passed through this field and the recording of the fluid-field's movements was then linked to both the physical position and the transitional state of each module. This allowed a series of iterative proposals for the bathing deck to accommodate specific activity combinations or a specific ground condition on the coast.

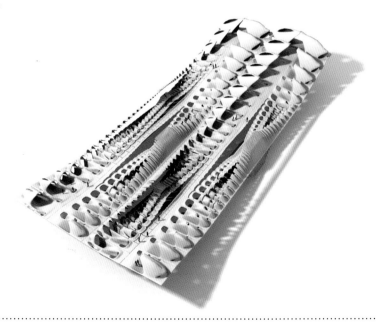

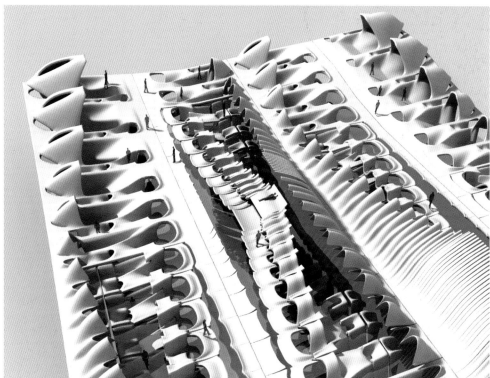

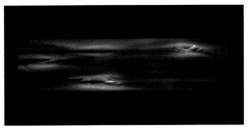

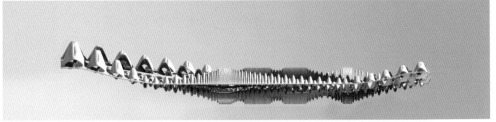

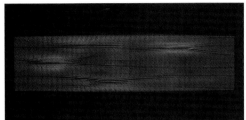

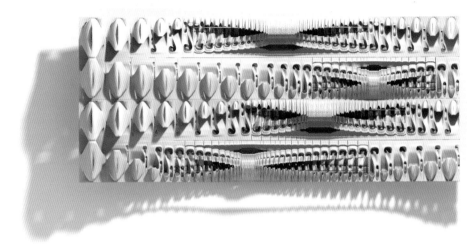

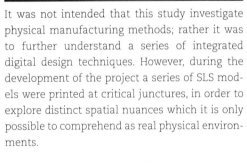

It was not intended that this study investigate physical manufacturing methods; rather it was to further understand a series of integrated digital design techniques. However, during the development of the project a series of SLS models were printed at critical junctures, in order to explore distinct spatial nuances which it is only possible to comprehend as real physical environments.

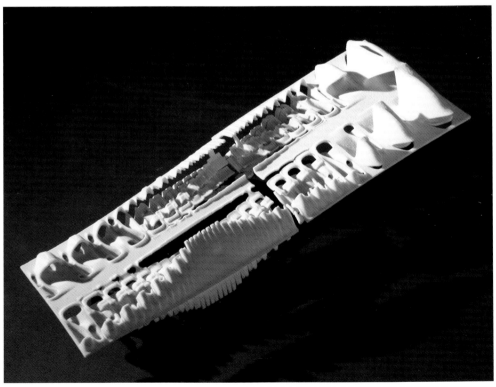

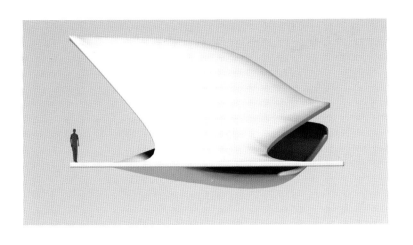

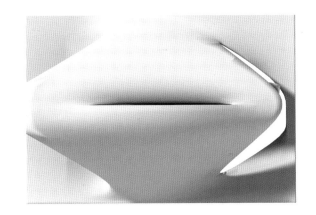

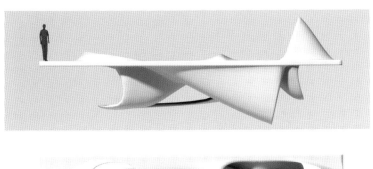

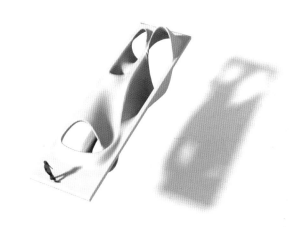

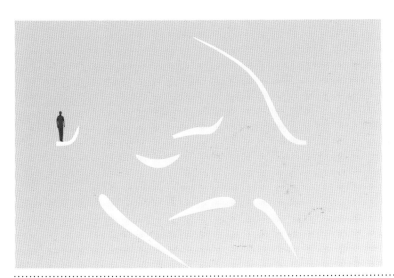

Elena Manferdini - Alexis Rochas
Vision Wall

Vision Wall is part of an extensive research on the role of scripting, fabrication and new material affect that SCI-Arc is leading in the field of architectural education.

Not dissimilar from Escher illustrations, the installation was designed following general rules of planar tessellation.

The design of the components was obtained running a script that blended two primitive figures along the axial plane of the wall with no overlaps and no gaps. A basic dia-grid anchored the size and the rhythm of each cell. The script was not based on the logic of the Penrose algorithm, which relies on 2 modules to tile the entire plane. Instead the script was engineered to follow a linear deformation of one cell into another. Therefore each component interlocked perfectly with each other into the grid but was different from the surrounding ones. As a result of this variation the final mathematical drawing displayed a tension between the visibility of the figure and the logic of the field. This initial two-dimensional plane was then used to create a system of three-dimensional cells and Boolean openings that constituted the final wall. Constructed by a total of 53 self supporting folded cells complexly connected together, each cell was obtained by 3 custom laser cut panels. The plastic used to build the components was laminated with 3M radiant foil, a light polarizing surface treatment that changes its color depending on the viewing angle of the surface. The highly faceted geometry of the wall along with the optical material laminated on its surface created a deep play of reflections and chromatic effects. The surrounding images that are reflected by the radiant facets interfere with each other to crate fantastic distortions of the light colors into an array of different shades.

Vision Wall was fabricated by a team of SCI-Arc students who contributed to the cost analysis, structural behavior, unfolding and laser cutting of the wall. Students were exposed to a broad range of experiences in this workshop leading to a better understanding of the potential relationship of design and fabrication logics.

Instructors: Elena Manferdini, Alexis Rochas
Students: Loke Chan, Christy Coleman, Robbie Eleazer, Sona Gevorkyan, Kristofer Leese, Jaitip Srisomburananont, Jairo Vives

Vision Wall was presented in Florence, Italy between the 9th and 17th of July 2009. It was created by a team of seven SCI-Arc students lead by Elena Manferdini and Alexis Rochas.

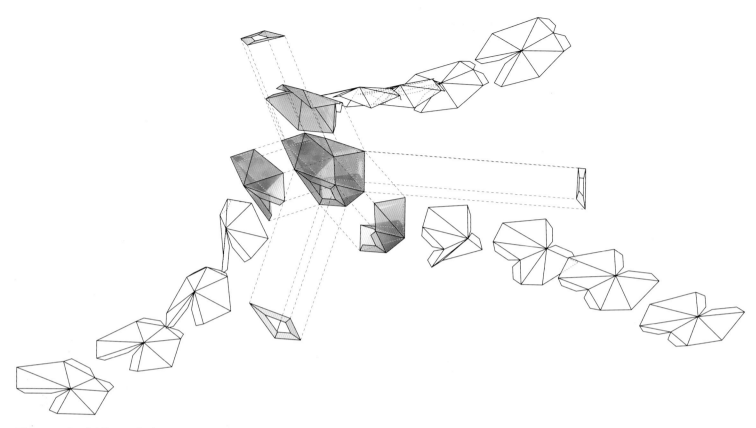

Diagram of unfolding techniques of each cell into planar elements

Assembly process of the 53 cells on site

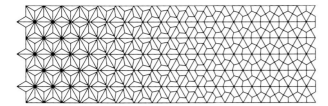

Original scripted line work

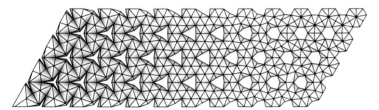

Initial three dimensional translation

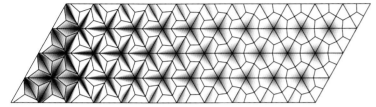

Final pattern with modular gems

Scripting blending primitive figures along the longitudinal axis of the wall

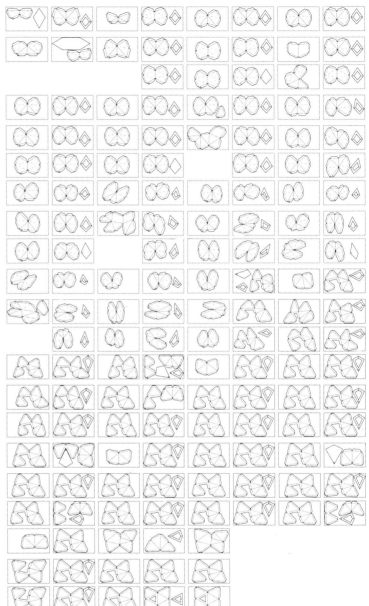

Unfold drawings of the 53 cells ready for the laser cutter

Caterina Tiazzoldi
Parametric Bookshelves

Parametric Bookshelves, designed by Caterina Tiazzoldi, uses advanced digital techniques developed by the designer as director of the Advanced Research Lab NSU at the School of Architecture at Columbia University to achieve a formal exploration of new configurations of the same bookshelf.

Parametric Bookshelves was presented at the Young Talent Selection by Giulio Cappellini at the Temporary Museum for New Design During Milano Design Week.

Each customer introduces data (length, height, preferred colors) and the parametric system responds by automatically changing some of the attributes (depth, thickness, color saturation). In this way each customer is assured of a unique configuration. Parametric Bookshelves helps develop and produce an infinite number of unique pieces, tailored to the customer's requirements, using a single model. Each element composing Parametric Bookshelves is defined by three attributes affecting Parametric Bookshelves' configuration. Each Parametric Bookshelf is provided with a code as a customer warranty of the uniqueness and originality of the piece.

The application of a large number of iterations to a limited number of rules leads to a level of formal complexity and sophistication which it is impossible to obtain from traditional processes. The vision is not only to customize a piece. Parametric Bookshelves transform the production process.

Desgin: Caterina Tiazzoldi
Design Team: Lorenza Croce, Dora Keller
Visualization and photographs: Lorenza Croce, Sebastiano Pellion di Persano

Given reality

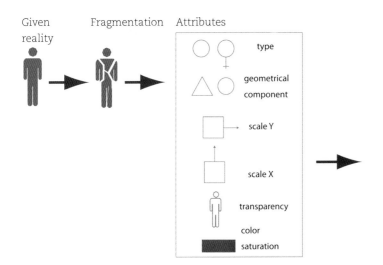

Fragmentation

Attributes

- ◯ ◯ type
- △ ◯ geometrical component
- ☐ → scale Y
- ☐ ↑ scale X
- 🧍 transparency
- 🧍 color
- ▮ saturation

Operation organizing the attributes

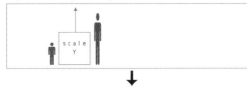

rotate
scale
change transparency
duplicate
change color
translate

rules organizing the opperations

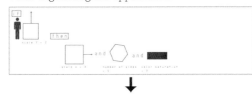

if / then
do / while
until
and

system organizing the rules

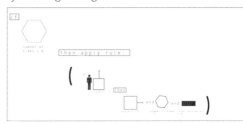

l system
neural network
complex adaptive systems
responsive devices

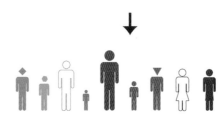

Concept - adaptable components

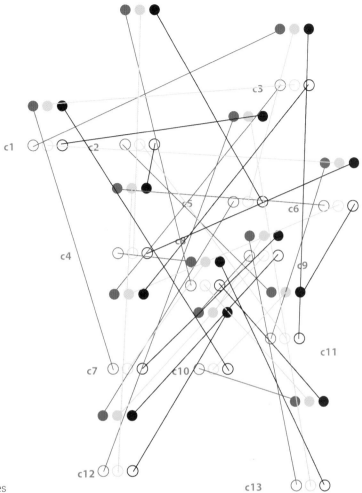

Legend:
- ● affecting
- ○ affected
- ● thickness
- ● length
- ● color

Node labels: c1, c2, c3, c4, c5, c6, c7, c9, c10, c11, c12, c13

thickness

c1 - c7	c8 - c4
c2 - c8	c9 - c13
c3 - c1	c10 - c9
c4 - c6	c11 - c2
c5 - c12	c12 - c5
c6 - c11	c13 - c10
c7 - c3	

length

c1 - c3	c8 - c7
c2 - c4	c9 - c10
c3 - c5	c10 - c11
c4 - c12	c11 - c2
c5 - c13	c12 - c9
c6 - c1	c13 - c8
c7 - c6	

color

c1 - c10	c8 - c13
c2 - c5	c9 - c7
c3 - c11	c10 - c12
c4 - c2	c11 - c6
c5 - c1	c12 - c9
c6 - c4	c13 - c8
c7 - c3	

Rules controlling the changes

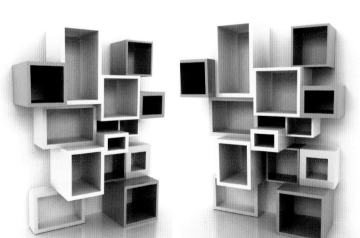

Caterina Tiazzoldi
Parametric Stalactites

Parametric Stalactites is the new design proposal from Caterina Tiazzoldi / Nuova Ordentra for a luxury Italian shoe brand. It has been conceived as an adaptable layout for a shoe store.

The Parametric Stalactites design derives from a unique parametric digital model that can achieve different configurations. All the surfaces are conceived as an assembly of 45 × 45 cm 'smart parametric tiles' responding to the different spatial requirements of the various store locations. Each tile can be more or less extruded according to the size of the store and the quantity of shoes on display.

The level of extrusion also defines the level of intensity and saturation of the space, and the entire surface is realized in a reflective resin, increasing the labyrinth effect of the space.

The model of Parametric Stalactite has been developed with a software application allowing the designer to connect the length and the density of the extrusion with the distance between the extremities of each stalactite.

Parametric Stalactites is a design tool developed to deal creatively with the complexity of today's cities. The project is characterized by Caterina Tiazzoldi's strong interaction between advanced digital research in architecture, developed in the academic and scientific field, with ten years' experience in the design of products and interiors.

Parametric Stalactites engages the concept of repeatability, adaptability, recognition and variation and develops a deep understanding of needs of contemporary commercial modules and their requirements to respond to different contextual conditions. It reflects the idea of adaptable components developed by Caterina Tiazzoldi in which a single component (in this case the stalactite module) is able to reconfigure itself to respond to different space conditions.

Desgin: Caterina Tiazzoldi
Interior designer: Caterina Tiazzoldi
Design team: Lorenza Croce
Visualization and
photographs: Lorenza Croce, Sebastiano Pellion di Persano

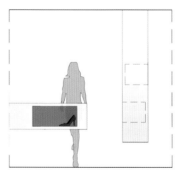

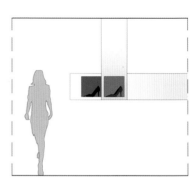

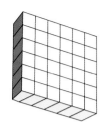
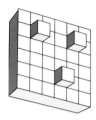
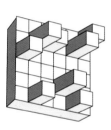
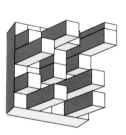
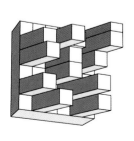

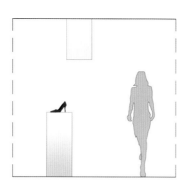
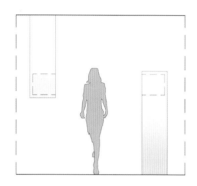
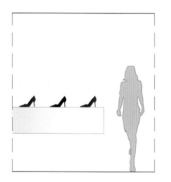
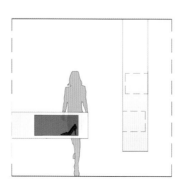

Caterina Tiazzoldi + Eduardo Benamor Duarte
Porcupine

Porcupine is an adaptable chair for waitng areas in hotel lobbies, restaurants and airports. Inspired in the fractal growth of a shell, it is realized in felt and fiber-glass.

Its design has been generated with a parametric logic (deriving from a Grasshopper application) that allows it to be reconfigured in accordance with the location and the user's inputs. Customers can control the form, the level of proximity between the different seats and the height modulation.

The prototype of the Porcupine configuration has been expressly designed for the reception space of the Altis Hotel in Lisbon. The installation emphasizes the question of the relation existing between the proliferation of abstract geometrical configurations and their becoming object or space through material implementation. It engages the difference between an iteration based on an abstract geometrical model that can be downloaded and repeated in any part of the globe, and the resistance of the specificity of material materiality to such a temporal contraction.

By taking a glimpse at the typical Rhino tool "Throw Curve along Curve", Porcupine transforms abstraction into design. Porcupine is realized with 40 sheets of felt supported by a fiber glass skeleton. The sheet heights vary from 68 to 30 cm while their spacing shifts according to the pressure of the body's weight or the proximity of a group of sheets.

The design for the porcupine seat is processed through the iteration and transformation of a single component. Porcupine Parametric Model varies in accordance with three inputs. The first controls the path and therefore the plan of the design, the second controls the height of the sheet of felt and the third input controls the spacing of the components.

The selection of the material become the unique condition to actualize geometry: It is by throwing felt, and not wood or steel, that the porcupine becomes a piece of design. What previously was an abstract procedure acquires the capacity to change the matter's performance.

Desgin: Caterina Tiazzoldi + Eduardo Benamor Duarte
Design team: Tania Braquino, Mauro Fassino, Katy Seaman
Photographs: Sebastiano Pellion di Persano

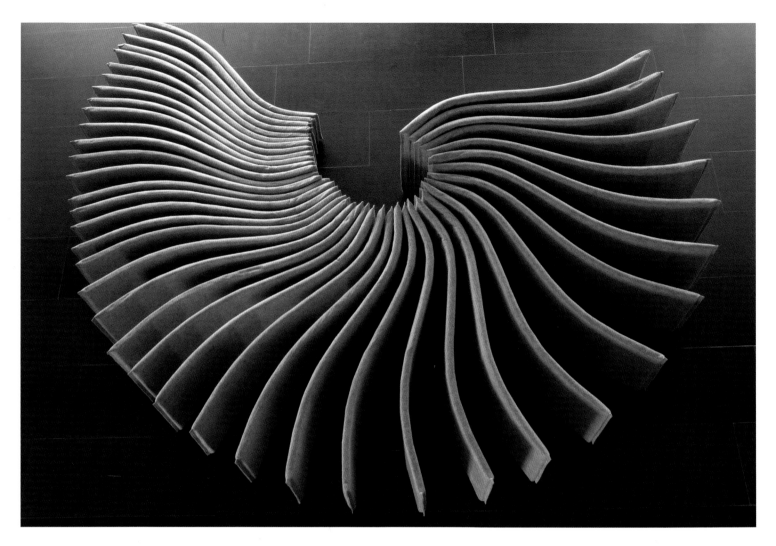

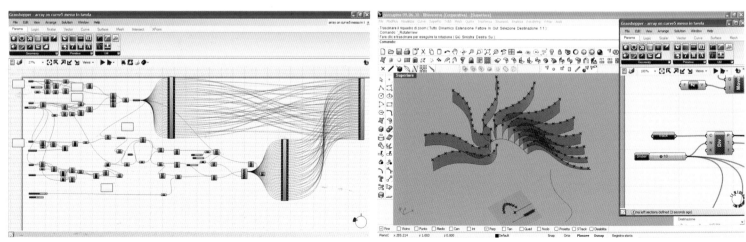

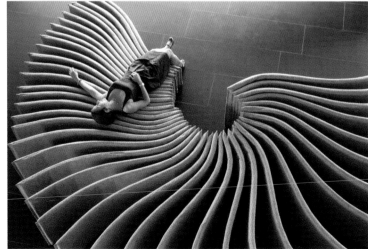

Emergent / Tom Wiscombe
Novosibirsk Summer Pavilion

This Pavilion design is the result of research into grid-stiffened shells. Grid-stiffened shells (a.k.a. gridshells), prevalent in 1950s-60s engineering masterworks by Nervi, Otto, Fuller and Candela, were part of a lineage of experimentation into material intelligence and analogue shape computation leading all the way back to the Gothic era. The elegance of these structures is a function of their controlled curvature which is generated using form-finding techniques as well as their patterned relief which reduces weight while increasing stiffness. These solutions, while efficient and elegant, were often limited by the modern paradigm and its tendencies toward formal purism on the one hand and structural expressionism on the other.

In the contemporary digital environment, the grid-stiffened shell is newly relevant. The re-examination of the grid-stiffened shell accepts the material sensibility of this earlier work while questioning its monotonous pattern geometry and tendency toward universal forms. This proposal for the Novosibirsk Pavilion is based on the simultaneous response of pattern to surface curvature and force pathways, generating a highly varied and informed structuration. Variability in pattern morphology, density, and depth allow for a localized structural tuning which would be impossible with an invariant pattern logic. Ultimately, limitations of traditional form-finding, where structures tend toward funicular forms, are lifted, and more complex surface shapes begin to be possible. Form-finding, no longer a determinant of global geometry, becomes a technique for optimizing regions of geometry in a larger structural ecology.

Design team: Tom Wiscombe, Kevin Regalado, Chris Eskew, Gabriel Huerta
Client: Novosibirsk Municipal Government
Location: Novosibirsk, Russia, 2007

The pattern logic of the stiffeners was critical for the spatial sensibility of this project and it was painstakingly developed as a hybrid of several shape grammars and computational techniques. A base subdivision of the surfaces was achieved based on curvature where pinched or twisted regions of the surfaces were broken down into smaller and smaller quadrilateral cells. A routine for transforming this subdivision into a branching logic was developed in order to generate a more complex and robust network of structural pathways, one which could be easily re-adjusted based on engineering information. Long beam-like regions of stiffeners began to emerge with less dense infill areas interconnecting them, together creating what we now refer to as beam-branes.

Beam-branes, first explored in Dragonfly, are smooth but highly varied structures which transform from beam to membrane and back again in response to local stress conditions.

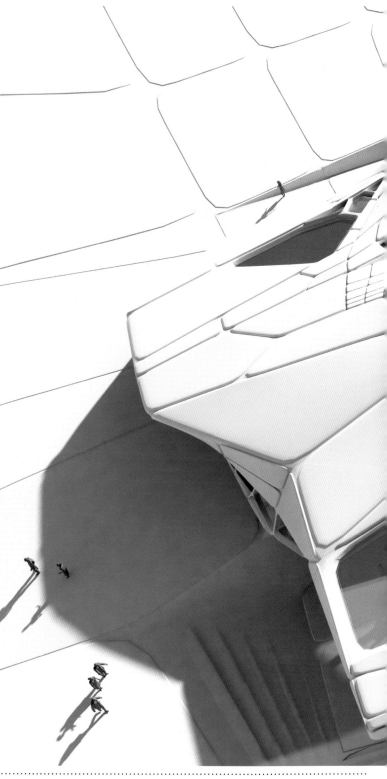

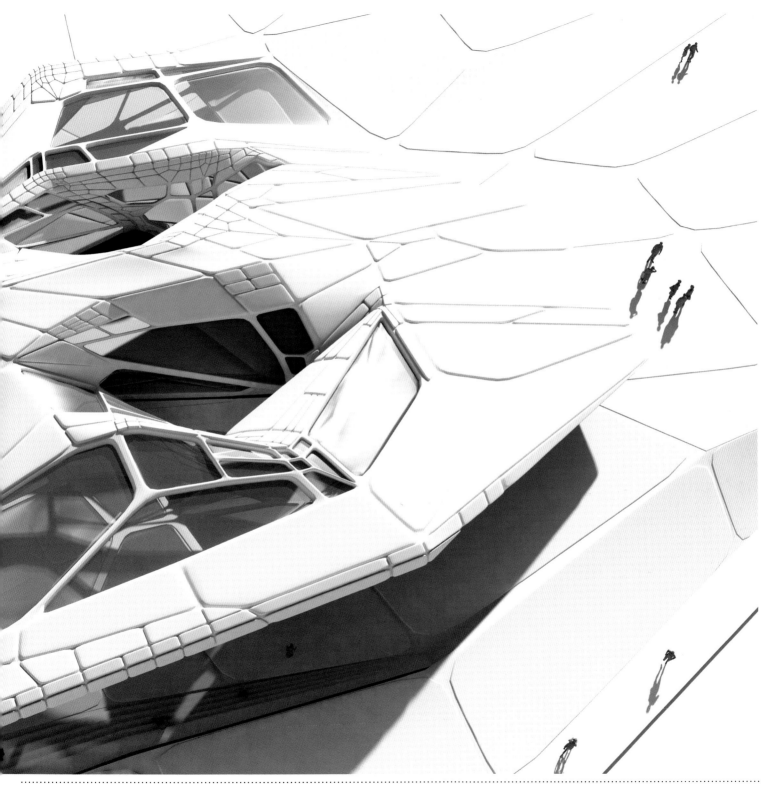

This project was conceived as an opportunity for two related but narrowly engaged techniques, geographic information systems analysis and digital fabrication, to be integrated in the production of architectural form and ornament through digital fabrication techniques and input from data environments. The assumption of such integration is that the result, rather than being a conceptual or otherwise generative idea that is realized through an accommodation of tool and technique to a projective end, would emerge from the combination of techniques, as a synthetic investigation of the ability of disparate tools to inform design. As such, the project was consciously situated within the bourgeoning climate of real-time, information-driven, communicative and digitally founded architecture.

This project investigated wireless internet connectivity and router usage across Columbia University's Morningside campus, using a sampled dataset of 270 router access points taken during the course of finals week (6-13 December 2008). The project had two primary goals. One was to design and fabricate a prototype architectural object that uses the environmental datascape produced by this space of wireless connectivity as a geometrical infrastructure for design, but also to contribute to this space in a reciprocal, public, physical alteration. Another is the further contribution to this space through an innovative approach to interactive representation of the dataset, using GIS to both produce the datascape informing fabrication and represent this datascape four-dimensionally. Techniques of investigation included GIS analysis and data representation, Flash animation with interactive components, parametric modeling, print-to-part modeling, and digital fabrication.

Design team: Brian Brush, Yong Ju Lee, Leah Meisterlin
Advisors: Phillip Anzalone, Sarah Williams

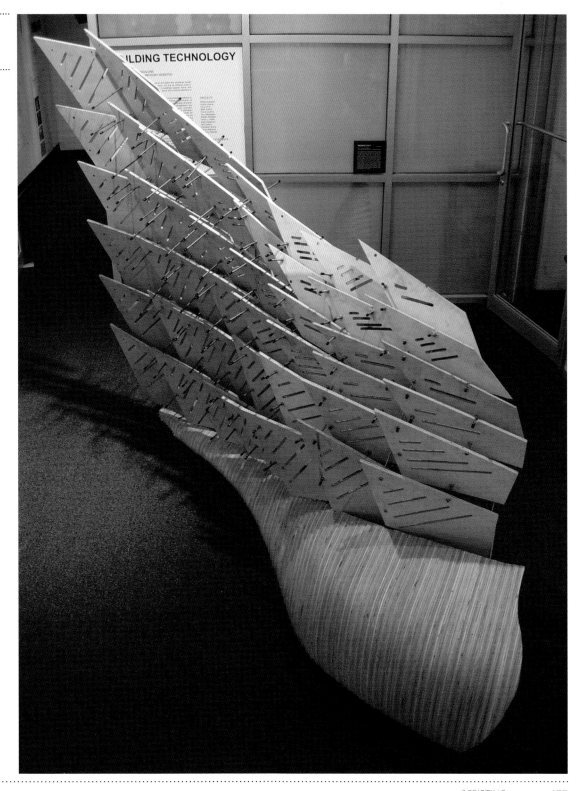

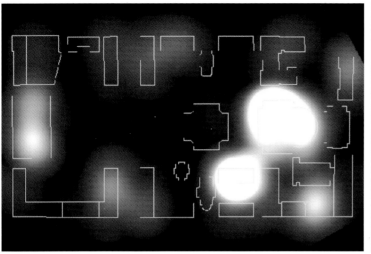
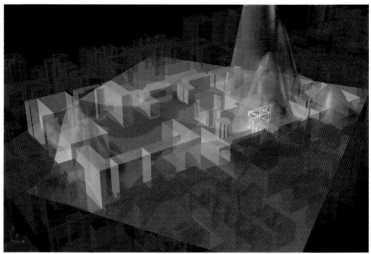
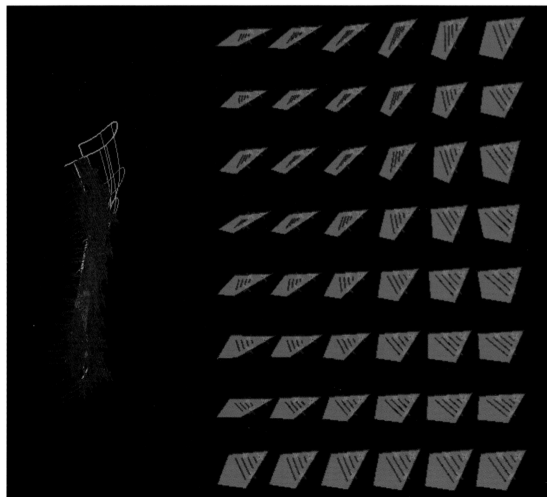

Brian Brush - Yong Ju Lee
Softshelf

Softshelf is inspired by the idea of creating a bookshelf that deforms the rational cellular grid in order to create a custom occupiable, differentiated, and soft space for the storage of books and other objects. It is fully customizable by manipulating five customer controls embedded in a parametric design system: overall size of the shelf, overall geometric effect of the shrinking and expanding of boxes, the strength of this geometric effect on the entire shelf system, the curvature shape of the shelf, and the stretched shape of the boxes. Softshelf takes advantage of the rigidity and fluidity of wood combined with the precision of CNC milling technology to create a monolithic and continuous form, sturdy yet geometrically complex, and ultimately innovative.

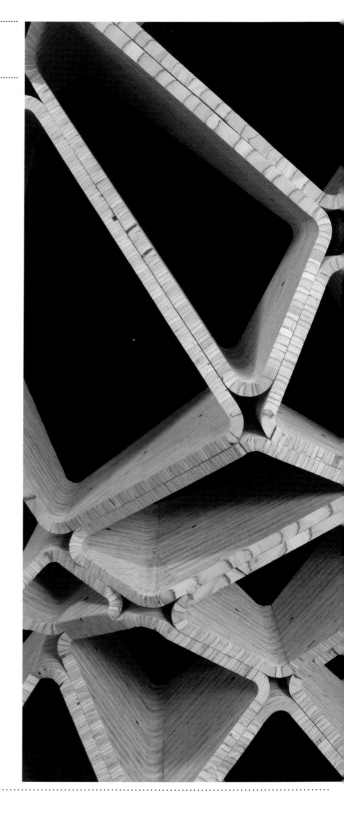

Elbo Group & Studio Lynn
Technicolor Bloom

Can construction enhance the sensuality of digitally designed architecture rather than compromise it? Technicolor Bloom, a kaleidoscopic construction prototype built from 1400 uniquely cut, flat plywood panels, proposes a potential answer. Designed and fabricated by Elbo Group: Brennan Buck and Rob Henderson with Studio Lynn at the University of Applied Arts, Vienna, Technicolor Bloom uses completely standard, scalable fabrication technology to produce doubly curved, digitally designed architectural form. It proposes a method and a set of aesthetic principles that extend the architectural potential of topological surfaces by incorporating traditional architectural parameters (structure, aperture, material) directly into the project's geometry. The result is a spatial study of the literal and phenomenal effects of a 3-dimensional pattern.

Given architecture's current obsession with all things iconic, the project produces more subtle relationships between figure and form. If an iconic building maintains a banal one-liner relationship between figure and form, Technicolor Bloom experiments with figure at its most undefined and indeterminate: patterns reinforce a certain geometry one moment and cloud it the next; figures emerge separately and simultaneously fuse together. The installation proposes a variation of architectural figure that never produces specific meanings, but evokes only loose, variable associations, remaining in the realm of affect.

Technologically, the project is comparable to the Technicolor film process which multiplied the visual intensity of film by superimposing three primary colors. The full saturation of the new technology and its short lifespan are both characteristics of contemporary phenomena which tend to shine brightly and burn out quickly. Technicolor Bloom embraces the "hot" geometry of subdivision surfaces and techniques of computation, but treats them as a given rather than as motivation. While adaptive tessellation algorithms were used to produce the initial patterns, parametric efficiency was suppressed in favor of precise control of visual effects. Generic structural efficiency was compromised as specific figures were identified and accentuated. Creases, converging centers, multiple scales of pattern and specific shapes were amplified through a series of iterations.

Elbo Group: Brennan Buck, Rob Henderson
Studio Lynn: Dumene Comploi, Elizabeth Brauner, Eva Diem, Manfred Herman, Maja Ozvaldic, Anna Psenicka, Bika Rebek
Photographs: Christof Gaggl

In addition to pattern variations, a series of techniques were used to multiply the affective qualities of the patterned surface. Surfaces were layered at various depths to produce moirés and other effects, while individual structural members were thickened or thinned to emphasize a network of figures which materialize and fade away within the overall pattern. The interior face and sides of each panel were painted gradient shades of magenta, blue and yellow, resulting in very different effects from each side and barely noticeable refracted colors on the white surfaces. The final three dimensional pattern shifts between alternating zones of sharp focus and vague blur, dense opacity and light porosity, or neutral whiteness and intense color, while surface curvature is alternately reinforced, suppressed, or conjured up from flat surfaces.

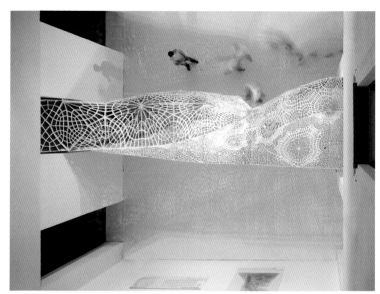

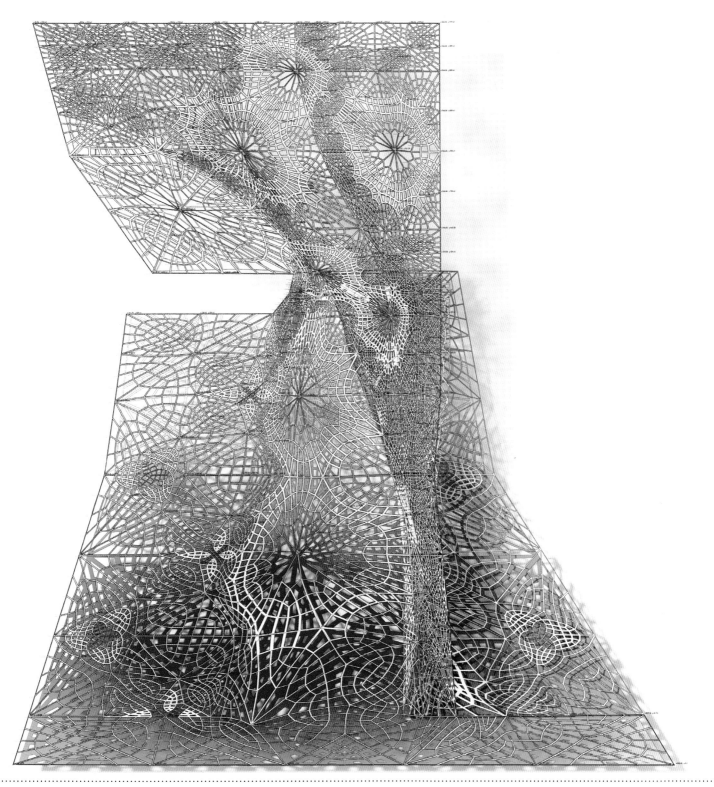

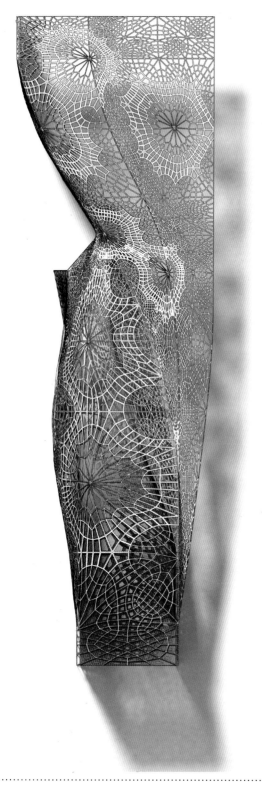

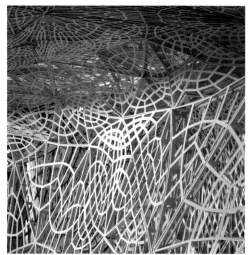

davidclovers & C.E.B. Reas
Yud Yud

Set within an old, medium density walking area of Wan Chai, Yud Yud stands in contrast to its surroundings. It builds upon the persona of the typical Hong Kong gate, pushing it toward the enigmatic. It is designed to be explored, touched and engage other forms of sight. Onlookers have been found rubbing it. It is an urban artifact not meant to be fully understood but to capture and interact with one's imagination.

Much of the visual and spatial ambiguity of the storefront lie in the tension designed between dimensions. They are blurred by both forming and etching an otherwise matte, Corian™ facade. The design engages the fourth dimension using animated LED lighting that produces a "twilight" effect. What appears a heavy, dense mass at moments reverberates between opaque, translucent and transparent; slowly pulsing etched lines appear and then fade out and disappear.

The storefront has both operable and fixed components. Each apply DuPont Corian Solid Surface™ to a wall sandwich composed of a welded steel frame and animated LED light system, sheathed in the front with treated plywood and in the rear with aluminum panels. The form of the storefront is simultaneously guided by the basic physics of door swings and a capillary-like plasticity. Mostly flat, the storefront uses 15cm to produce a very subtle pucker-like formation that spans across the doors. Each leaf is symmetrical and comprised of three facing pieces of Corian Solid Surface™ that are seamlessly joined together using a liquid form of the same material.

The unique application of Corian™ lies not only in its exterior use and translucency but the combination of techniques overlaid and oscillating across one another; each adroitly executed by SpeedTop Hong Kong. At one scale – the scale of the door – sheets are thermoformed, a pressure reflected in the subtlety of the design. At a smaller scale – that of the ornamental texture – CNC tool paths swim through the substrate to produce calligraphy-like formations. Each scale was designed three dimensionally and rides the limits of both the material and their processes.

Architects: davidclovers
Collaborating artist: C.E.B. Reas
Design team: David Erdman, Clover Lee, C.E.B. Reas, Fei Mui
Client: DuPont China/davidclovers
Location: Wan Chai, Hong Kong

Similar innovation is explored at the level of software programming. C.E.B. Reas' algorithmic line work (done with the Processing software) was a launching point for the collaboration with davidclovers. These dense, animated, line networks (typically shown in prints or on screen) evolve endlessly. They are software process as art.

Materializing these processes is the intersection point between Reas artwork and davidclovers' architecture. Line quantities are reduced and edited, but they are anything but stabilized. Each line is reactivated in multiple ways. First, by forming tool paths three dimensionally shadow lines vibrate and translucency varies. Cut into flat sheets of Corian™ prior to forming, each line is designed to capture artificial light and shadow; to snap in and out of focus. The overall "tooling" (using large 1.5 × 2 m wood molds) and forming was calibrated in relation to the CNC milled texture. Rather than encapsulating the texture between seams, it moves across them, bending and cornering. This requires an intricate three dimensional choreography of the CNC texture with each corresponding, formed, Corian™, sheet. Once they are aligned, this detail allows the texture to at once flatten the overall form (moving across edges), as much as augment it (deepening, drifting and fading in and out within it).

Finally, the wall section cavity and depth is regulated with each of these parameters. Where the texture is the furthest from the lighting it is the deepest and most intense, where it is the closest it fades out. This adds a delicate, effulgent quality to the slowly dimming and brightening LED's as their light courses through each three dimensional line – appearing as if the texture itself were phosphorescent.

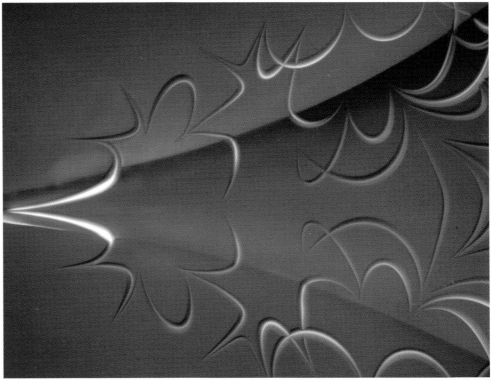

Tang & Yang Architects
Geno-Matrix

The central feature of this project is the development of a deformable structure that exhibits characteristics of a living organism, with the potential for evolution in a manner similar to the larger cityscape. It is named Geno-Matrix, a genotype driven structure for skyscrapers, which, according to the changing spatial requirements, can produce potentially infinite scenarios. It can deform itself at the molecular level, compatible with the unstable fitness of current inhabitation cultures. Rather than using the conventional architectural design process to generate the form, Geno-Matrix comes from genotype, phenotype, mate, crossover, morph, mutation and selection process. Geno-Matrix can be adapted to any context and multiplied throughout the urban space. In the design process, genetic computing and evolution techniques have been applied with the emphasis on their potential of creating forms that are useful in the production of architectural novelty and originality.

Inspired by Lego blocks, the strategy of Geno-Matrix is to do as much pre-fabrication as possible, under controlled factory conditions. Within a modular building system, large quantity of cubic units are fabricated and assembled into a lattice system.These units can be "pulled", "pushed" or "combined" in the lattice grid along the axis and form infinite typological features.

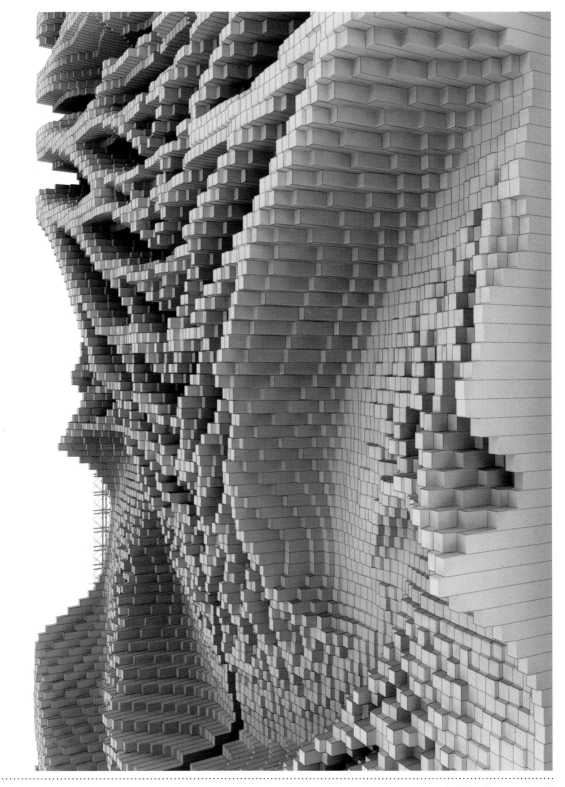

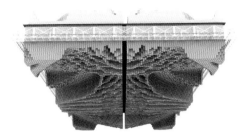

By changing local relationships of individual units, Geno-Matrix can achieve an emotional response similar to that realized by the culture icon or national symbol, though on a much larger scale. For instance, to reflect the social value, an ordinary "tree" pattern can be generated by moving the units along the normal axis. Organization patterns emerge at varying scales and hierarchies. Another example, the chaotic pattern of an "ocean wave" can be generated for a skyscraper, to function as a hotel on the beach.

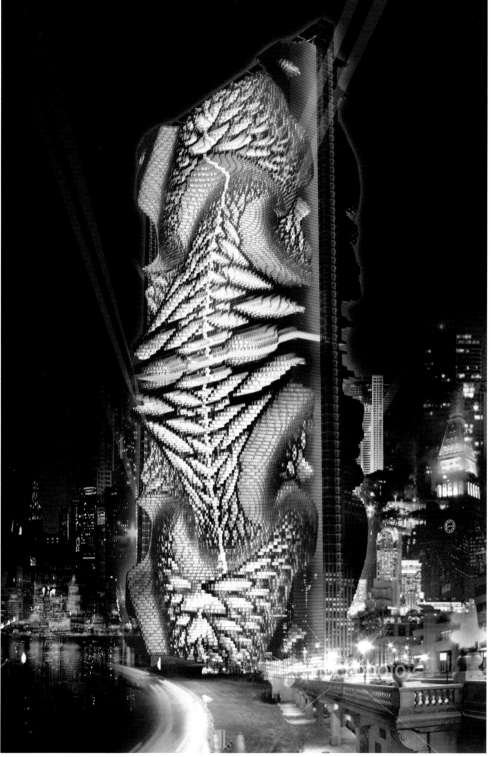

Generation 3
Offspring 126

Generation 4
Offspring 371

Generation 5
Offspring 406

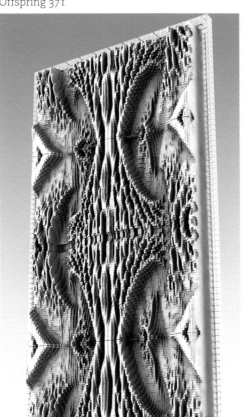

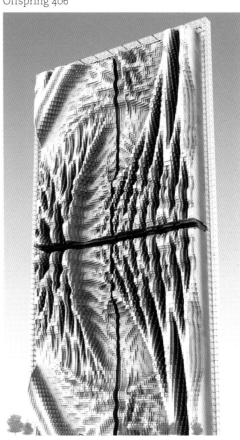

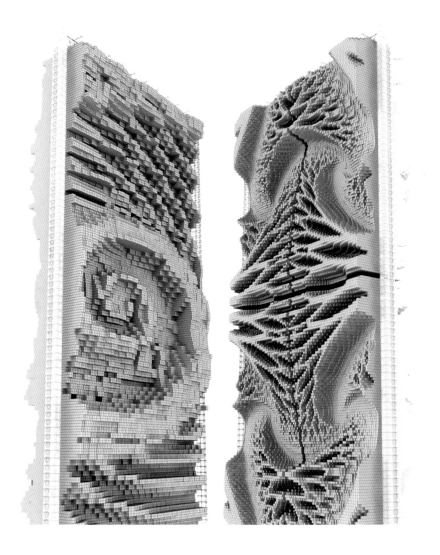

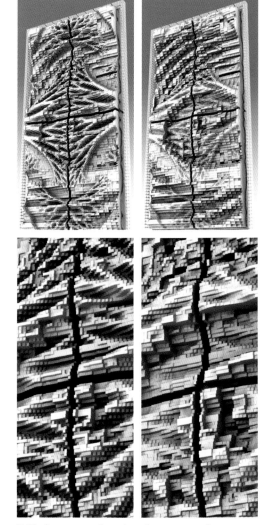

Stills from an animation that captured 500 spatial arrangements in 5 generations.

Assembly of cubic units into lattice

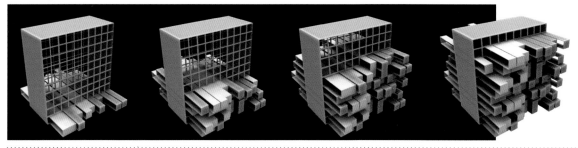

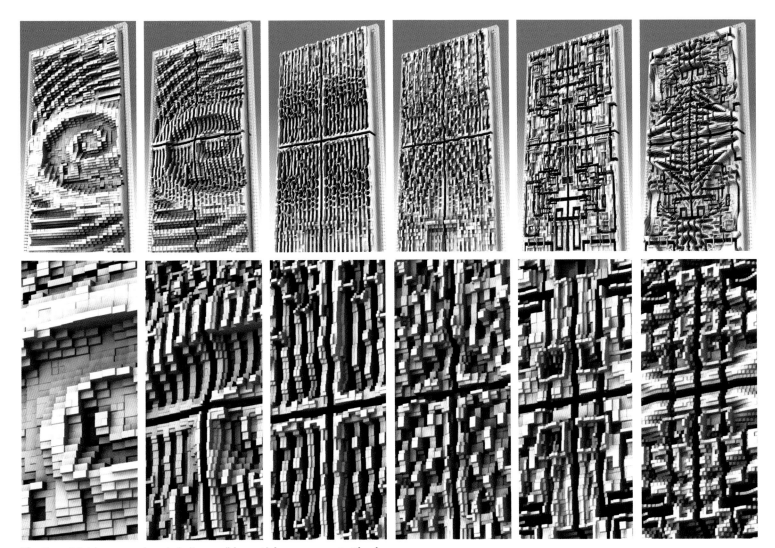

The Geno-Matrix can produce infinite possible spatial arrangements. The designers have applied evolutionary techniques allowing the design to evolve.

MESNE
Strange Attractor

This project, a wine tasting pavilion in South Eastern Victoria, is part of an ongoing study into the re-purposing of optimization and analytic tools as generative tools for architectural form-finding. The departure point is the idea of a Lorentz Attractor, which is an oscillation between two discrete points. The design team has used the Lorentz attractor as a diagram to organize and evoke a spatial experience of intimate distance that folds tasting into dining as a means to lubricate purchasing.

The interest in this project was to re-appropriate an engineering algorithm, bi-directional evolutionary structural optimization (BESO). The BESO process, which finds optimally-directed structural designs, begins with the provision of a maximum building envelope, design-specific points of loading and restraint, and the definition of 'non design' geometry that cannot be removed. An iterative process of structural analysis then begins followed by the deletion of under-utilized elements, during which the residual structure gradually evolves towards an optimum. In this way, the form of the pavilion emerges through the actions of a guided feedback loop. While recognizing the limits of optimization as a tool for architectural design, the designers believe that the outcome of this process does not reflect the single optimal response to a set of constraints but rather illustrates one possibility amongst an unspecified number of ways of not entering into fatal conflict.

What is most interesting about this process of form discovery is the negotiation between the positioning of structural "boundary conditions" and the design constraints of concept, planning strategy and site. The pavilion takes on form via the continual refinement of this negotiation through the incremental "tuning" of exogenous forces. A consistent connection is thus maintained between the artefact and the processes that bring it into being. Angular and tectonic on the exterior, internal spaces seamlessly unfold from floor to bar, wall to ceiling and structure.

Project team: Paul Nicholas, Tim Schork, Jerome Frumar, Scott Crowe, Matthew McDonnell

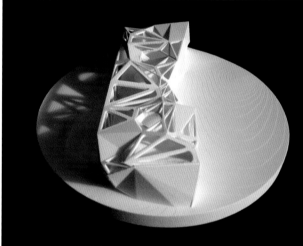

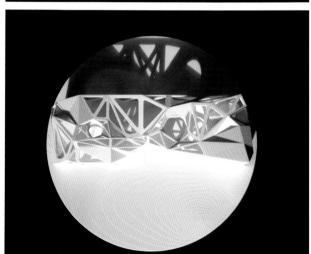

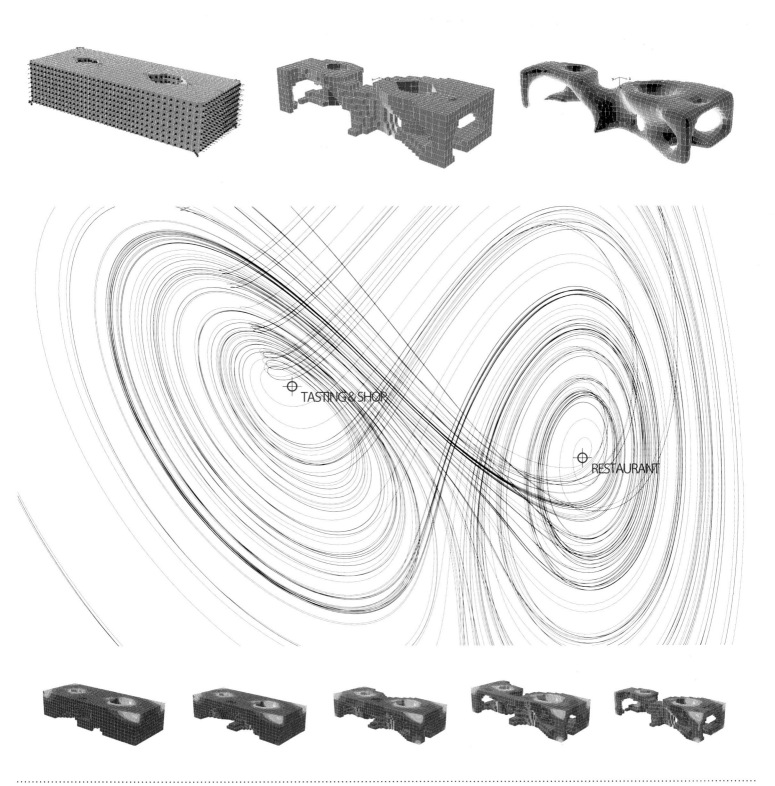

TASTING&SHOP

RESTAURANT

Digital Origami

A Japanese proverb says: *"If you encounter someone making many different things out of folded sheets of paper, do not lightly pass him by, but learn."*

The "first wave" of digital architecture broke in the mid nineties. 90 percent of all final projects at Chris Bosse's faculty consisted of hand-drafted plans on tracing paper and balsa wood models. Three years later, for his masters project, 90 percent of the projects presented were digital. The digital revolution happened fast. However, this first wave had no gravity, nothing for the senses and few constraints. Architecture was split between the digital visionaries and the 'real' architects who build. In today's second wave, 'the digital' is enabling designers to conceptualize and build in an entirely different way. The computer has bridged the rift between conceiving and building. Stuttgart's Mercedes Benz museum, for example, is no longer based on elevations and plans, but on a 3-dimensional, movement based, spatial experience. Skills at the interface of digital design and manufacture are what must be transmitted to the next generation of architects, as an experience. Anthony Burke's digital masterclass program at UTS has been doing this for several years now. They regularly invite guest lecturers for short but intensive masterclasses. This year's guest was Chris Bosse.

His masterclass avoided being another crazy flythrough rendering and concentrated on realizing concepts. The students were asked to research current trends in parametric modeling, digital fabrication and materials and apply this knowledge to a space-filling installation. The aim was to test the potential of a given module, copied from nature, to generate architectural space, assuming that the intelligence of the smallest unit dictates the intelligence of the overall system. Ecosystems such as reefs act as a metaphor for an architecture where the individual components interact in symbiosis to create an environment. In urban terms, the smallest homes, the spaces they create, the energy they use, the heat and moisture they absorb, multiply into a bigger organizational system, whose sustainability depends on their intelligence.

Design: UTS master class students with Chris Bosse
Lighting installation: ERCO
Chris Bosse
Partner /Architect
LAVA
Location: 72 Erskine, Sydney, Australia, 2007
Photographs: Contributed by the designers

Out of 3500 recycled cardboard molecules of only two different shapes the students created a mind-blowing reinterpretation of the traditional concept of space. The ordeal of dealing with pragmatics (including gravity), translated so dynamically that the project exceeded all expectations. Lighting by ERCO and an Acoustic installation by Joanne Jakovich enhanced the event. At the time of writing, 25 young architects were climbing through it upside-down, exploring the Cartesian space and interpreting their own 3d drawing into real 3-dimensional and physical space. Isn't that what architects do? Utilitas, firmitas, venustas... digitalitas. Vitruvius kept quiet about that one!

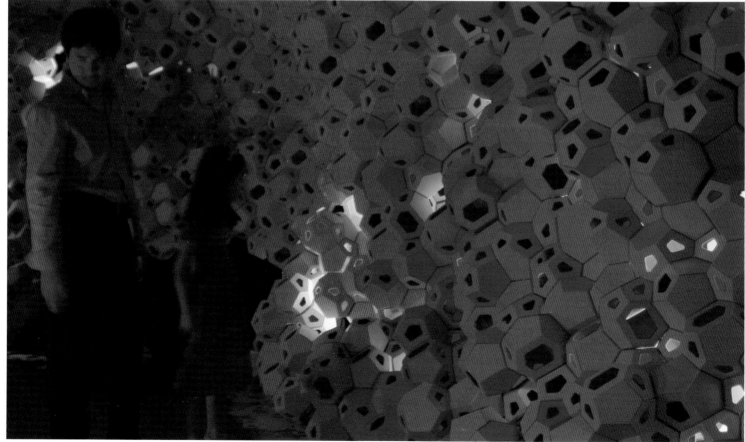

Supermanoeuvre + Kokkugia
Morphogenetic Lattice

A collaboration between supermanoeuvre and kokkugia, this project is an experiment in the effects created by morphogenetic algorithms. These algorithms are designed to generate ornamental distortions within geometry through the internal logic of cellular automata. A technique where a population of self-similar elements in space continually change their state based on the states of their neighbors in a feedback loop, giving rise to emergent patterns. The project is driven by a series of encoded procedures which build a hex-grid cellular automaton and a network of springs which drive the distortion of the more geometrically complex screen. The springs respond to the changing CA states and enable a non-hierarchical distortion of the network through the use of a non-linear physics solver. Accordingly the influence of an individual CA cell trickles through its neighbors influencing the geometry beyond its immediate adjacencies.

Design: Dave Pigram, Roland Snooks
Thanks to: Cory Clarke

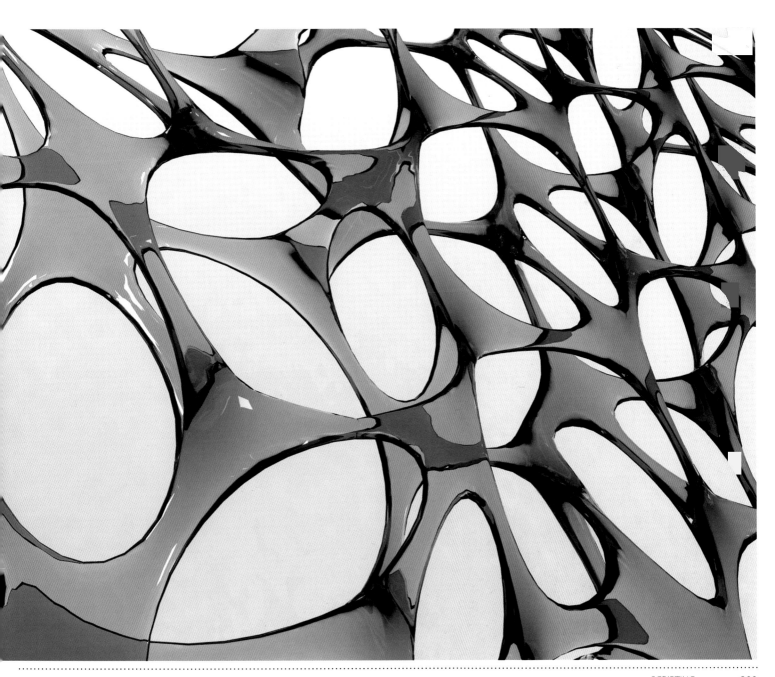

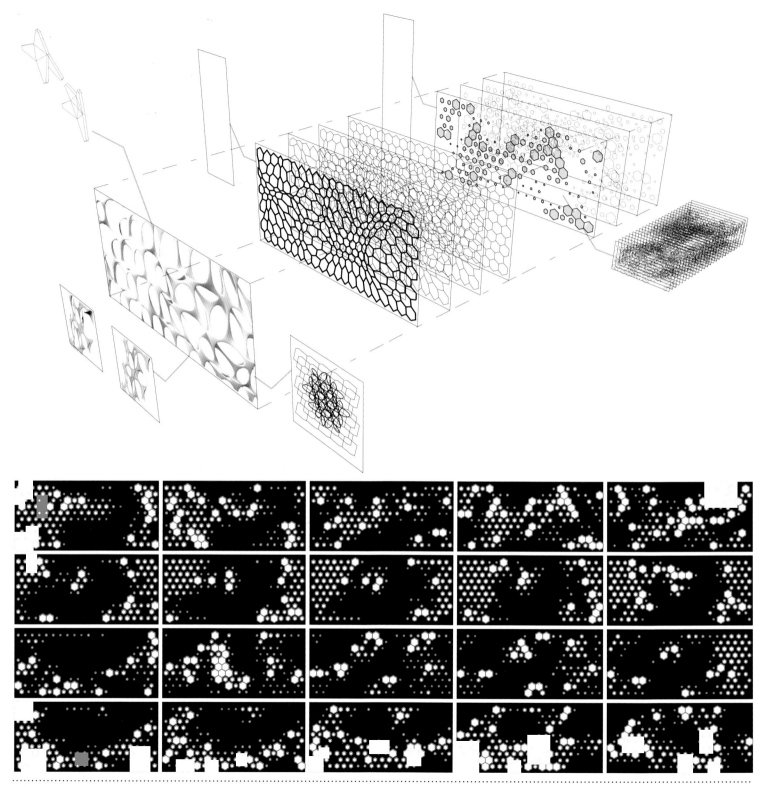

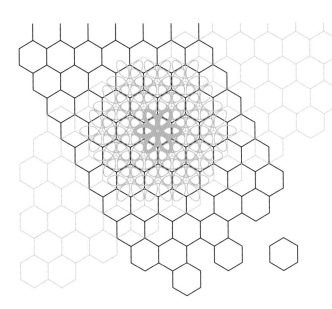

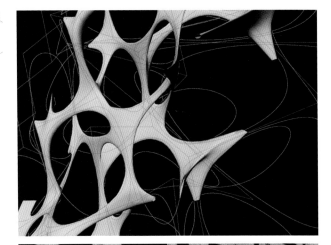

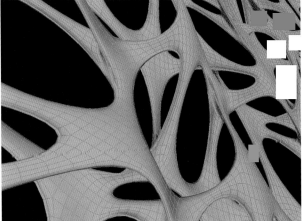

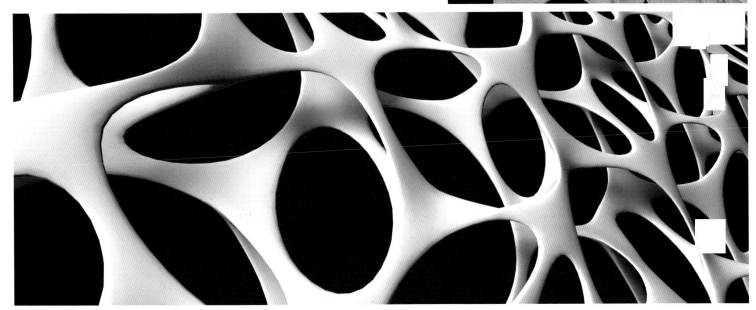

Supermatter

'Supermatter' is both a continuation of supermanoeuvre's broader research interest into systemic processes of formation, and an assessment of the capacity of contemporary prototyping technologies to elaborate thousand-year-old processes of fabrication.

Conceived as a family of objects cast in bronze, Supermatter explores the algorithm as a geno-typical morphology, where similarity across the collective is instilled through the instructions of assembly embedded within the algorithm as it operates on a discrete set of geometric aggregates. The input of geometry enables a speciation of each resultant object as the rules of growth and assembly are applied to the specific geometric constraints and potentials of connection particular to each aggregate primitive. Through changing either one or all of the primitives, or the generative rules of the Lindenmayer (L-System) combinatorial algorithm itself, differentiation across the population can be instantiated. The resultant objects, are indexed to both the rules and geometric laws of aggregation, and as such the character of similitude is enacted.

To this end, the project facilitates a shift to a new definition of the architectural model to be inclusive of comprehensive methodologies of spatial, formal and material distribution.

In realizing the final cast objects, samples of the computational process were selected for rapid prototyping (SLS). These 1:1 outputs were then used as positive forms in the preparation of casting moulds, a process which combined an accurate translation of the formal character and intricate detailing of the digital model with the specific material behavior of first molten and then thawed bronze.

Project team: Dave Pigram, Wes McGee, Iain Maxwell, Paulis Austrins, Zack Jacobson-Weaver, Brandon Clifford

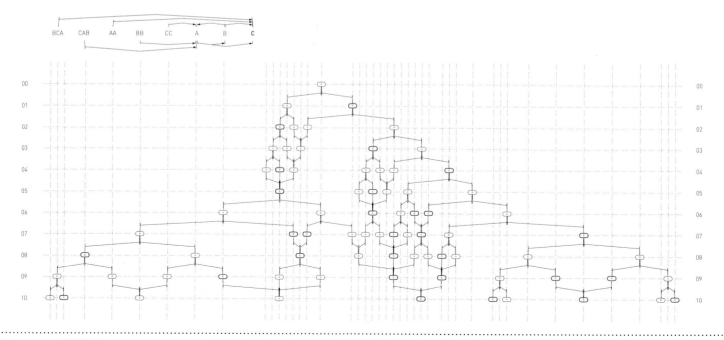

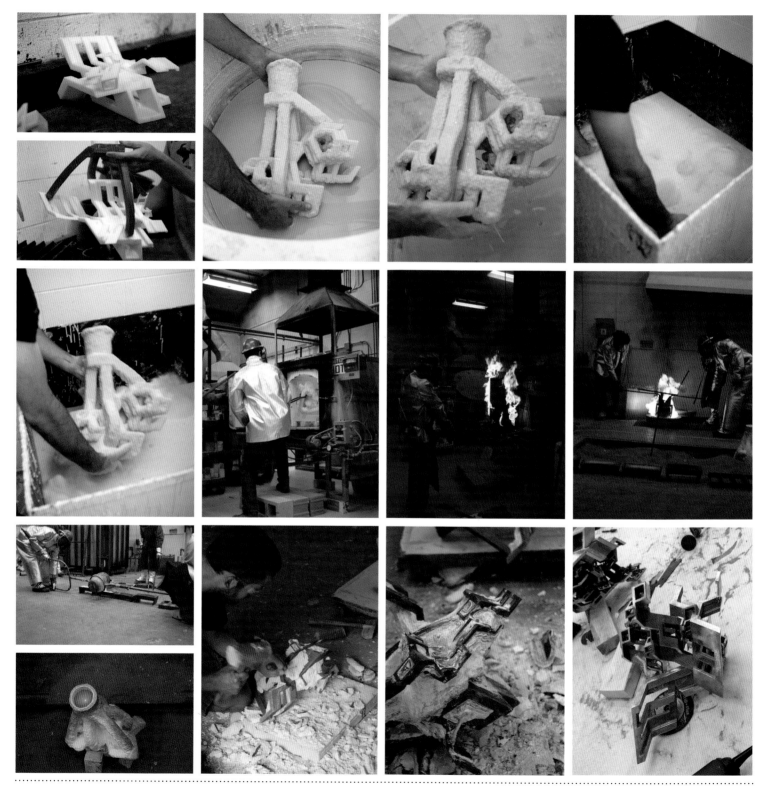

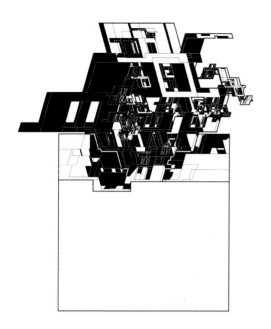

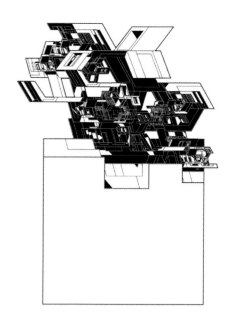

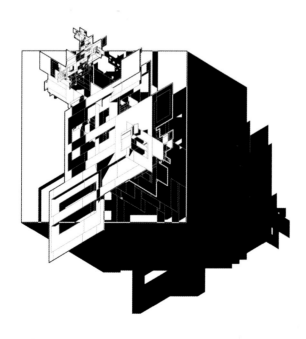

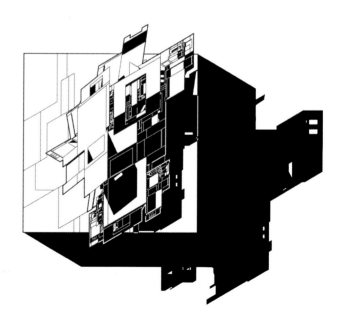

Supermanoeuvre
Proto-Synthesis & Trabeculae

The two projects, Proto-synthesis and Trabeculae, are here presented as a pair and respectively illustrate the genotypical and phenotypical aspects of supermanoeuvre's design approach.

Proto-synthesis (the genotype) is not a singular design project or curated artefact; rather it is an algorithmic strategy for the elaboration of a topologically rich and highly networked architecture. It is also the genome or operative-framework for the latter architectural project – Trabeculae. But here, Proto-synthesis has not been encoded with specific programmatic protocols to engender a specific programmatic effect and therefore remains typologically-free, and capable of multiple possibilities. Within the system, the very construction of architecture; position, scale, displacement, density, thickness, length and so on, are deeply embedded within the decision-making mechanisms of the algorithm, and are stimulated through both internal logics, and the discrete sampling and feedback of stimuli within the local environment.

Trabeculae (the phenotype) is an instantiation of the Proto-synthesis algorithms, achieving specialization enabled through embedding qualitative programmatic, situational and environmental design aspirations toward the reimagining of the central atrium office tower. Replacing the traditional operation of repetitive extrusion, the heliotropic branching system actively seeks out those areas within the zoning envelope with greatest access to daylight. Forking and swelling in response to varying light conditions the atrium is thus conceived as a site-specific network that traverses intelligently and freely from one façade to another. The atrium becomes the defining element of differentiation within otherwise normative floor plates.

Within the atrium a second order proliferation of the same system at a finer scale develops a structural meshwork - the Trabeculae. The swellings and coagulations of this topologically free structural network-within-a-network accommodate meeting & function rooms, bridges and communication stairs as well as supporting the atriums glazing.

Project team: Dave Pigram, Iain Maxwell, Brad Rothemberg, Ezio Blasetti, Jared Olmstead, Matthew Hall, Susan Teal

$$vect[Node_a] = \int_0^n unitVect[Member_n] \times EA[Member_n] \times \Delta L[Member_n]/sL[Member_n]$$

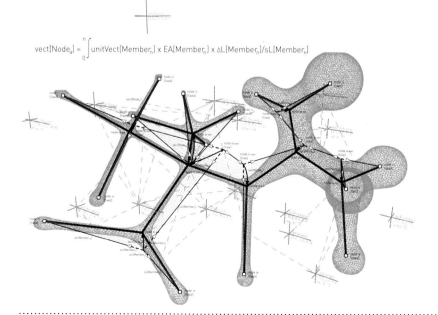

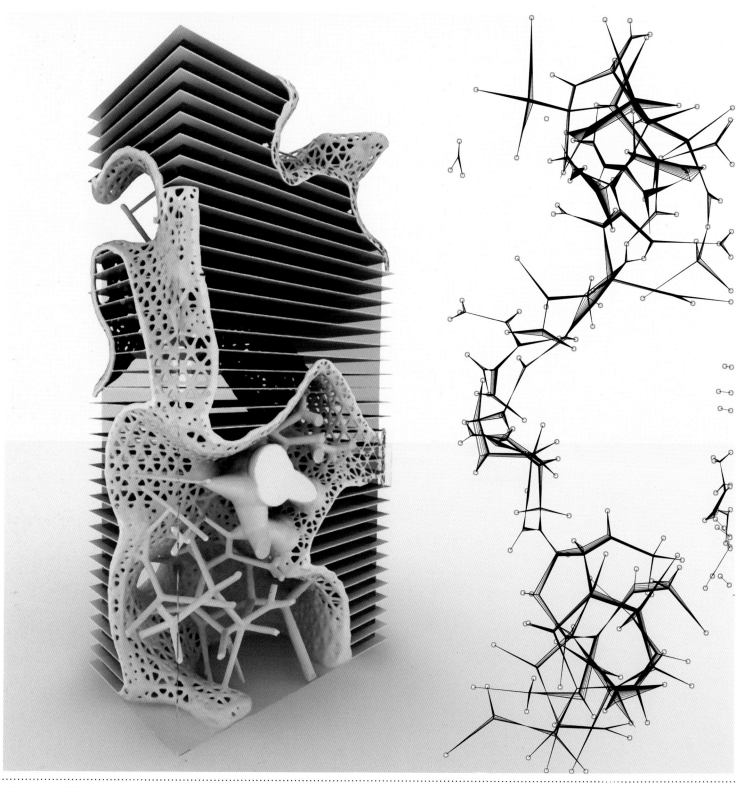

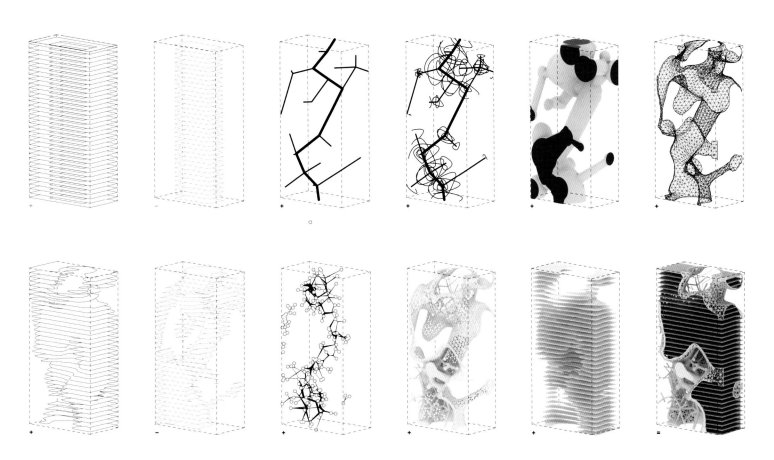

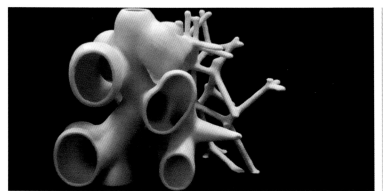

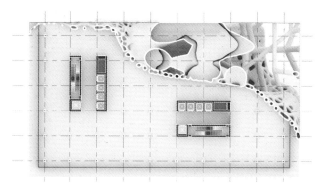

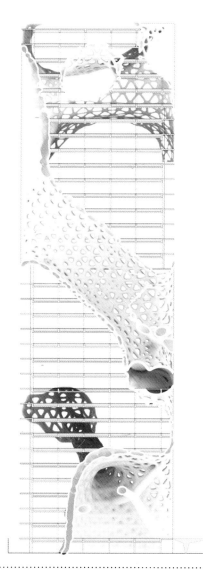

Inorganic Speciation: Matter, Behaviour and Formation in Architecture

Form is the primary instrument through which architecture engages with the world. It is this firmly held position that motivates supermanoeuvre to develop custom methodologies of formation that allow for the explicit and open-ended negotiation between multiple architectural intentions and the complex milieux within which they will operate. These methodologies are algorithmic in nature, primarily digitally enacted, and extend the capacities of the form-finding tradition within architecture through a decoupling of its processes from the limits of physics, enabling a broader examination of the number and nature of negotiable inputs. The abstract notation underlying these algorithms enables a meta-analysis of the formational processes, which has an accelerating influence on their evolution, as experienced within other fields of intellectual and artistic endeavour. Through the application of algorithmic notation, the conception of form-production within design shifts from object-centric applications of typology, to the speciation of mutable architectural models.

Architectural form is concerned with organization across multiple scales (programmatic, material and structural) enmeshed in a complex feedback loop with the forces, events and behaviors that simultaneously drive and are driven by them. The description of 'formation' through causal processes (morphogenesis) has been convincingly articulated by D'Arcy Thompson. He posited that 'form' could no longer be understood as an isolated, inert, or solely genetic event; but rather a generative process of transformation negotiated through an organism's internal constitution (DNA) and its adaption to a situation via the sampling of environmental, physical or material forces (feedback). The gift of form is both a *"diagram of the forces"*[1] that gave rise to it, and a critical, selective and adaptive process through which morphology sheds its 'generic' nature and attains a higher order of specialization. The more stable or recurrent of these specializations can be understood to have achieved the level of 'speciation'.

Matter, like architecture, is traditionally conceived of as benign, an underestimation that generally extends to all things lacking the motivations for life. In accordance with the contemporary understanding of formation, as exhibited in soap-film aggregations, snowflake crystals, and bee-cell morphologies, the property of 'body' is in fact driven by the action, or 'agency', of one molecule upon another while simultaneously negotiating internally produced (surface tension) and externally imposed (surface pressure) influences. Formalness is therefore not a latent property of the single molecule, but a collective and intelligent behavioural event. Thus, *"matter can no longer be seen as passive and 'dead.' it can sense and respond, in unpredictable ways, to its own condition and to external influence. The intimacy of the interaction of material with these fields is forcing a revision of the conception of matter and form as a separable duality."*[2] Supplant the term 'matter' with 'architecture' to yield a framework for supermanoeuvre's approach to design.

Collaboration with matter's computational abilities is a well-established trajectory within architecture; Gothic Cathedrals, Antonio Gaudi's hanging-nets and Frei Otto's seminal work on minimal surfaces all serve as preeminent examples. Similarly, traditional design methodologies frequently take advantage of the positive formal constraints of specific design mediums. Charcoal sketches, clay models and procedural methods such as folding, cutting or weaving, all provide a consistency of character via a delimited 'phase-space of possibility'. However, the limitation of analogue modes of computation in relation to broader architectural speculation is precisely their fixed relationship to immutable physical laws and material properties. Without the ability to expand, intervene-in or tune the parameters of form-finding techniques, architects are either forced into subservience to imperfect analogies between these factors and a larger set of extrinsic design intentions, or, must remain content to limit themselves to structural and material investigations. When executed digitally however, form-finding processes enable a greater incorporation of architectural constituency; programmatic as well as material design goals in negotiation toward the elaboration of architectural effect; spatial experience, ornament and performance.

Digital techniques, specifically algorithmic as opposed to parametric (associative) processes, allow for the non-hierarchical and non-linear (feedback) negotiation between mul-

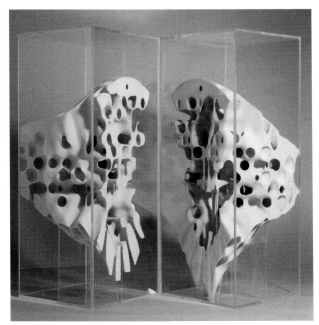

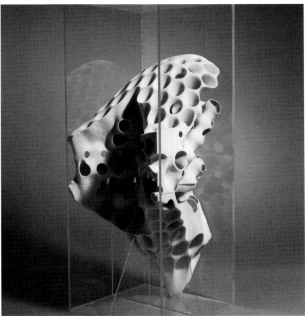

Iain Maxwell, Marga Busquets, Sebastien Delagrange
Adaptive Ecologies. AADRL. 2008
Housing protoype realized through reverse-engineering the
planning, spatial and circulation logics of Unite d'Habitation.
Increasing the proto-systems internal and context sensitive
behaviours, enables an expansion of the systems capacity
to produce more diverse apartment outcomes, whilst
embedding Le Corbusier's circulatory heirachies.

tiple factors; the topology of the system, its network of connections (physical, virtual or both), remains open and is able to self-organize. The conception of architecture as a collective organization driven through multiple agencies is more akin to the dynamics of complex natural systems than to conventional modes of design. For this reason, supermanoeuvre is consciously drawn to the modelling of the algorithmic processes that underlie biological and chemical phenomena, as opposed to the emulation of pre-existing geometries found within nature. Such fixed references, serve only to limit the capacity of the design process before it has even begun. Our interest therefore, rests firmly in the description of behaviors such as growth and change, mechanisms of feedback, and the transformative agencies such entirely syntactical models elaborate. This is a critical and conscious departure from graphical systems of representation, toward an active engagement with the protocols of 'making' that exist deep within all complex behavioral systems. The algorithm becomes the operative medium (descriptive environment) through which intentions are first encoded, then negotiated and ultimately enacted.

The application of algorithmic processes presents architecture with a set of descriptive and accelerating possibilities akin to those embedded within mathematics via its systems of abstract notation. Similarly, music enjoys rapidly enhanced evolution with each successive creation of new symbolic notational systems. As John Holland has observed, *"anyone with a bit of effort can appreciate quite complicated music, but there are musical subtleties that are difficult to convey without notation. The sophisticated compositions of Bach, Beethoven, and Prokofiev depend on the discipline that produces that musical notation. To know musical notation is to enrich one's understanding of the music and of the process of composition."*[3] Here the delimiting frame of syntactical protocols, enables rather than inhibits the space of formal possibility. The 'fugue', *"a type of contrapuntal composition or technique of composition"*[4], famously adopted by Bach, is a prime example of cultural production literally inconceivable without symbolic grammar. Thus, notation enables a medium for the systematic meta-analyses not only of the artefact (theorem, composition or building), but also of the processes that have brought it into being. In short, it enables the creation of theories of making, which can then form a foundation for the elaboration of a design methodology. Within architecture, it is our precise ability to relay, quantify and query design speculation and aspiration through computable terms, that allows *"architectural concepts [to be] expressed as generative rules so that their evolution may be accelerated and tested."*[5]

Advocating architectural form as a synthesis of internal motivations and their response to situation requires an expansion of the framework through which it is theorized. Analysis of commonalities across and between architectural forms is critical to their generation, evaluation and positioning. Historically, typology has been both a practical and theoretical apparatus to this end. Premising architectural organization upon established typologies, however, can be a reductive and external practice that unnecessarily pre-conditions and limits the act of design. The difficulty is that established typologies have conventionally been viewed as fixed, and are primarily articulated in programmatic and/or semantic terms without explicit reference to the forces and processes that generated them. There are exceptions; Zaera-Polo, Tschumi, Kipnis and Frampton have each articulated models of typology that are active to various degrees. What such models do not provide however, is an adequate meta-analysis or operative grammar through which a productive and empowering design methodology could be structured.

It is within this context that we advocate the adoption of an alternate conceptual framework, speciation: *"the evolutionary process by which new biological species arise."*[6] When applied to architecture, speciation offers a series of analytical tools and terms that redress the aforementioned deficiencies of typology and as such it presents a more open and robust vehicle through which to qualify architectural formation. Of particular value is the conceptual distinction between genotypical and phenotypical variation. Analyzing formational processes and internal motivations separately to formal characteristics and context sensitive behaviours enables the discernment of a much larger and richer set of affiliations between projects. This in turn allows for more sophisticated systems of evaluations of fitness, both for purpose (the traditional domain of type), and of adaptability to a host environment. Fitness is here measured not against assumed global orders, but is evidenced through the realization of a persistent, entirely local, and specialized instantiation of the genome. By advocating speciation over typology we do not seek to abandon the organizational diagrams of type, rather to enrich and elaborate them through their exposure to additional influence and the establishment of operative meta-models.

As a design practice, supermanoeuvre implicitly values richness and diversity and privileges complex and aperiodic forms of order; the heterogeneity and flux of the outside world are welcomed collaborators in the design process. Organizational, spatial and material characteristics arise from a synthesis of their own network of internal logics and their environmental,

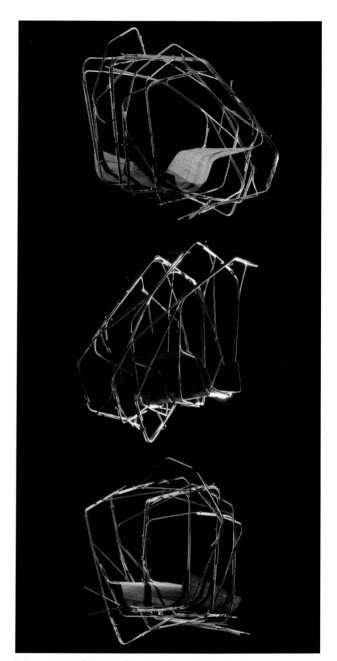

"Pipe Dreams" by Nicolas Rebeck and Kendra Byrne. 1:2 scale prototype fabricated with custom-built pipe bending attachment to KUKA 6.5 axis robot arm utilizing custom written software.
Research into Robotic Fabrication directed by David Pigram and Wes McGee, University of Michigan, Taubman College of Architecture and Urban Planning

social, political, cultural and technical contexts (both existent and desired). Architecture, seen in this way, is neither a neutral substrate, mapping external influence without resistance, nor is it an inert exercise in the explicit production of shapes without reference to their environment. Instead it is an active participant with agency across multiple domains. Algorithmic techniques enable non-hierarchical, non-linear and explicit negotiations between an enlarged set of architectural intentions. Computation is employed to extend the form-finding traditions of architecture beyond the limitations of material substrates, while abstract notational systems enable a meta-analysis of the processes of form generation allowing them to be better understood, tuned and deployed, thus accelerating their evolution. Through the conceptual apparatus of speciation, fitness can be qualified through the persistence of specific formal differences, attained through the mutability of deeply embedded architectural logics. Supermanoeuvre's work is dedicated to the critical exploration and invention of strategies, methodologies and grammars of architectural formation.

1. Thompson, D'Arcy. Edited J T Bonner. *On Growth and Form.* Cambridge University Press, UK, 1961. p11
2. Jachna, Tim. Postscript Essay. in; *"An Evolutionary Architecture"* by Frazer, John. Architectural Association Publications. 1995. p110.
3. Holland, John H. *Emergence: From Chaos to Order.* Oxford University Press, UK, 1998. p 15
4. http://en.wikipedia.org/wiki/Fugue.
5. Frazer, John. *An Evolutionary Architecture.* Architectural Association Publications. 1995. p 9.
6. http://en.wikipedia.org/wiki/Speciation

The influence of digital technologies does not stop with the building's design or construction. Many technologies can be incorporated in the building and significantly alter its performance and appearance. The idea of the "intelligent" building has gained a lot of ground and found many applications. Sophisticated building systems can monitor the interior and exterior conditions of a building as well as the presence of humans and modify the internal environment (temperature, light, etc) accordingly. Buildings become not so much static objects as changing machines able to respond to different conditions.

The idea of a non-permanent and non-static architecture has its own history. At least since the 60s theorists like Reyner Banham and groups like Archigram and Superstudio have explored the possibilities of a mutable, transportable architecture that works as a machine for environmental control exchanging energy and information with its environment. More recently, Toyo Ito with the Tower of the Winds and NOX with the SonOhouse and other projects have explored these possibilities in practice.

Responsive systems for buildings are already available as commercially available products in many forms. Domotic systems composed of networks of sensors and actuators permit the remote control of a building's environment as well as the optimization of the performance of its heating and lighting systems and the establishment of security zones. Interactive panels can provide ambient lighting responsive to human presence and movement or touch. Now we are able to move from the simple practical tasks of domotic systems to the more complex ideas of providing pleasant and stimulating environments where interaction can go beyond the registering of human presence or simple entertainment games. The possibilities are now limited only by the designer's imagination. In this section we have focused on few projects by designers who are aware that the big questions about responsive environments do not lie with the technological application but with our own expectations and desires about technology.

All responsive systems consist of three main parts, sensors, actuators and controllers. In technical terms a sensor is a device that measures a physical quantity and transforms the result to a signal that can be further processed or used by other machines. A thermometer that can translate its measurements to some form of electric signal will thus be a temperature sensor. Sensor exist today for most kinds of physical phenomena; temperature, humidity, light, pressure, movement, many chemical elements and substances, wind, speed, orientation can all become objects of a sensor's attention. Depending on the type of activity that needs to be detected and the necessary accuracy and range, a sensor can be very simple and inexpensive or very sophisticated. Sensors of many types exist on the market and they can be custommade according to specific needs.

The controller is the part of the system that receives the information from the sensors, processes this information and gives the corresponding commands to actuators. Like sensors, controllers can be very complex systems of specialized hardware and software but they can be almost (or completely) non-existent in very simple systems. In many cases a normal computer with the necessary hardware for connecting to sensors and actuators can be programmed to function as a controller.

The actuator is the part of the system that takes the signals from the controller and transforms them to action. In most cases the actuator will receive an electrical signal and transform it to motion, light or sound. Many common pieces of machinery such as motors and loudspeakers can function as actuators but complex systems may require custom-made robotic elements.

Lattice Archipelogics

The Lattice Archipelogics project is the result of a commission from the Steirischer Herbst in Graz, Austria for the Latent Utopias exhibition curated by Zaha Hadid and Patrik Schumacher in November 2002. Addressing conditions of emergent behavior, Lattice Archipelogics integrates digital design, computer-numerically-controlled fabrication, and interactive motion technologies to create an interactive scripting device within a gallery context. A suspended cellular archipelago of vacuum-cast elements embedded with motion sensors, LED lighting, and speaker technologies responds to, as well as influences, a wide range of circulatory and conversational patterns throughout the installation. Conceptualized as spatial and programmatic software, Lattice Archipelogics captures the viewer to engage in its performance. An archive of movement patterns is generated and recorded by the proximity sensors as the gallery space is populated. When left in its inert state the algorithmic interface will sample from this catalogue of stored movement patterns to perform them iteratively. Depending on the participants' movements the performance is never the same with no beginning or endings, rather emergent, and unfolding. A three dimensional luminous drawing is sketched by visitors through their bodily manipulation of the digital interface. Once engaged with the work the exchange within the gallery environment is no longer passive. The spatial hardware of lattice archipelogics is a thick atmosphere of 150 vacuum cast polyethelene cells, each of which interlock with a twin cell in the formation of the larger system. The cells are vertically staggered in a pattern of self-counterbalance and double as conduit for the distribution of various cables and wires specific to its programming system. The spatial software of lattice archipelogics is an intricate web of interactivity generated by computer programming which effectively allows the system to observe the circulatory patterns of its users and translate that movement by way of algorithmic filters into a variety of lighting and sound patterns which, in turn, affect the behavior of its users, generating a feedback loop.

Author: Servo in collaboration with Smart Studio - Interactive Institute Stockholm

Servo: David Erdman, Marcelyn Gow, Ulrika Karlsson, Chris Perry

Smart studio - interactive institute stockholm: Ingvar Sjöberg, Tobi Schneidler, Fredrik Petersson, Olof Bendt, Magnus Jonsson, Pablo Miranda

Design team: Daniel Norell, Clare Olsen, Jonas Runberger

Special thanks: IASPIS (International Artists' Studio Program in Sweden), KTH Royal Institute of Technology, SSARK medialab, White arkitekter, CARAN

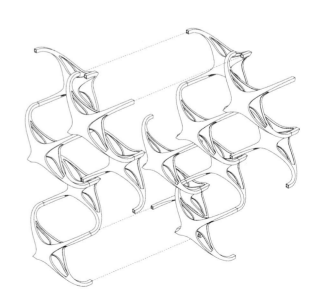

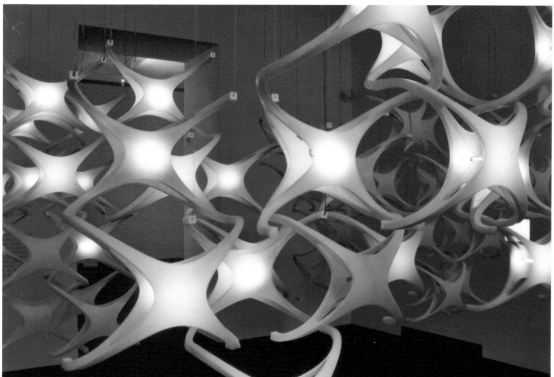

Still sequence of sensor-LED algorithm

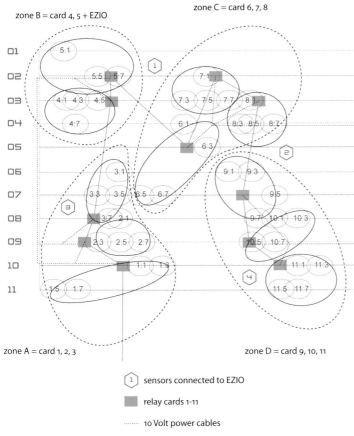

zone B = card 4, 5 + EZIO

zone C = card 6, 7, 8

zone A = card 1, 2, 3

zone D = card 9, 10, 11

1 sensors connected to EZIO

▪ relay cards 1-11

······ 10 Volt power cables

Sensor relay to cluster network diagram

Plan of the installation

Lattice structural assembly

The Semi-Porous-Operable-ORGanism takes its name from a primitive, usually unicellular, often environmentally resistant, dormant or reproductive body produced by plants and some microorganisms. These microorganisms are capable of developing either directly or indirectly after fusion with another spore, producing a new individual which is, in some cases, unlike the parent. In the context of this project, each spoorg cell is embedded with local intelligence, enabling it to communicate with other adjacent spoorgs. It is, to a specified degree, responsive to selected local and regional environmental changes. The spoorg aggregate is locally in fluctuation but also produces larger scale atmospheric effects in the specific region in which it is located. Materially, it is equal parts architecture, decoration, hardware, and software.

The spoorg system is a cellular system which interfaces with the interior and exterior of glass building skins. It is essentially a demonstration project, exploring the potentially productive effects of integrating contemporary material, geometric, sonic, and photo-sensing technologies. The intelligence of the system is distributed (as opposed to being centralized) and based on wireless radio communication. Spoorg reacts to local as well as regional environmental changes of light and responds by generating various forms of ambient sonic output. The behavior of each spoorg individually, and the network of spoorgs collectively, evolves over time through the modulation of sound textures based on a series of algorithmic rules. Each spoorg cell is comprised of a thin-skin plastic shell with hollow regions for embedding local infrastructure such as PCBs (microcontrollers), photo transistors (sensors), small-scale speaker elements, and RF (wireless radio communications technology) for local communication between the cells. The shells are manufactured through sintering and vacuum-casting. The local infrastructure combines wired and wireless technologies.

Installation design: Servo: David Erdman, Marcelyn Gow, Ulrika Karlsson, Chris Perry

Design team: Erik Hökby, David Erdman, Marcelyn Gow, Ulrika Karlsson, Chris Perry

Electronic and algorithmic design: Pablo Miranda, Åsmund Gamlesæter

Sound design: Leif Jordansson, Martin Q Larsson

Location: MAK Center for Art and Architecture, Los Angeles, USA, 2006

Special thanks: Jonas Barre, Sue Huang

Support from: Konstnärsnämnden, Sveriges Bildkonstnärsfond, Stiftelsen Framtidens Kultur, BSK arkitekter, White, Wingårdhs, Royal Institute of Technology (KTH), Atmel Norway AS

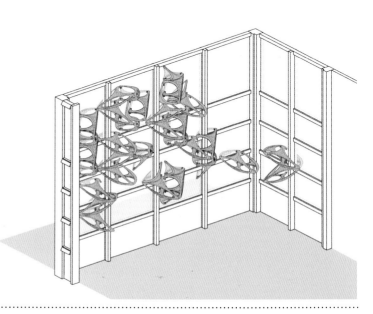

The Spoorg system allows one to cultivate and decorate domestic space by distributing and expanding shading and sound into a cellular, semi-porous membrane. Through this form of cultivation (the user's interaction with the spoorg system) new behavioral patterns emerge. A lack of cultivation will result in a certain decay of the spoorg system's performance. The difference between decay and growth renders the domestic space with subtle changes of atmospheric moods. Varying states of transparency emerge as the spoorg interfaces with natural lighting. Shifts in the density and the pace of ambient sound become apparent through the spoorgs' modulations of frequency. Sensitivity in the spoorg cells can be programmed and adapted for specific forms of monitoring and interacting with the environment.

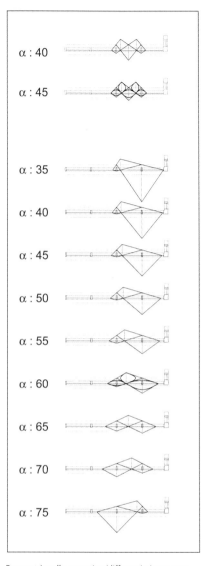

$\alpha : 40$

$\alpha : 45$

$\alpha : 35$

$\alpha : 40$

$\alpha : 45$

$\alpha : 50$

$\alpha : 55$

$\alpha : 60$

$\alpha : 65$

$\alpha : 70$

$\alpha : 75$

Parametric cell generation/differentiation system

typical cell division

transition from rhombic dodecahedron to inscribed curves

transformational studies: from bounding box to surface geometry

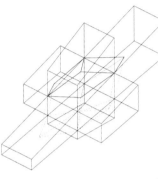

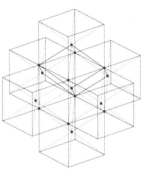

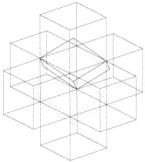

1. Suction cup for attachment to glazing
2. Audio speaker (40 mm)
3. Audio speaker (50 mm)
4. Computer chip

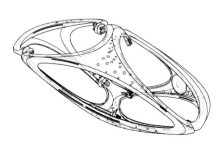

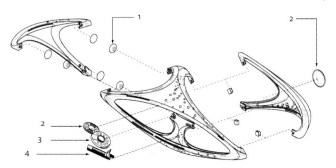

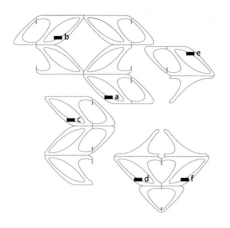

```
readSensor()
updateActivityLevel()
mapActivityLevelToSoundParameters()

if(ActivityLevel)
            outputSound()

evaluateFitness()
```

Example:
All nodes in their default state responding to changes in local sensor readings by modulating and outputting sound. Fitness is evaluated as the integral of fluctuations in sensor data.

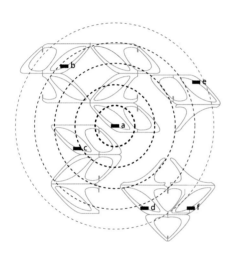

Pseudocode:

```
if(fitness > adaptive_fitness_threshold)
            broadcastGenotype()
```

Example:
Node a is successful and broadcasts its genotype over RF. The radio transmission is short range and the signal loses accuracy and strength beyond its nearest neighbors.

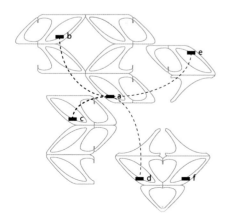

◌⁓ RF signal

▬ Node

Pseudocode:

```
if(receivedData())
            checkCorruption();
            crossOver()
else
            mutate()
```

Example:
Node b and c receive the full genotype unaltered. Node d receives the data with one corrupted byte (which is included in the evolution of the gene pool as any random mutation). Node e receives the data with one or more bytes missing and disregards the rest of the data. Node f does not receive any packages at all.

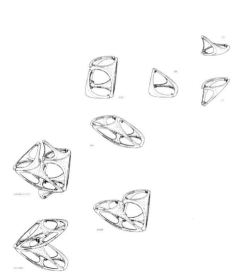

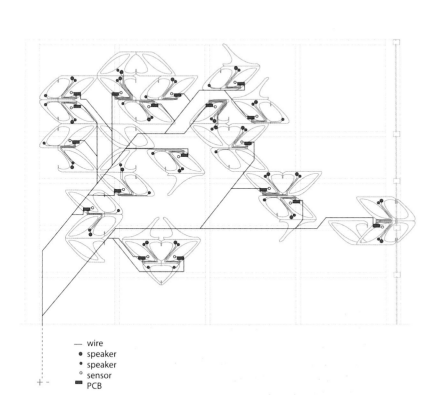

- — wire
- • speaker
- • speaker
- ° sensor
- ▬ PCB

Seeing the aesthetic code of industrial society as one based on simplicity, repetition or the assembly of additive systems, the architects of this project propose an architecture that is not concerned with its apparent figure but is characterized by a certain incorporeality;. an architecture of energy in which the visible form is simply the materialization of environments through mere energy dissipation. A building will be nothing more than the material form adopted by a particular energy configuration: a system that exchanges energy with the medium in different ways.

The project consists of a system of objects installed through the Venice lagoon. Each one works capturing and emitting energy. The pieces mainly work in two directions, on one hand, they reactivate public space through energy and production of private use spaces, and on the other hand, they try to reclaim, from the biological point of view, the lagoon through micro organism cultures.

Each object is a technical system that, through the capture and emission of energy, induces spatial, environmental and visual effects. What we understand by space becomes a set of perceptions linked to environmental effects generated through the management of various forms of energy. Thus, architects become genuine specialists in special effects, linked now to a sense of expanded perception.

Architecture becomes an artificial atmospheric system on a reduced scale. With its unstable equilibriums, its transitory states, its complex internal relationships and associated visual effects. Everything technically induced: artificial atmospheric effects.

Architects: cero9 (Cristina Díaz Moreno, Efrén García Grinda)
Collaborators: Luis Cabrejas, Íñigo González-Haba, Aritz González
Location: Venice Lagoon, Italy, 2002

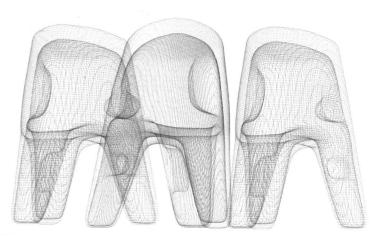

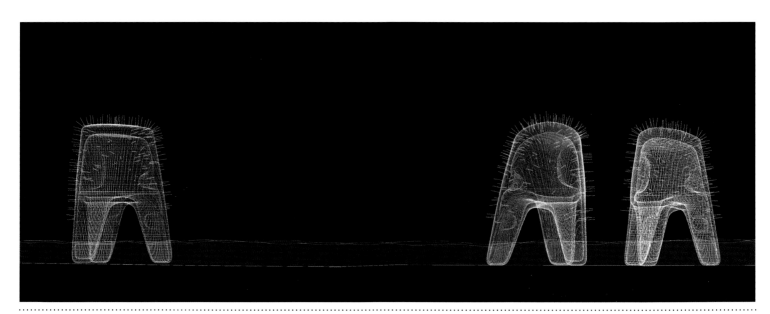

Venice is a city that is slowly dying, absolutely suffocated by tourism. A city that is visited by more than ten million people a year, although the population is fewer than forty thousand people. The sweet water lagoon connected to the sea where Venice is placed has been progressively altered by a process of change in the level of salinity due to the enlargement of its canals.

Then the target would be to reactivate the city from its public condition, avoiding a sterilization of the urban tissue produced by the industry of tourism and biological changes, and accelerated by the creation of an appropriated habitat for the changes in the level of salt in the water.

This proposal turns the city towards the exterior borders of Venice trying to balance all the activities around the Grand Canal. The aim is to extend the city by means of working on the exterior limits: to enlarge the city without adding a single cubic meter of sand.

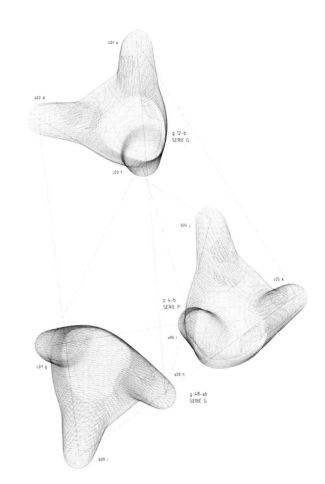

Site plan of the lagoon

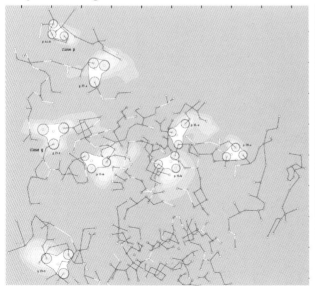

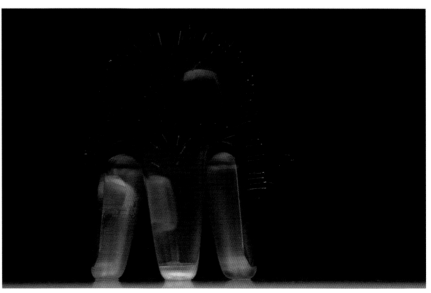

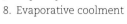

1. Cloud nets
2. Drinking water deposit
3. UV-A
4. Hydroponic cultivation
5. Solar colectors
6. Photovoltaic panels
7. Capillary microtubes
8. Evaporative coolment

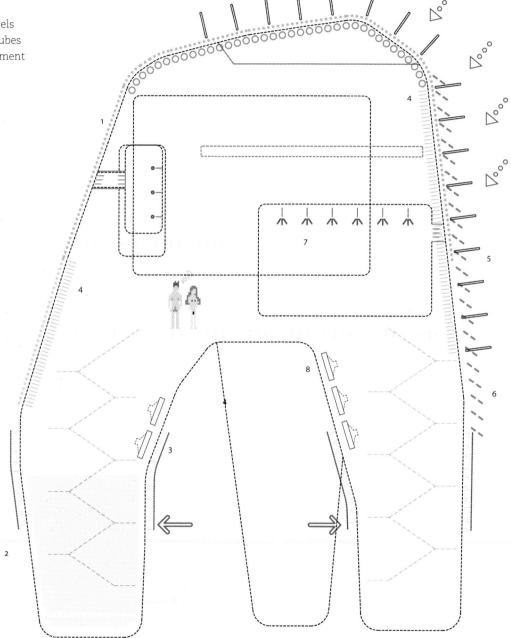

collectors

cloud nets

water trajectories

infrared

trp

capillary microtubes

UV-A

marijuana

PV silicone

sensors

evaporative cooling

Autonomous systems

Emergent / Tom Wiscombe
Flower Street BioReactor

The point of departure for this project was to engage the nascent cultural paradigm shift from thinking about energy as something which comes magically from distant sources to something which can be generated locally in a variety of ways. The goal was not, however, to undertake an engineering experiment, or to simply express material processes, although this is certainly one dimension of the project. The primary goal was to create a sense of delight and exotic beauty around new technologies by decontextualizing them and amplifying their potential atmospheric and spatial effects.

The project is an aquarium-like bioreactor inserted into the façade of the building, which contains green algae colonies that produce oil through photosynthesis. The aquarium is made of thick transparent acrylic, molded to create the intricate relief on the front. This relief tracks along with and supports an internal lighting armature which is based on the Bio-feedback Algae Controller, invented by OriginOil in Los Angeles in July of 2009. This new type of bioreactor uses tuned LED lights which vary in color and intensity to support algae growth at different stages of development, maximizing output. According to OriginOil, "*this is a true bio-feedback system… the algae lets the LED controller know what it needs as it needs it, creating a self-adjusting growth system.*" At night, when this system intensifies, it generates a simultaneously urban and jungle effect: glittery reflections on acrylic combine with an eerie élan vital of glowing algae.

A solar array, used to collect energy during the day, spirals and winds up into the branches of an adjacent tree, jungle-style. This energy will be stored in a battery and used during the night to run the various systems.

Design team: Tom Wiscombe, Bin Lu, Chris Eskew, Ryan
Client: Macyauski
Location: Dept. of Culture and the Arts, LA
Los Angeles, USA, 2009

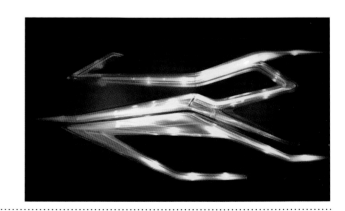

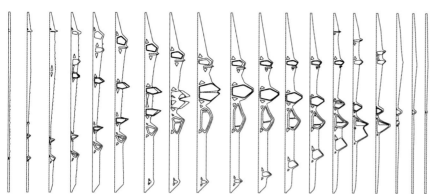

Sections

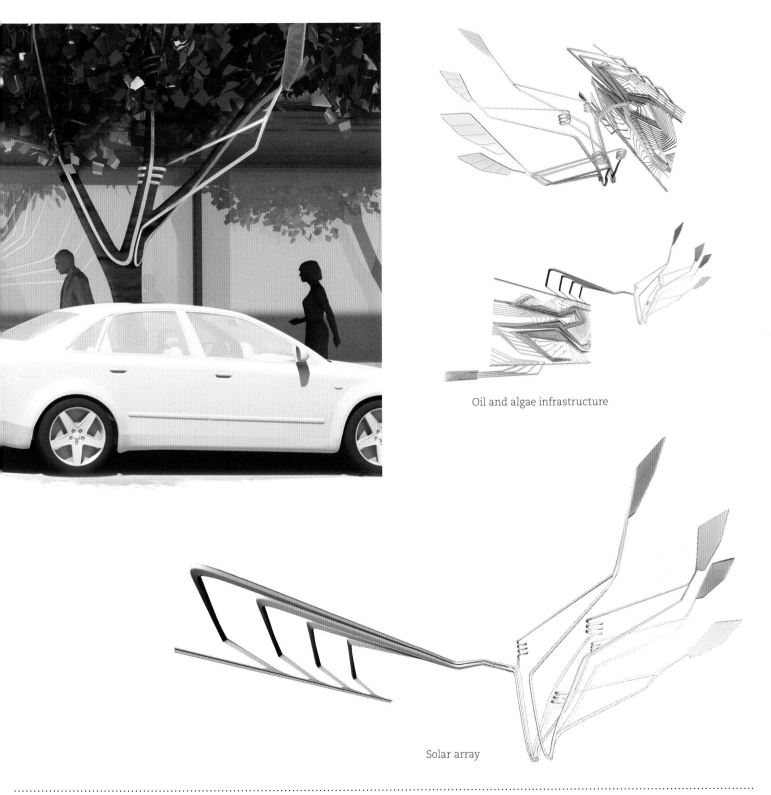

Oil and algae infrastructure

Solar array

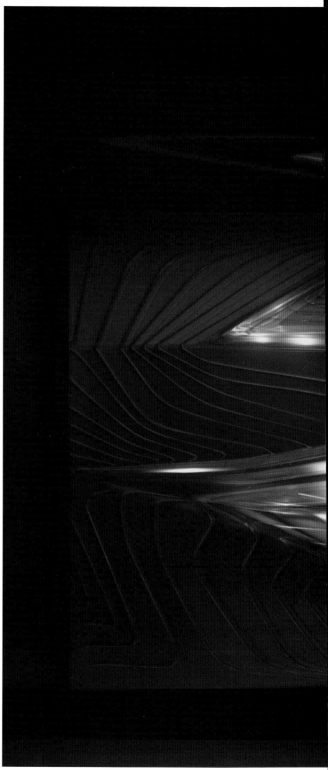

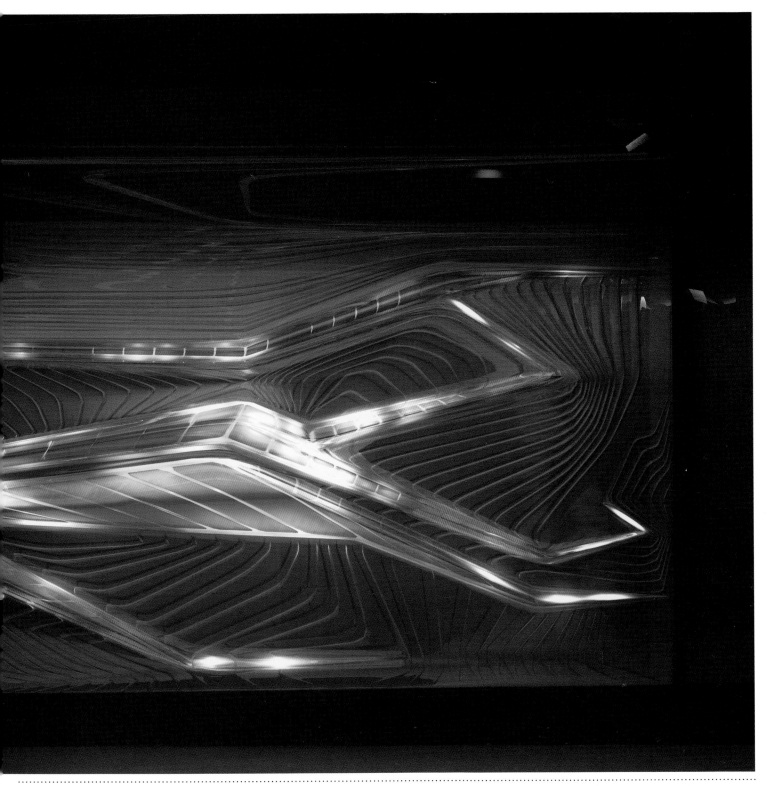

Philip Beesley
Hylozoic Soil

Hylozoic Soil is an immersive, interactive sculpture environment made of many thousands of custom-made components. The sculpture's global VIDA 2009 award for art and technology stated *"the glass-like fragility of this artificial forest, built of an intricate lattice of small transparent acrylic tiles, is visually breathtaking. Its frond extremities arch uncannily towards those who venture into its midst, reaching out to stroke and be stroked like the feather or fur or hair of some mysterious animal.In keeping with Beesley's own description, his enchanted environment complies with the laws and cycles that determine the millennial assembly of a coral reef, with its cycles of opening, clamping, filtering and digesting. Capacitance-sensing whiskers and shape-memory alloy actuators create a diffuse peristaltic pumping motion, luring visitors in to the eery shimmering depths of a forest of light.*

Hylozoic Soil implements a distributed sensor network driven by dozens of microprocessors, generating waves of reflexive responses to those drawn into its vast array of acrylic fern stalagmites. Different levels of programmed activity encourage the emergence of coordinated spatial behaviour: thirty-eight controller boards produce specific responses to local action, while a bus controller uses sensor activity collated from all the boards to command an additional "global" level of behaviour. The forest thus manifests a haunting, breathing organicity, as it stirs to envelop and charm its human explorers. In keeping with the tradition of biologist artist Ernst Haeckel's Riddle of the Universe (1899), which traced actions of organic and inorganic nature alike back to natural causes and laws, Beesley's Hylozoic Soil stands as a magically moving contemporary symbol of our aptitude for empathy and the creative projection of living systems" [VIDA 11.0, Fundacion Telefonica]

The work is an evolving series, designed by sculptor-architect Beesley with his partner Rob Gorbet, an expert mechatronics engineer and custom-manufactured using digital fabrication machinery within their Toronto and Waterloo studios. Seven installations have been completed to date, initiated at the Montreal Beaux-Arts Museum in 2007-8, traveling to Matadero-Madrid 2008-9, and incorporated into a permanent installation at Ars Electronica's Museum of the Future in Linz for the Cultural Capital of Europe festival 2009. An expanded version employing new modular meshwork elements and adding a suspended lower filter stratum was developed as the lead exhibit for SIGGRAPH 2009 in New Orleans, and was subsequently mounted in Enschede, fall 2009. Versions of this work are currently in development for the Meduse facility, Quebec City, a chapel installation in Mexico City for the Festival de Mexico, and a new version is slated for installation as the Canada pavilion, Venice Biennale, 2010.

Hylozoic Soil uses the technical system of an interactive geo-textile mesh that senses human occupants and responds with caressing and swallowing movement, in peristaltic waves within distributed fields of lightweight pores. Hylozoic Soil 'breathes' around its occupants. The relationship is, on the surface, gentle. Proximity sensors detect movement, and respond with caressing and swallowing motions. Waves of breathing motion ripple out from individual encounters.

Author: Philip Beesley
Photographs: Philip Beesley Architect Inc

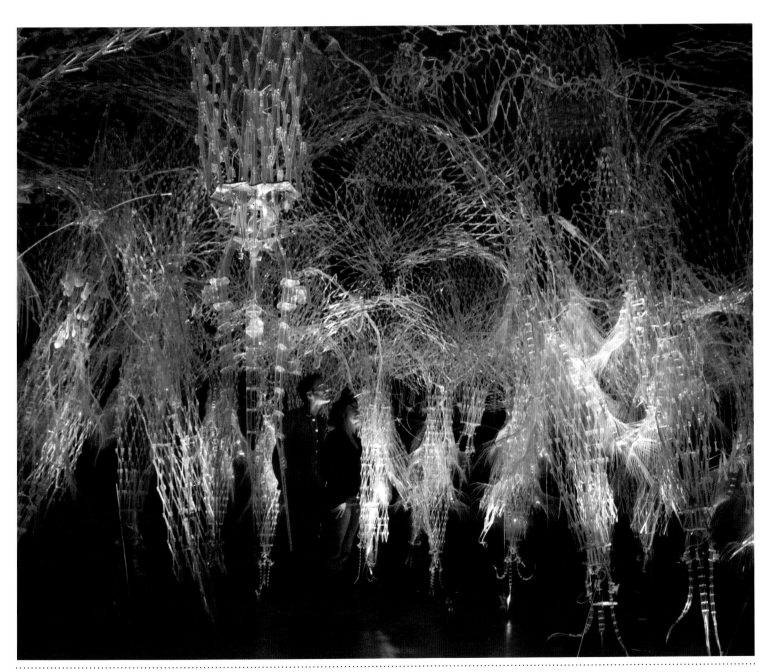

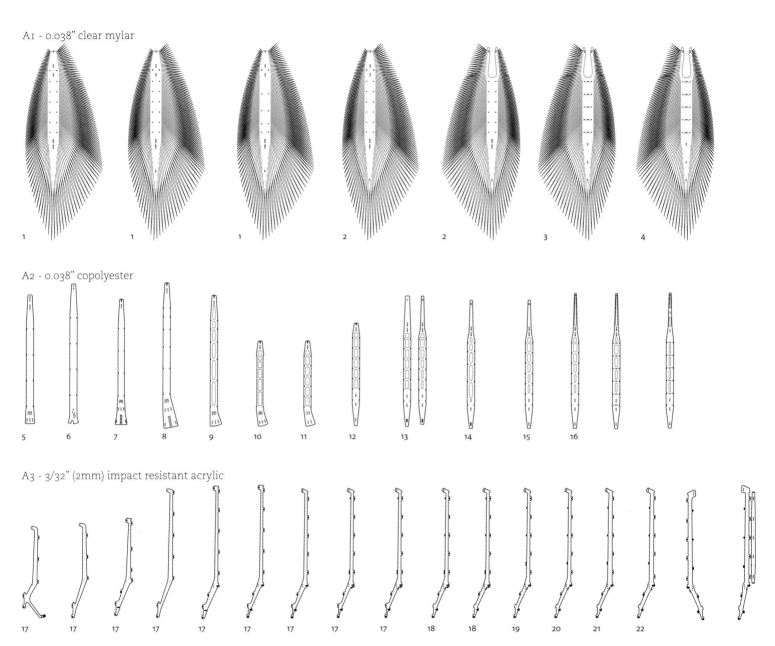

A1 - 0.038" clear mylar

1   1   1   2   2   3   4

A2 - 0.038" copolyester

5   6   7   8   9   10   11   12   13   14   15   16

A3 - 3/32" (2mm) impact resistant acrylic

17   17   17   17   17   17   17   17   17   18   18   19   20   21   22

1. breathing pore - tongue a
2. breathing pore - tongue a - Aug 23
3. breathing pore - tongue a - LINZ
4. breathing pore - tongue a - Jan 7
5. breathing pore - tongue a
6. breathing pore - tongue b
7. breathing pore - tongue c
8. breathing pore - tongue d

9. breathing pore - tongue e
10. breathing pore - tongue f
11. breathing pore - tongue g
12. breathing pore - tongue h
13. breathing pore - tongue i
14. breathing pore - tongue i test - July 31
15. breathing pore - tongue i - July 30
16. breathing pore - tongue i - Aug 1

17. breathing pore - spine a
18. breathing pore - spine a - July 30
19. breathing pore - spine a - Aug 1
20. breathing pore - spine a - Aug 2
21. breathing pore - spine a - Aug 7
22. breathing pore - spine a - Aug 8

Previous pages: Hylozoic Soil, Montreal Museum of Fine Art, 2007
Right page: Evolution of individual components.
This page, top: Montreal Museum of Fine Art, 2007: Detail view of Kissing Pore actuated sensors.
This page, bottom: Diagrammatic sectional view

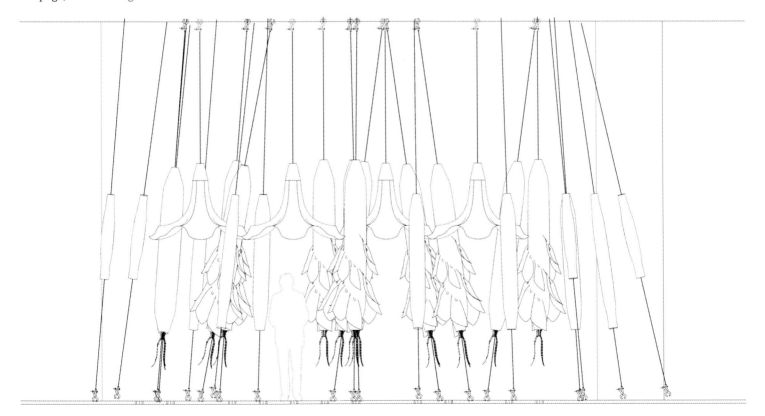

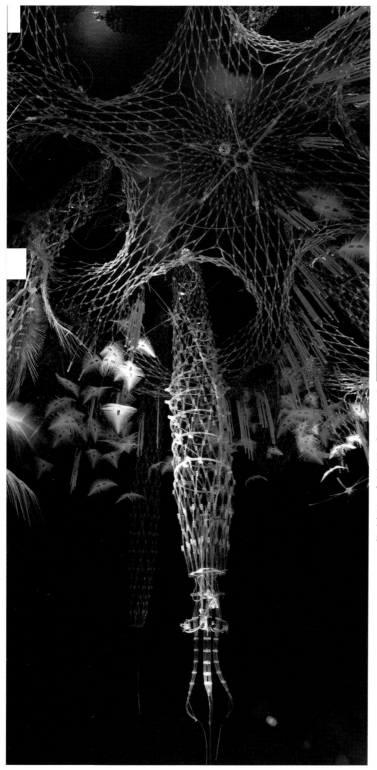

This page,left: Hylozoic Soil, VIDA 11.0, Matadero, 2009: general view of canopy layer,

Top: Hylozoic Soil, VIDA 11.0, Matadero, 2009: detail view of Weed layer.

This page, right: Hylozoic Series: 3D model of a Breathing Column.

Next page, bottom: 3D model of top and bottom column ends.

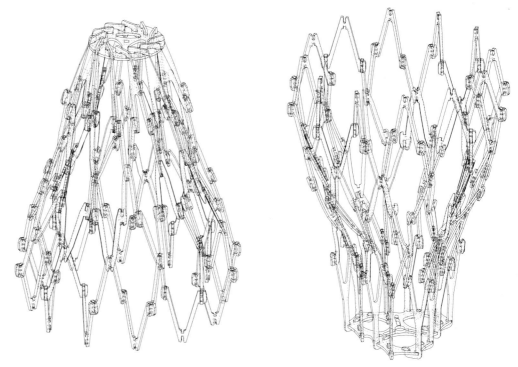

Philip Beesley
Cybele

Cybele is a self-assembling framework made of delicate laser cut components connected and oriented by miniature rare-earth magnets. A barbed cellulose membrane covers the structure. The membranes ride upon individual snap-fit acrylic frames and create a continuous topography. The rhombic tesselation of this system is reinforced by intertwined felting created by intermeshing of the serrated cellulose material.

Through flex and movement in the system the system knits itself together. Tiles are supported by a precarious scaffold akin to a tangled forest canopy whose structure is concentrated at upper and lower levels. Upper spring-clip wire mounts are configured for insertion into quarter-points of the cellulose tiles. Lower tripod sets include paired needle-stakes that work in concert with a lead counterweight encouraging free rotation prior to settling into final orientation. These details encourage jostling, flexible negotiation between tiles and the development of densely interwoven formations in the upper layer.

Each tile carries a brace of suspended elongated bladders. Funnel-shaped openings for each bladder are oriented upward, for drainage and collection. Salts prime the bladders, anticipating dilution and exchange.

Author: Philip Beesley
Photographs: Philip Beesley Architect Inc
Location: University of Waterloo, Cambridge, Ontario, Canada, 2005

Right page:
Detail view of cellulose membrane with bladder openings and felted cellulose fronds.
This page:
Bottom view showing bladder arrays.

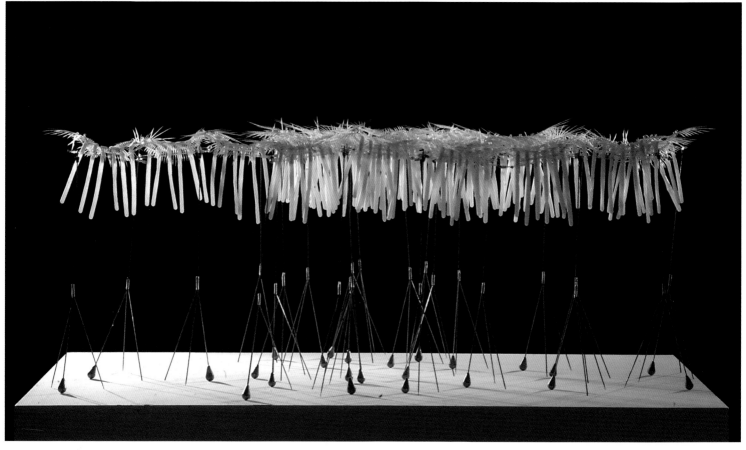

Top:
Front view.
Left:
Model view showing cellulose tile
and bladder units.
Right:
Plan diagram.

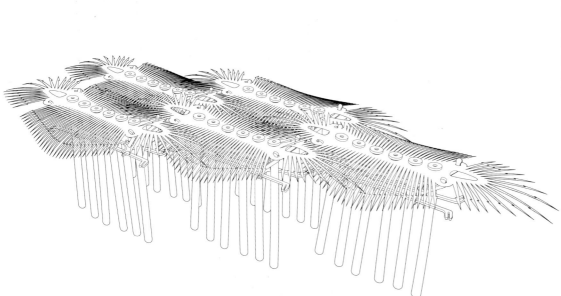

Left page, top:
Detail of upper side of cellulose tiles.
Left page, bottom left:
General view of underside.
Left page, bottom right:
Detail of support feet showing sharpened bipod and lead weight.
This page, top:
Side view.
This page, right:
Plan details showing alternate tessellation systems.

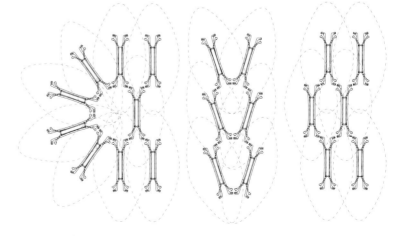

Philip Beesley
Orgone Reef

Orgone Reef is an artificial reef that could support a living skin. The project is a hybrid geotextile, a new class of materials used for reinforcing landscapes and buildings. The details of this structure are designed to catch and hold the things they contact, accumulating a thick, porous mass. The project functions with aggression, clamping and cutting into neighbors, draining and digesting the things contacted and converting this material into fertile soil. The structure would help a scarified landscape heal and grow new layers.

Several kinds of rhombic pyramidal structural tiles make this textile, connected by vinyl links that allow flexing and shifts in local relationships. The interlinking system creates a billowing space-truss that alternately arches upward and hangs in catenaries, adapting to locations of intermittent suspended supports. A primary tile, repeated hundreds of times within the topography, includes a pyramidal skeleton that supports a deeply serrated mylar filter configured to provide one-way trapping flows within a fluid medium. Fronds of adjacent tile filters intermesh, yielding a coarse felted membrane.

Cutting patterns are designed to release embedded stresses within roll-formed mylar, producing oriented curling of frond-rows within the filter material. Curled elements are arranged in opposing pairs, producing passive mouth-like pores that encourage passage in one direction while resisting reverse passage. This hybrid osmotic function is employed as a design principle at varying scales within the installation. Motions telegraphing through the matrix allow this system to function as a distributed pump acting upon the environment.

Author: Philip Beesley
Photographs: Philip Beesley Architect Inc
Location: University of Manitoba, Winnipeg, Manitoba, Canada, 2006

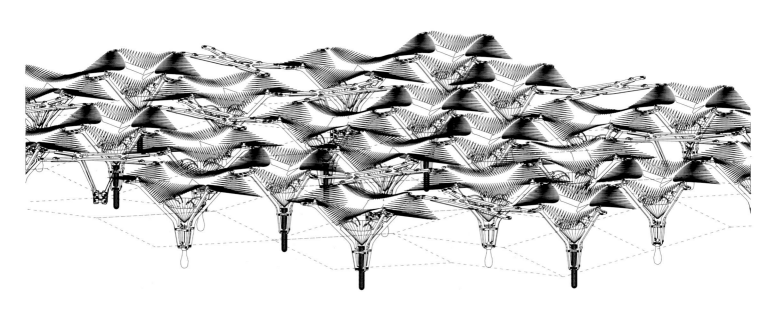

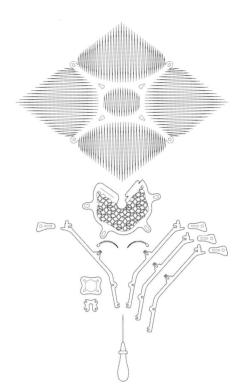

Top: General view of the Orgone field.
Left: Model views showing collection unit, plasma receptacle, and structural rhomboids.
Top right: Assembly view of collection unit.
This page, bottom: Plan diagrams showing Penrose tessellation variations.

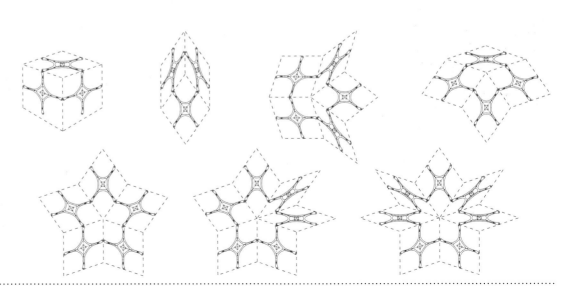

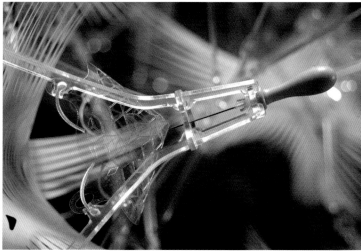

Left page, top: Top view of the rhombic filter units.

Left page, bottom left: Detail of barbed collection nest and bladder.

Left page, bottom right: View of geotextile edge.

This page, top left: Detail view of collection unit arm junctions.

This page, bottom right: Penrose tessellation ordinance system.

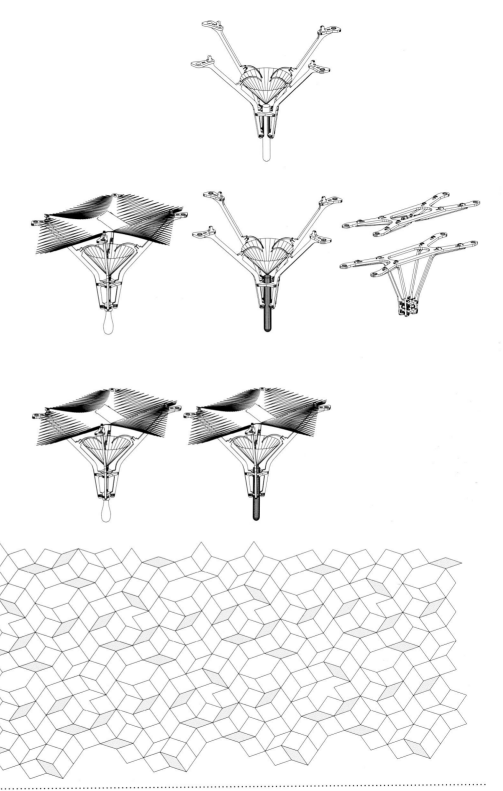

Poetics

The influence of the development of digital technologies does not stop at the technical level of architectural practice. These technologies shape the entire social and cultural environment in which architecture operates. The role of digital architecture does not stop at exploring the new possibilities offered by CNC fabrication, algorithmic design and interactive technologies. Architecture remains, as always, partly an art and as such it has to address how humans engage with their environment not only functionally but also aesthetically and symbolically. Most architects present their work in the form of drawings and models, whether as construction drawings or objects to be published and exhibited. Construction practice and law require of these representations to be accurate and unambiguous. A complete set of drawings is always thought to act as an objective representation of a building. Although technical necessity has always promoted this functionalist view of architectural representations there have always been alternative practices where architects have used drawings and other representations as symbolic mediums capable of expressing more than the dimensional and material properties of buildings. The etchings of Giovanni Battista Piranesi are an obvious early example. The work of the Futurists and Constructivists was also in the form of drawings and models that explored possibilities far beyond the immediate functional needs and technical abilities of their time. Alberto Perez-Gomez has described the symbolic potential of architectural drawings comparing it with musical notation: *"Like music, realized in time for a more or less "open" notation and inscribed as an act of divination for a potential order, architecture is itself a projection of architectural ideas, horizontal footprints and vertical effigies, disclosing a symbolic order in time, through rituals and programs. The architect's task, beyond the transformation of the world into a comfortable or pragmatic shelter, is the making of a physical, formal order that reflects the depth of our human condition, analogous in vision to the interiority communicated by speech and poetry and to the immeasurable harmony conveyed by music."*

Digital media have expanded the expressive potential of architectural representation. Today the architects have at their hands a number of powerful tools for the creation of images. In most cases these tools are used to create photo-realistic images and videos of proposed buildings, images of a nature and "objectivity" similar to that of the architectural drawings. In the projects presented below, the architects have used these tools to explore the creative and symbolic potential of architectural representations. They have incorporated in their work techniques from different fields (like MRI scans) and they have addressed issues of history (both architectural and political), ritual and religious practice, ecology and medicine. Their work demonstrates that digital technologies can be incorporated and offer a lot in architecture not only in its construction and morphogenetic ability but also in its symbolic and poetic potential.

Xefirotarch / Hernan Diaz Alonso
Lautner Redux

On the occasion of the retrospective exhibition of John Lautner, the Hammer Museum and the Getty Center invited Xefirotarch, as well as three other architecture firms, to create an
addition to four of Lautner's radical houses. Xefirotarch worked
on designing an addition for the Chemosphere, a house that
stands on the San Fernando Valley side of the Hollywood Hills,
just off of Mulholland Drive. The house is perched atop a concrete pole nearly 9 m (30 ft) high. This innovative design was
Lautner's solution to a site that, with a slope of 45 degrees,
was thought to be practically unbuildable.

Design: Xefirotarch / Hernan Diaz Alonso
Project architect: Steven Ma
Design team: Edward Kim, Jordan Kanter, Thorne Ransom,
Doug Wiganowske

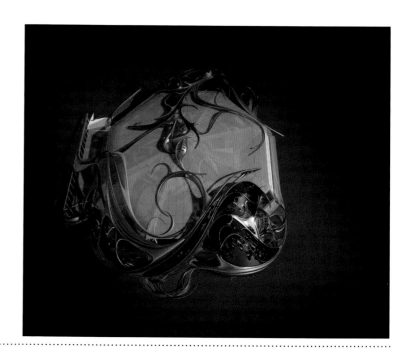

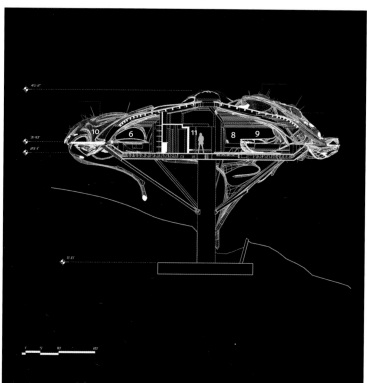

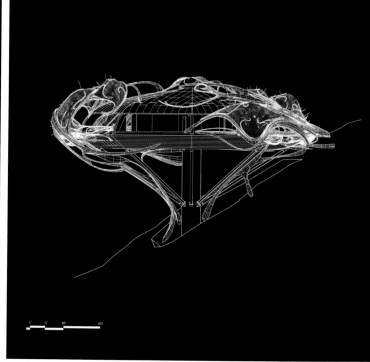

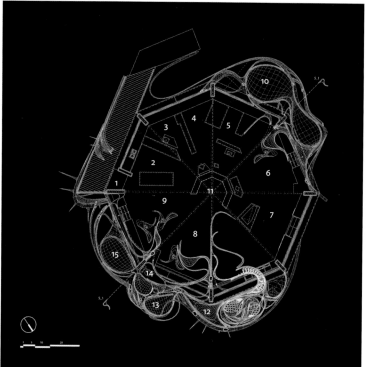

1. Entry
2. Kitchen
3. Laundry
4. Bedroom I
5. Bedroom II
6. Bedroom III
7. Bedroom IV
8. Living room
9. Dining room
10. Torture chamber
11. Lounge
12. Jacuzi
13. Balcony
14. Bathroom
15. Observatory

A. Skin membrane system
B. Structural framing system
C. Circulation/program system
D. Existing building

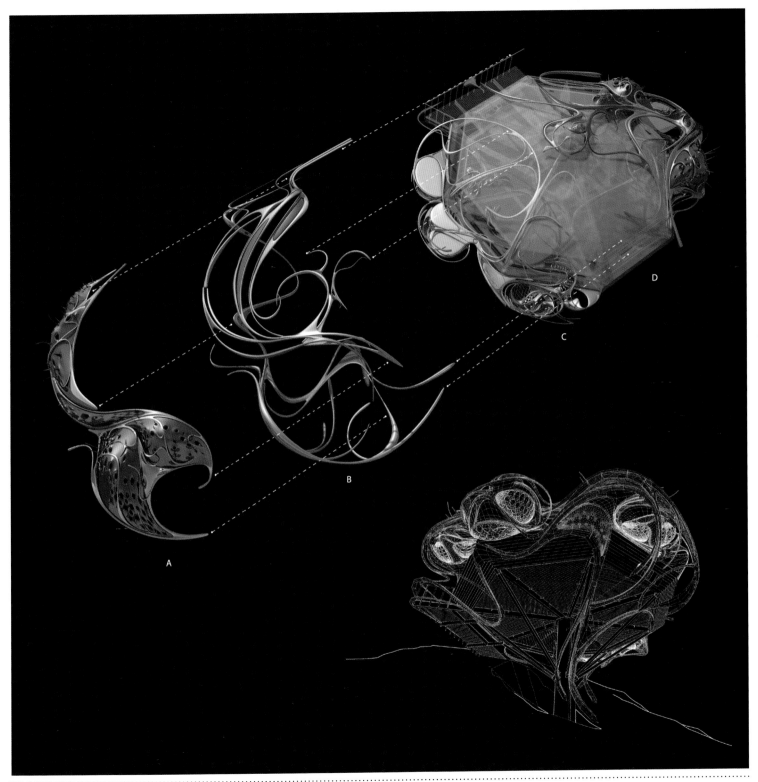

A

B

C

D

Xefirotarch / Hernan Diaz Alonso
Tabakalera - International Contemporary Culture Centre

Tabakalera is the project that will change the former tobacco factory of San Sebastian into an International Contemporary Culture Centre, specialized in visual culture.

Contemporary art, television, video and cinema, design and sound will converge in the same space. A unique venue of exhibitions and audio-visual programs. And, above all, a place to work, to produce, to create. An image factory. The logic of the project does not work on the idea of building types, but developing a concept of "species", creating a new dynamic logic to allow the project and the city to develop a relationship based on play and joy. The project is not based on an organization of functions but in the generation of sensations through multiplying cells that are the generators of the building. The addition also operates as a prosthesis, adding, transforming but not completely replacing, producing a dialogue between history and the past. Museums, it has been said, are the cathedrals of today, a concept that is of concern to the architects since the project maybe a new icon for the city and also a place where the interior creates an atmosphere that involves the visitor. Space is conceived as continuous, and the proposal is to underplay the separation between exhibitions and service areas. The art of digital media is in constant evolution and transformation, and the designers want the building to be an element of dialogue with art and not just a framework. The ambitions are clear, to produce beauty in terms of the future and not a condition that we already know, a city like San Sebastian is always surprising, such is life, such is love ...

Design: Xefirotarch / Hernan Diaz Alonso
Location: San Sebastian, Spain

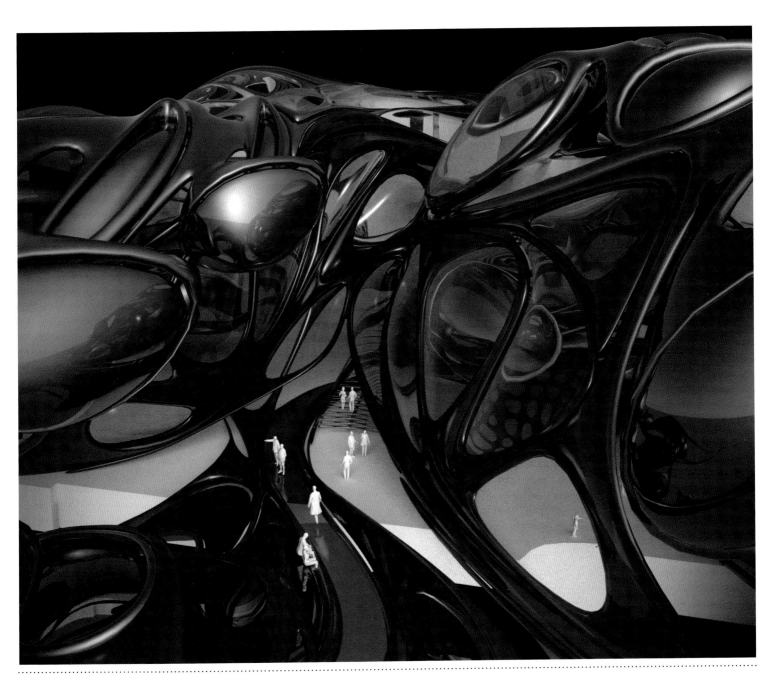

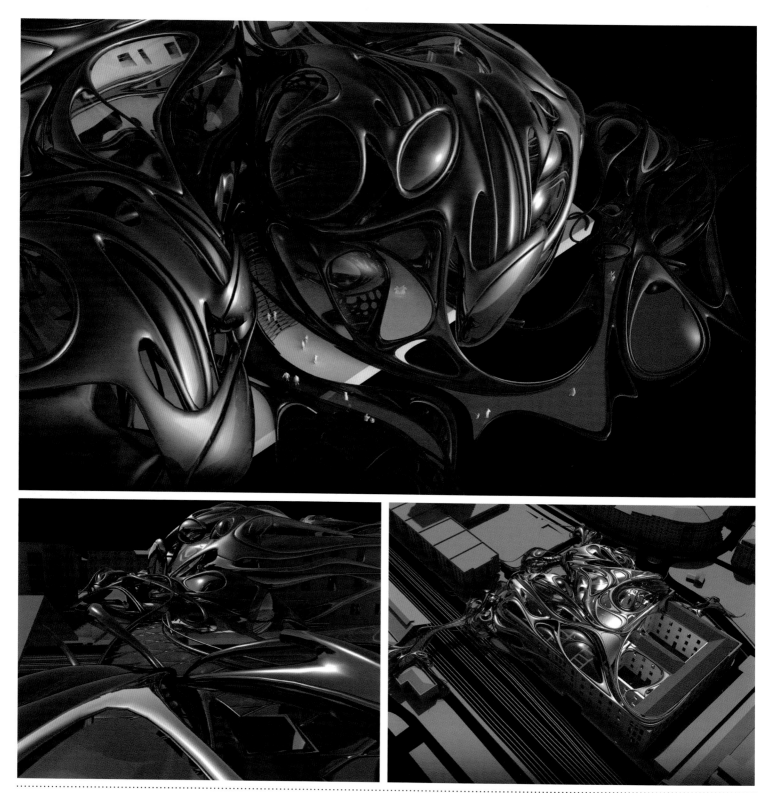

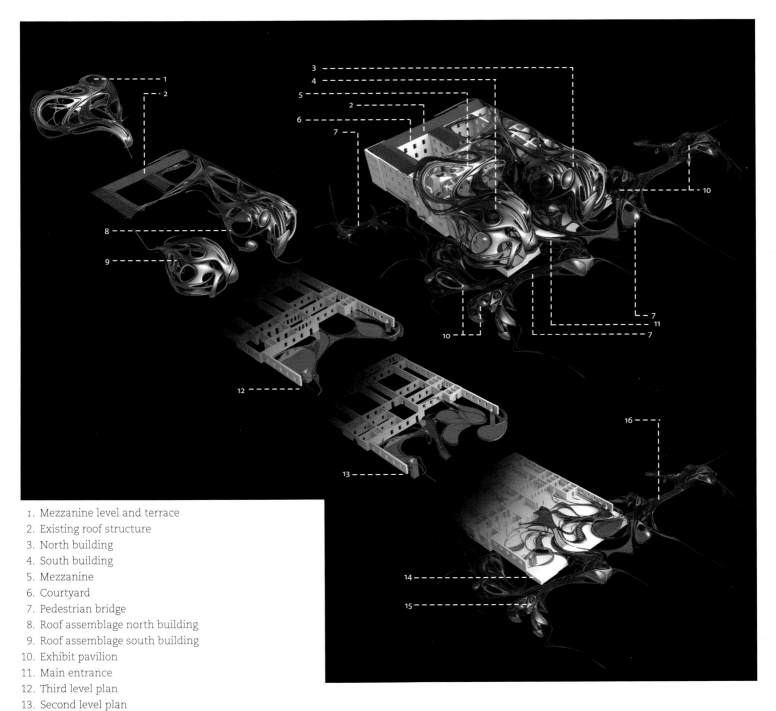

1. Mezzanine level and terrace
2. Existing roof structure
3. North building
4. South building
5. Mezzanine
6. Courtyard
7. Pedestrian bridge
8. Roof assemblage north building
9. Roof assemblage south building
10. Exhibit pavilion
11. Main entrance
12. Third level plan
13. Second level plan
14. Ground level plan
15. Pedestrian bridge south direction
16. Pedestrian bridge north direction

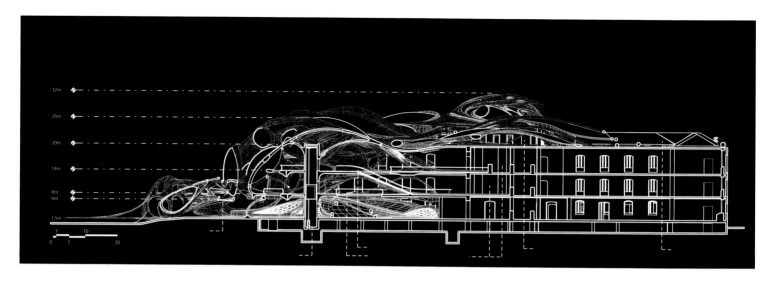

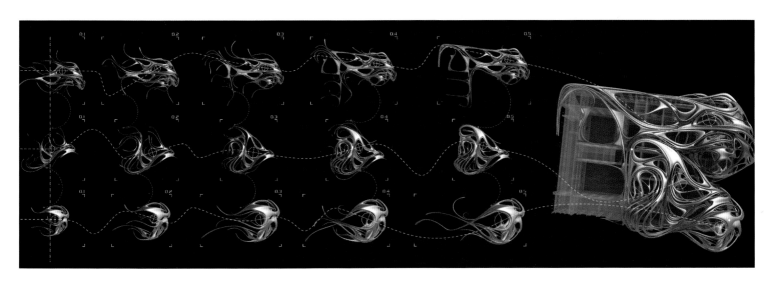

Xefirotarch / Hernán Díaz Alonso
Warsaw Museum

With the flair of the "Fabergé eggs" and the ambience of a park, this project activates city feelings and sensations. A mode of playful urban organization and absorption is created as familiar spatial vibrations are stimulated through unfamiliar figures with emerging aesthetics that define a beautiful and sparkling new condition in the city.

As a bejeweled elegance, the space intensifies mood and play. By means of contortion and exuberance, the space becomes dense and textured. The space is not loud but incisive, and overwhelming.

The project functions as a cinematic game: where there is no narrative, only active behavior and emergent interactive aesthetics between the city and the building... Behavior is in a constant state of re-actualization.

By unleashing the geometric performance suppressed by the unyielding orthogonality of the site's environment, the cultural populus attracted to this new form will be capable of challenging their own identities in reference to the contemporary and historic forms of the city itself.

The project serves as an anchor upon which this new architectural strain can act. The flows of movement channeled through the structure through various trajectories are in constant flux, resisting accordance with classical or traditional modes.

The fundamental difference asserted in this proposal rests in the notion that the form and image of the project attempts to embody "how" one might engage information and culture itself as opposed to explusively repeating familiar forms of the past rather than representing a static permanence within the body of the city.

Design: Xefirotarch / Hernan Diaz Alonso
Design team : Nick Kinney, Louis Koehl, Terry Gibbs
Engineers: Bollinger + Grohmann
Location: Warsaw, Poland

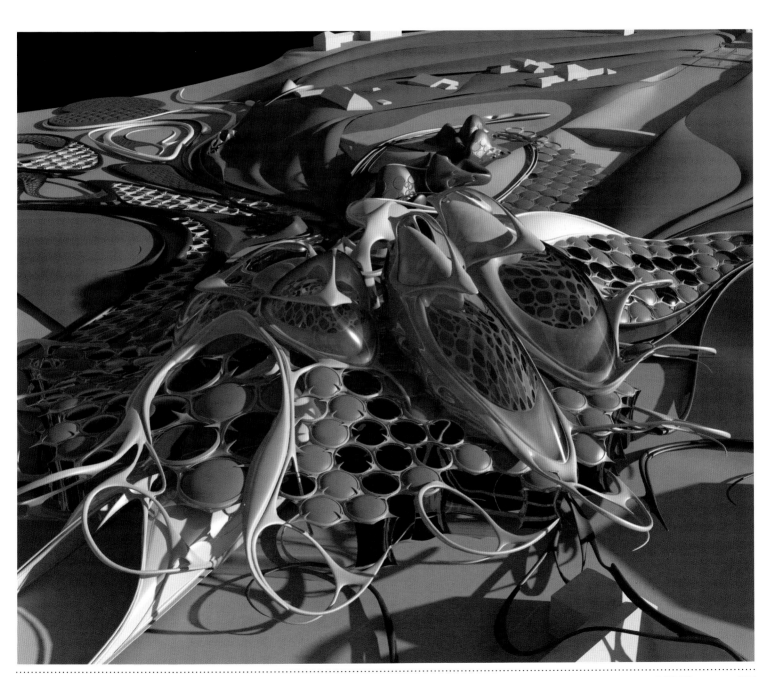

1. Primary private program
2. Secondary semi-public program
3. Noise barriers at tunnel entrance
4. Semi-dense public program zones
5. Walking / bike paths

Dense public program zone
Semi-dense public program zone
Preservation/restoration zone
Tree transplantation zone
Highway noise distribution

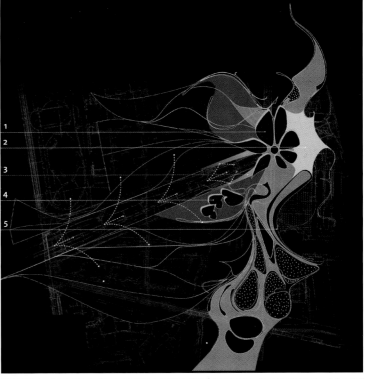

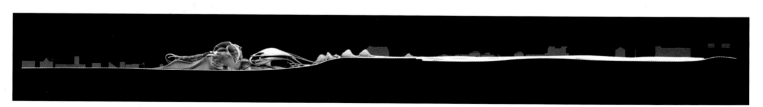

S. Chen - N. Cook - M. Sanes
Suspended Distention

Undeveloped land is scarcely available in Hong Kong. In the dense Western, Central and Wan Chai districts, this has historically led to the in-fill of Victoria Harbor and the creation of an artificial shoreline. This continued way of development replaces harbor with hardscape, further compounding the negative ecological consequences of unintelligent waterfront development. Historical waterfront development segregates commercial uses into dense towers and public space into large single-surface organizations - rather than take up large quantities of land, here the park multiplies the public uses into a vertical recreational system, full of vistas, pedestrian activity, open air galleries and exhibit spaces, and access to interior retail spaces and public services. As the programmatic repetition of towers has historically created laterally oriented, prosaic spaces, the tower strives to create repetitive zones of program with a new kind of spatial dynamism, achieved by the vertical mixing of various densities of open space, gallery and hotel uses coupled with the organizational oscillation of the structural system.

A series of preliminary structural explorations led to the development of initial programmatic opportunities and constraints - the basic structural part of an oscillating system was formulated based on iterative massing models. Structural components were accumulated to fill out the general massing of tower height and width, and then modified locally to increase stability. Elements of the structural system were then thickened, multiplied, eroded, or atrophied based on a series of physical modeling experiments designed to expose structural redundancies and weaknesses. As such, a materially efficient structural design emerged, that was then mined for accumulative potential. Areas of greatest promise and latent multivalence were selected and explored as detail areas. The entire tower was then revised and reaccumulated based on micro-scale structural and enclosure principles, site and contextual concerns, and overall vertical and lateral gradients of density, porosity, and opacity.

The tower's primary structural system is conceived of as a lattice of alternating space-frame elements (pods) and planar elements (fins). The primary vertical structure oscillates between the interior and exterior of the tower, changing at moments of movement between spatial zones; the primary lateral structure has two components – the structural sleeve of interconnected pods dealt primarily with rotational stability, and the crisscrossed lateral "braid" deals primarily with swaying and overturning. The systems are attenuated to their contextual situation – on the northeastern, harbor-facing side of the tower the surfaces of the lattice multiply and expand vertically to create larger areas of contiguous façade, sheltering the interior open space from the strong prevailing winds. On the southwestern, urban side, the lattice surfaces pull back from each other, exposing the interior gallery and park system, and opening views between the interior of the tower and the city.

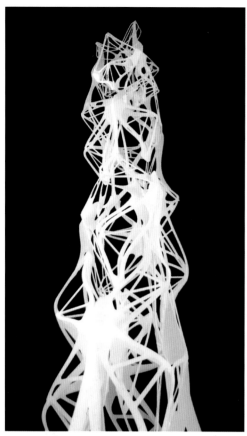

The tower operates as a vertical urban park for Hong Kong – the independence of the structural system from traditional masonry logics allows the tower to separate itself from the traditional datum, allowing the harbor to be reclaimed at its base to serve as a model for future development.

The circulatory system is composed of axial banks of elevators meeting periodically at universal floors – floors which connect to all banks laterally around the tower. At these floors, one may proceed into the localized circulatory systems or switch elevators to continue vertically up the tower. The local systems are composed of gallery stairs, egress stairs and localized elevators - a loop of exterior stairs, galleries, and interior pavilions winds its way vertically through the tower, attaching itself to the primary vertical fins and the lateral braid. These gallery stairs become the vertical pathway system of the park, allowing access to the park from selected floors, and closing down at times for security.

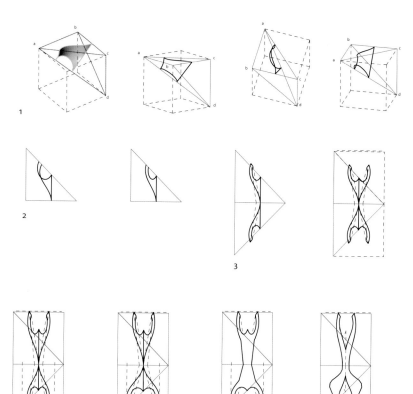

1. Schoens Manta - rotation of the fundamental region with the bounding geometry.
2. A section through one orientation of the fundamental region - modified into one surface.
3. Taking the mirror of the surface in two directions creates a larger symmetrical surface
4. Elongating one half or two regions creates assymetry in the overall surface.
5. Widening the opposite half develops the assymetry further.
6. The natural tendency of the piece pinches towards the middle - thickening this becomes more structural.
7. Blending the curves to read as one assymetrical piece.
8. One component is constructed from two perpendicular pieces interlocking on their central axis forming one component.
9. The component rotates 15 degrees about the x-axis.
10. The 15 degree rotation allows the component to then rotate in 120 degree increments about the central z-axis. 3 components then form a sleeve.
11. Each sleeve is rotated on itself and then rotated 60 degrees about the z-axis to form a connection between multiple components and sleeves.

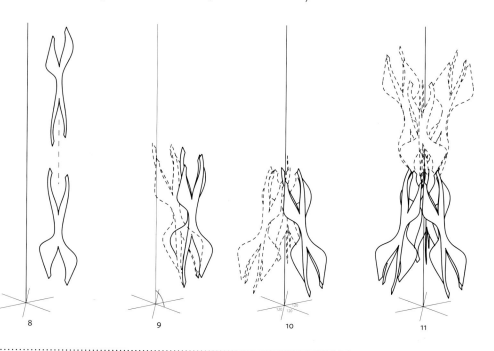

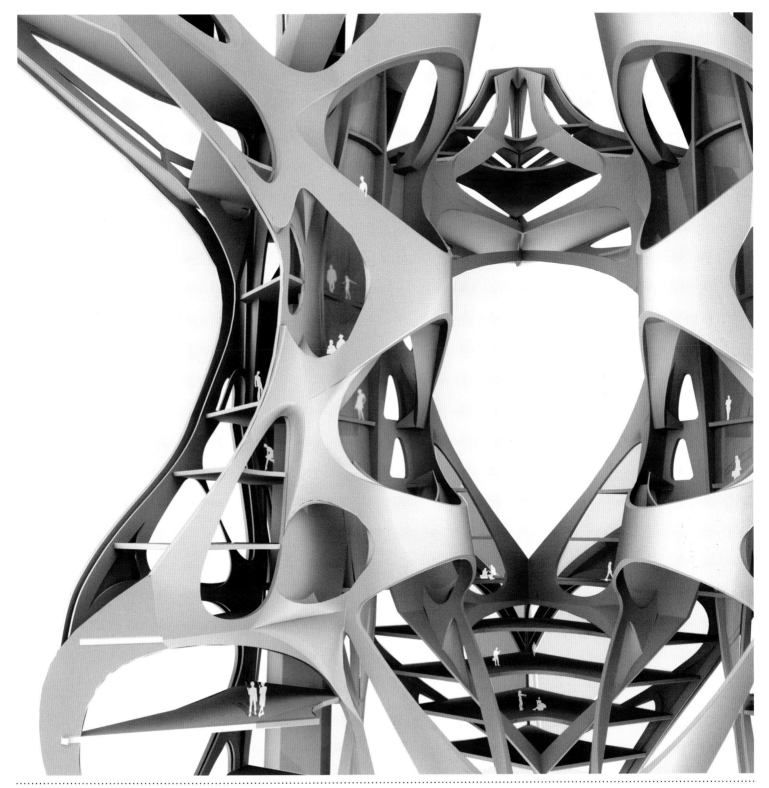

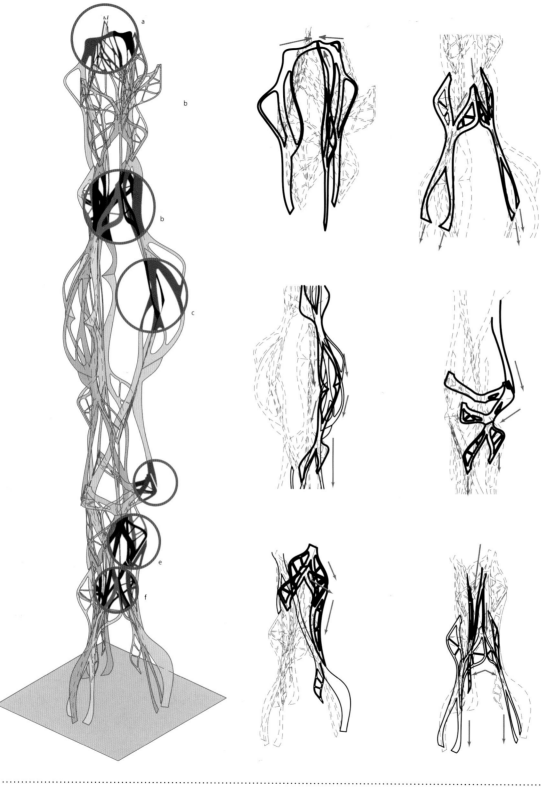

a. **dome enclosure:** the dome at the top of the tower is in compression with each other, as structural stability is achieved at the top.

b. **edge connection:** as the edges of the individual side of the profile press against each other, it creates a tripod design where the lateral force on each other stabilize the unit and allow the vertical load to travel down.

c. **edge connection:** since the edge curves does not allow the load to travel in a straight line, a secondary member that split the vertical member is introduce in order to alleviate the stress.

d. **1 to 2 connection:** as the verticals travel from top to bottom, they are divided from one member to two and directed down; the horizontal members function as structural beams.

e. **2 to 1 connection:** as the verticals travel from top to bottom, they are fused from two members into one; in this instance, this particular connection mainly supports lateral loads.

f. **braiding & one to two connection:** at this particular point, there is a total of 9 connection points, three from braiding (prevents overturning and act as cross-members), three from 2 to 1 connection (lateral stability) and three from the 1 to 2 connection, which is in line with the continuous vertical load as a straight line

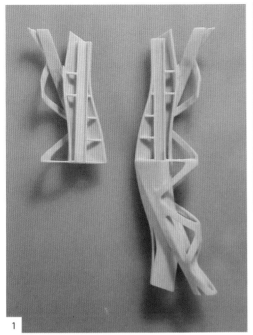

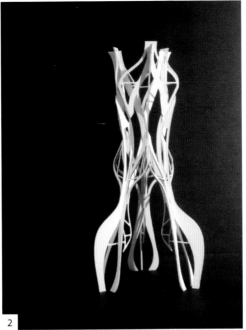

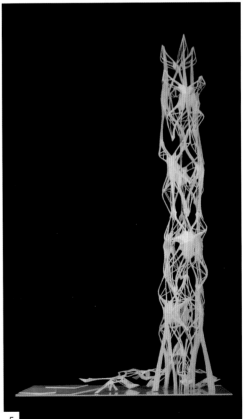

1. 3D print study model.
2. Laser-cut cardboard study model.
3. Rendering, exterior.
4. Rendering, exterior.
5. Model of the complete tower.

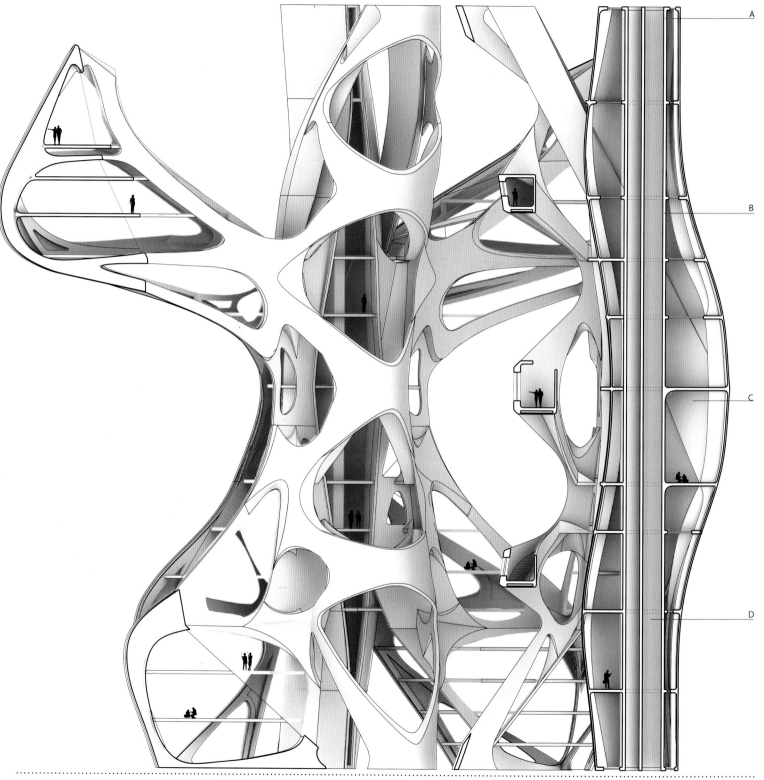

A

B

C

D

1. Gallery
2. Office
3. Outlook
4. Boutique
5. Circulation Core
6. Hotel Suites
7. Hotel Rooms

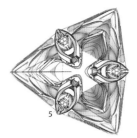

Floor plan A

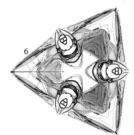

Floor plan B

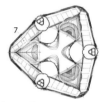

Floor plan D

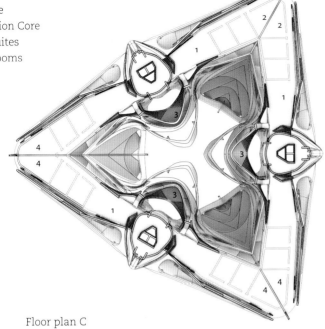

Floor plan C

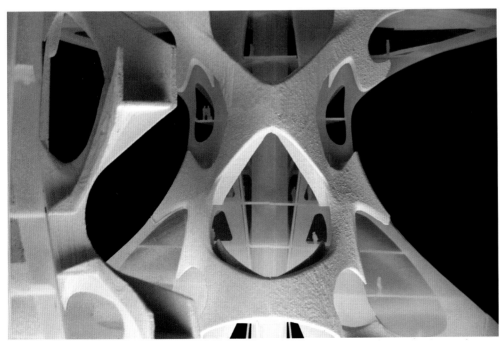

Tobias Klein
Synthetic Syncretism

The project's narrative background is based upon the hybrid Cuban religion of Santeria (a mixture between Catholicism and the African Yoruba tribe beliefs). As a result of this unusual syncretism an altered kind of religion evolved which hybridizes Catholic Saints with animals and Sakralraum with sacrifices.

The shortage of burial space at the Christobal Colon necropolis, the main cemetery, originated the proposal for a processional route through the city of Havana for ceremonial funerals in the sea. Along this processional route the 'Chapel of Our Lady de Regla' acts as the architectural highlight. Slotted inside an existing cross shaped courtyard, this inverted chapel contains a series of Santerian relics and utensils condensed from the virtual into the actual. Tweaked to the max, skeleteral and visceral at the same time, these 'cybrid' objects, 3D modeled and 3D printed in order to perfectly fit animal bones found on the site in Cuba, and 3D scanned into virtuality and re-moulded into actuality in London, provide, on a smaller scale, the formal expression for the larger architectural intervention.

The project provides an example of syncretism of contemporary CAD techniques and CAM technologies with site specific design narratives, intuitive non-linear design processes, and historical architectural references. The project shows the architect as the creator-craftsman that finally has the chance to overcome the fifteenth- and sixteenth-century schism of intellectual from manual labour, as well as the nineteenth-century gulf between automatic mechanization and poetic creation. The work tries to re-enact a very challenging architectural conversation on ritualistic objects, pre-Modern typologies, and religious ornaments.

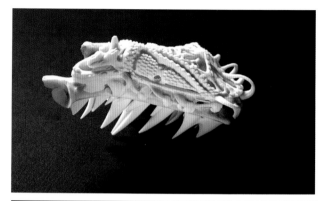

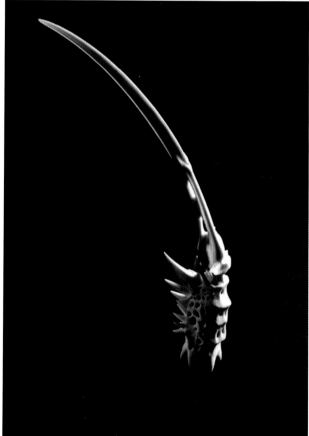

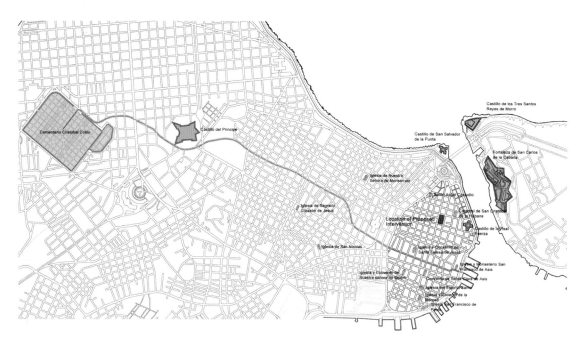

Existing fortifications
Existing places of worship
Existing necropolis
Proposed intervention

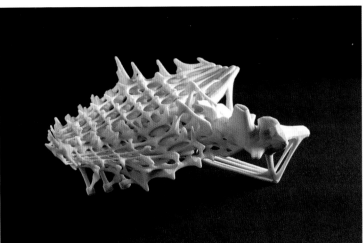

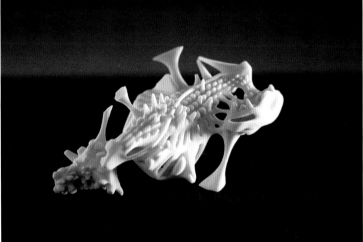

"Vacillating objects" - in this case the Chelonian Urn are spatially consistent structures immersed from the physical into the realms of virtual. For that purpose, similar to the process of a magnetic resonance image, the geometry of the physical object is 3D-laser scanned. The method of sculpting virtual based organs on a scanned real grown bone is similar to the work of a butcher in reverse gear, who must also fit the once-coexisting parts back together. The difference between such work and this modelling of virtual possibilities is the non-existence of the parts in the first place.

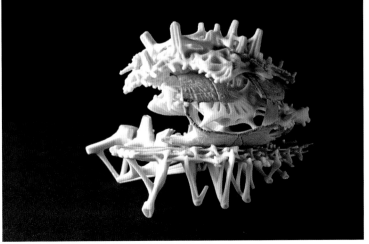

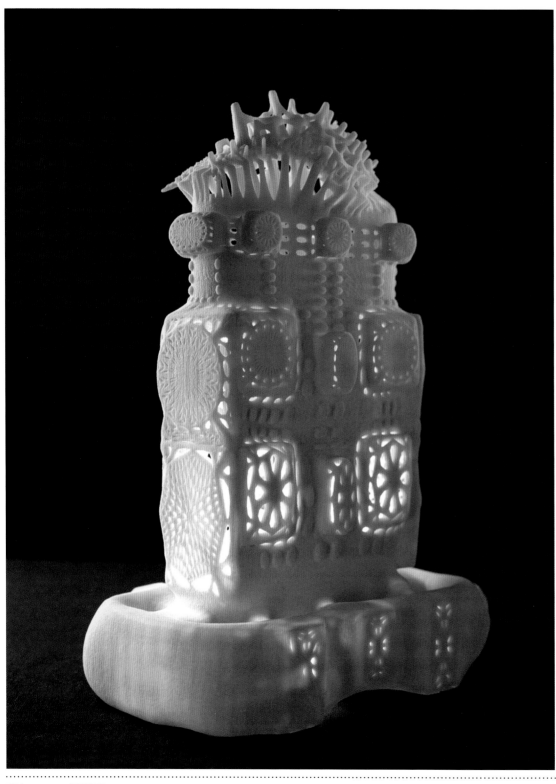

The Inverted Sacristy - overloaded with spiked virtuality, and bounded by convoluted surfaces of an intricate nature.

The dismantled physicality projected to the virtual allows the connection of any element to its bony heritage. Volumes of real beauty reunite with the spiked illusion of organs connected to real bodies. The skin becomes a tissue of multilayered structural integrity held by a shell of organic growth. Small eruptions of cellular distortions form a zoomorphic epidermis that will scatter light over the surface.

a - a

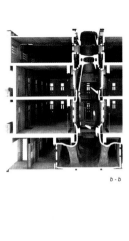

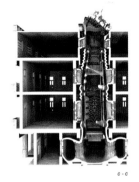

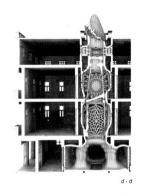

b - b

c - c

d - d

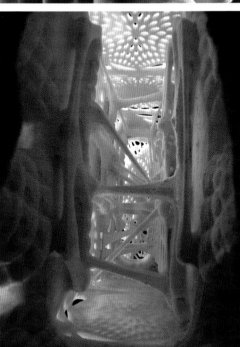

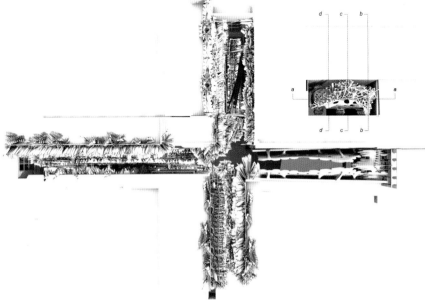

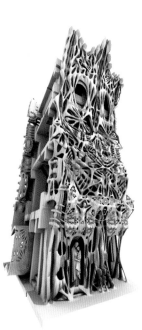

Usually a relic is made of the remains of a holy person. In the case of this temple the relic itself is the bone and its artificially grown attached organs. The relic consists of a hybridization between the remains of reality and their custom grown cyber-organelles.

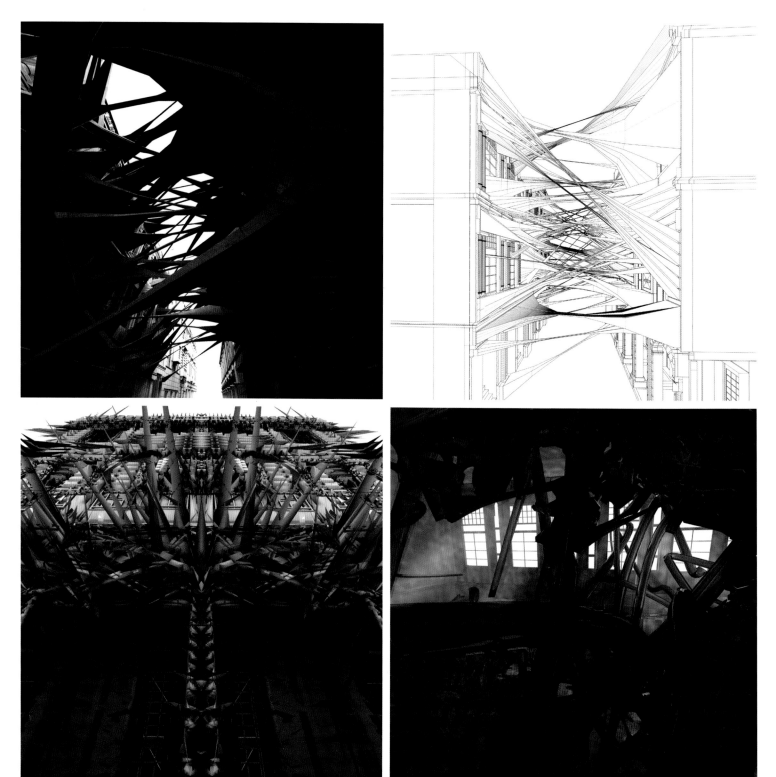

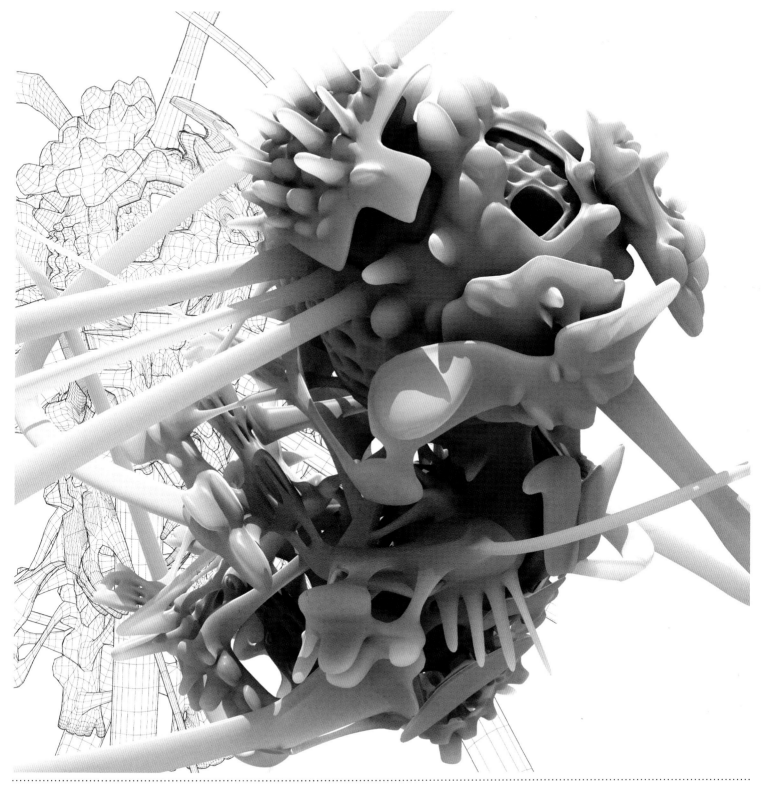

Tobias Klein
Soft Immortality

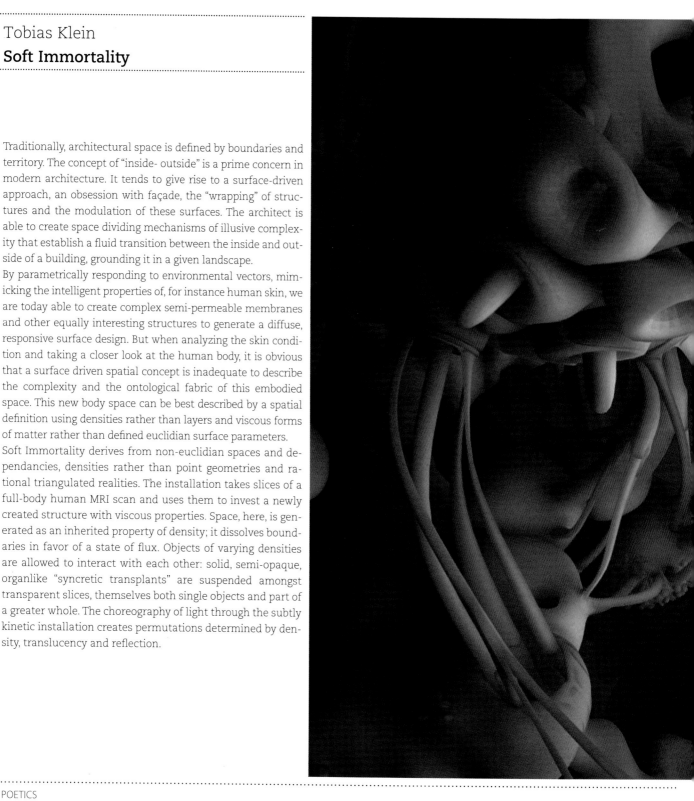

Traditionally, architectural space is defined by boundaries and territory. The concept of "inside- outside" is a prime concern in modern architecture. It tends to give rise to a surface-driven approach, an obsession with façade, the "wrapping" of structures and the modulation of these surfaces. The architect is able to create space dividing mechanisms of illusive complexity that establish a fluid transition between the inside and outside of a building, grounding it in a given landscape.

By parametrically responding to environmental vectors, mimicking the intelligent properties of, for instance human skin, we are today able to create complex semi-permeable membranes and other equally interesting structures to generate a diffuse, responsive surface design. But when analyzing the skin condition and taking a closer look at the human body, it is obvious that a surface driven spatial concept is inadequate to describe the complexity and the ontological fabric of this embodied space. This new body space can be best described by a spatial definition using densities rather than layers and viscous forms of matter rather than defined euclidian surface parameters.

Soft Immortality derives from non-euclidian spaces and dependancies, densities rather than point geometries and rational triangulated realities. The installation takes slices of a full-body human MRI scan and uses them to invest a newly created structure with viscous properties. Space, here, is generated as an inherited property of density; it dissolves boundaries in favor of a state of flux. Objects of varying densities are allowed to interact with each other: solid, semi-opaque, organlike "syncretic transplants" are suspended amongst transparent slices, themselves both single objects and part of a greater whole. The choreography of light through the subtly kinetic installation creates permutations determined by density, translucency and reflection.

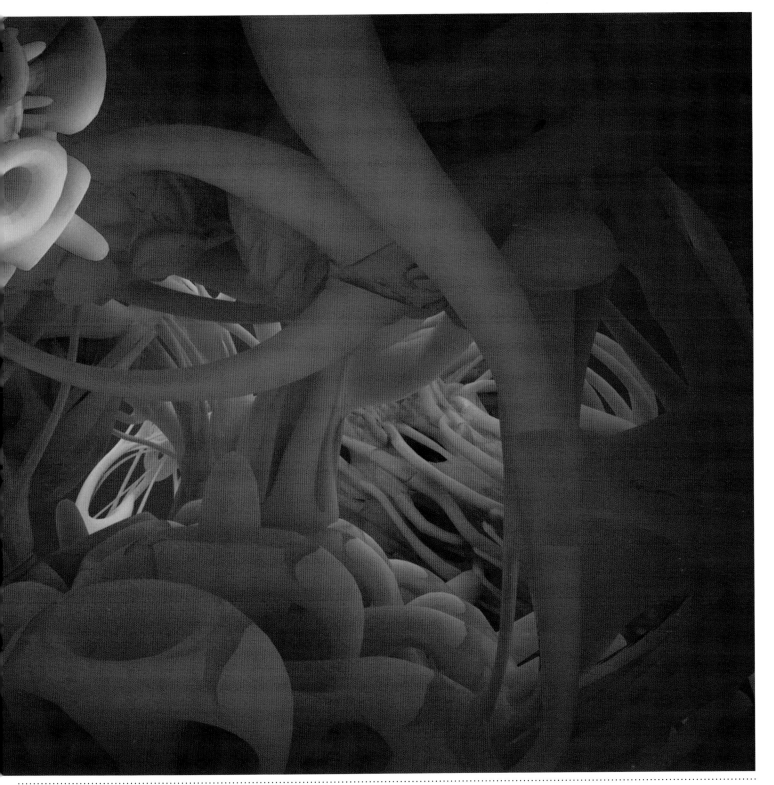

Derived from the use of non-invasive visualization techniques, it attempts to reverse engineer the understanding of the body within the emergent immersive environment of a virtual continuum. The raw data of a human MRI scan are taken as a starting point. Here, digital processes are used to create three-dimensional images from the inside of the body, as a result of interactive static and variable gradients of magnetic fields. In addition, data are generated and assembled with the use of the 2DFT (Two-Dimensional Fourier Transform) technique that incorporates slice selection, in which a magnetic gradient is applied during the radio frequency pulse.

The installation consists of two main elements; acrylic laser cut slices through the MRI data-set and a series of rapid prototypes (light sensitive resin that is CAD/CAM manufactured in an additive subtrate).

In a second step the installation was transformed, creating a more culturally embedded fragment. The model stands on a plinth of solid black Belgian marble – generating an atmosphere of reliquary architecture, subtly calling to mind a display of anatomical parts of holy men and saintly patrons. The material juxtaposition between light sensitive resins and the reflective surface of the solid black marble darkness explore a further dimension of the sacred digital flesh.

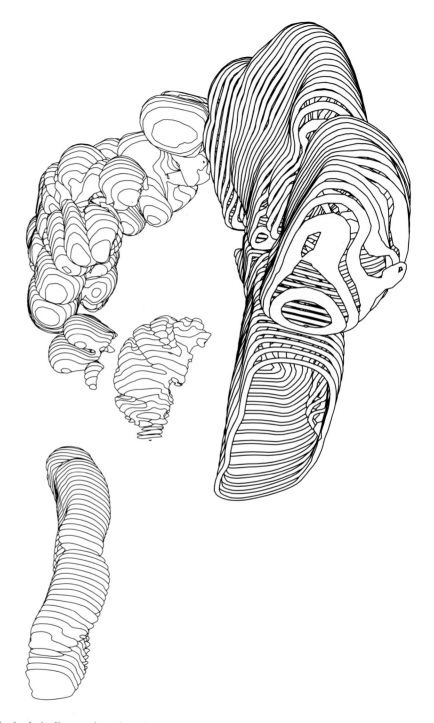

The body is dissected, projected and analyzed in a gradient of density fields generated from the MRI scans.

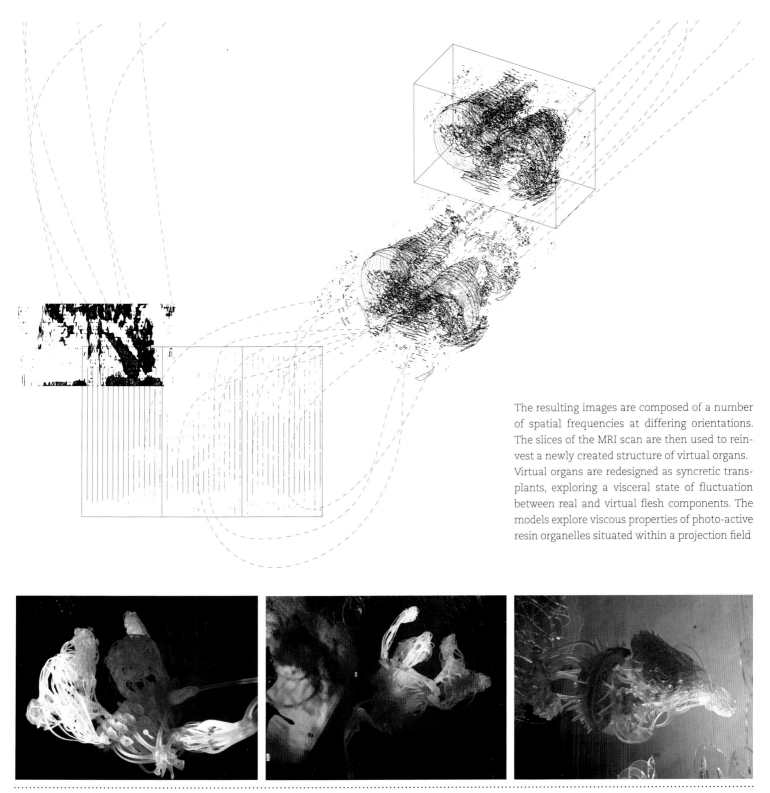

The resulting images are composed of a number of spatial frequencies at differing orientations. The slices of the MRI scan are then used to reinvest a newly created structure of virtual organs. Virtual organs are redesigned as syncretic transplants, exploring a visceral state of fluctuation between real and virtual flesh components. The models explore viscous properties of photo-active resin organelles situated within a projection field

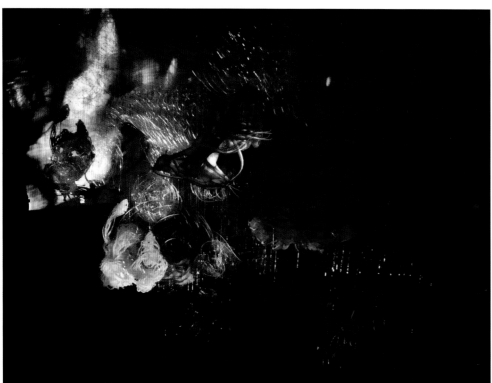

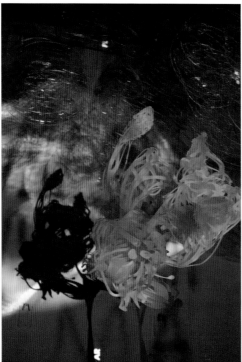

Left: Choreography of the various syncretic transplants within the embodied projection to generate the notion of body and field.

Right page, top: Virtual experimentation within a sub-surface scattered light environment. This is one of the states of viscous digital flesh, a conglomerate of MRI datasets, and density-driven celestial architecture.

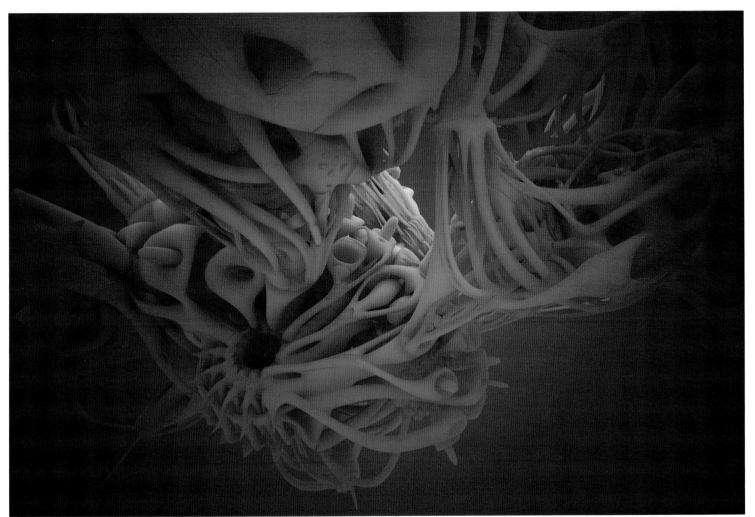

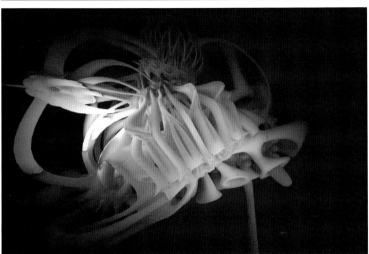

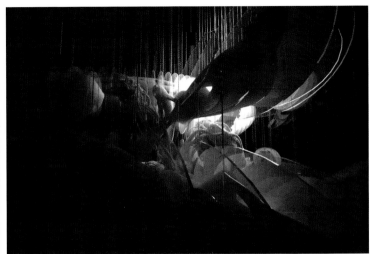

Minimaforms
Archigram Revisited

Minimaforms was invited by Archigram's David Greene to rethink and evolve his seminal projects the Living Pod and High-Rise Tower as part of his exhibition 'Imperfect Works'. The project took the form of a conversation, one that would be enabled through the construction of a series of models that would speculate on alternative forms of living.

These new models would be constructed as thought-experiments, highlighting time-based proto-systems that could demonstrate animal and collective orders of organization. These systems where developed as a response to transform the discrete 'plug-in' autonomy of the high-rise pods and their deterministic mega-structural (structure and circulation) systems of organization. This strategy looked towards the development of generative computational processes to privilege evolutionary and self structuring forms of interaction. Units where designed as behavioural agents that would take on the identity of their inhabitants, each agent understood as an autopoietic machine.

The project articulates three evolutionary stages in this conceptual metamorphosis.

Stage 1
Pods will evolve self-structured shells articulated through a taxonomy of skeletal spicules. These spicules will allow for complex interlinking that affords variable structuring of unit-to-unit relations. From discrete self-contained units the project will evolve as interactive agents that are co-dependent.

Stage 2
Pods will evolve tails. These tails are computational paths that allow access to each pod. The tails are paths that trace their history over time, allowing high-population agent interactions to be defined. As the computational agents find dynamic stability, scanning radii optimize paths in range and bundle neighboring tails, constructing internal and external access networks.

Stage 3
Systemic correlations evolve through unit-to-unit interactions; behavioral environments form as collectives giving rise to connective neighborhoods. Self-structuring principles govern in an animalistic architectural machine.

Exhibited: Mega-Structures Reloaded, Berlin (2008)
Imperfect Works, London (2008)

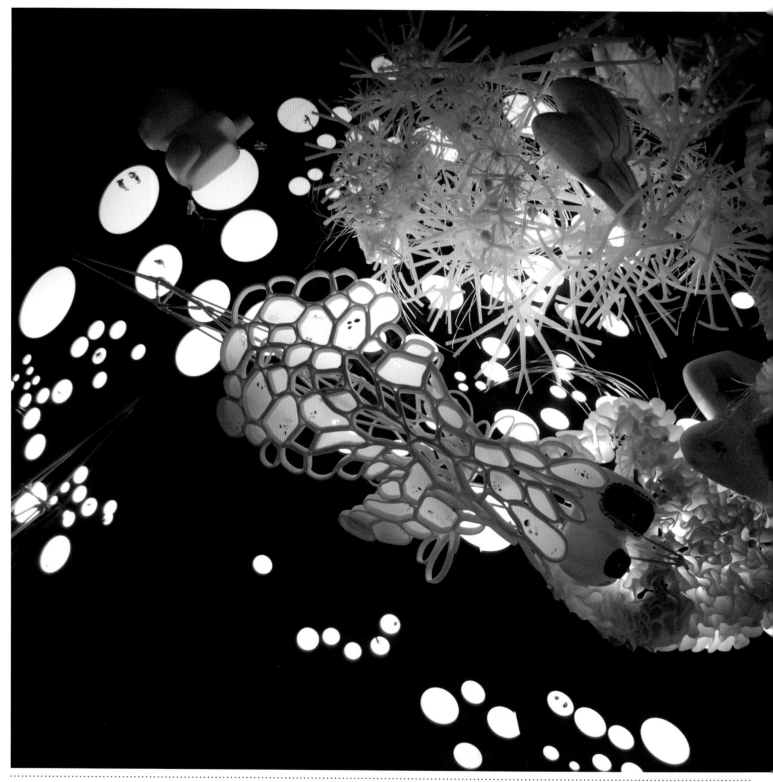

Tobias Klein, Dietmar Köring, Philipp Utermöhl
Cultural Mutations - Urban Permaculture, London, 2020

Permacultural adaptation deals with the fictional but very real scenario of global catastrophes and their cultural impact and transformative influences.

The scenario predicts that a global impact will at one scale not lead to the reconstruction of the existing urban structure but radically alter our perception of urbanism and will lead to a self-sustaining new form of communal agricultural living. This prognosis is taken to develop an evolved, urban concept of farming based on the idea of a traditional, self-sufficient family farm situation.

The narrative background or scenario is London after the Thames Barrier has broken and the center of the former British Empire lies in ruins. At this point the British government decides to abandon the former capital. The former territory of the city of London is divided amongst the new settlers who's project is the transformation of today's cultural buildings into a projected situation of urban farming, mutations of use and symbiotic relationships between culture and functionality.

One of these sites is St. Paul's Cathedral, which becomes a self sufficient algae farming unit. The construct follows the ideas of permaculture where *"The only ethical decision is to take responsibility for our own existence and that of our children."* The intent was that, by rapidly training individuals in a core set of design principles, those individuals could become designers of their own environments and able to build increasingly self-sufficient human settlements.

The term permaculture initially meant "permanent agriculture" but this was quickly expanded to also stand for "permanent culture" as it was seen that social aspects were an integral part of a truly sustainable system. Within this concept of self sufficiency the permacultural habitat is following a systematic of layering similar to a forest that reaches from the canopy, the low tree layer (dwarf fruit trees), shrubs, Herbaceous, Rhizosphere (root crops), Soil Surface (cover crops), the vertical Layer (climbers, vines) and finally the 8th layer, or Mycosphere (fungi).

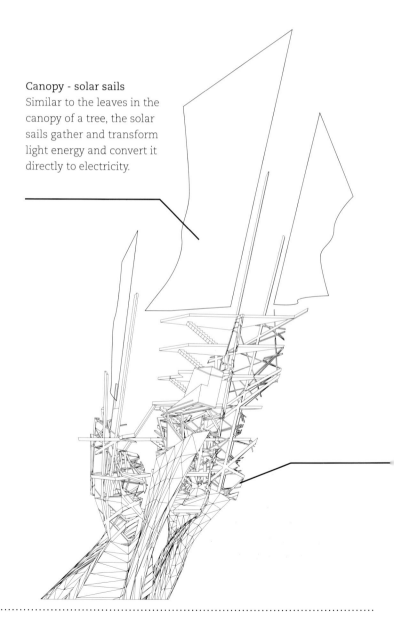

Canopy - solar sails
Similar to the leaves in the canopy of a tree, the solar sails gather and transform light energy and convert it directly to electricity.

Low tree layer (dwarf fruit trees) - thermal energy

The lower layer in the permacultural garden concept is worked out as a passive solar energy gain, using traditional waterfilled pipes to collect and transform solar energy indirectly.

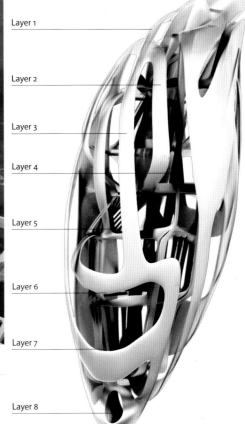

Layer 1: Outpost
Layer 2: Bedroom
Layer 3: Master Bedroom
Layer 4: Bathroom / WC
Layer 5: Livingroom
Layer 6: Kitchen / Community
Layer 7: Studio / Lobby
Layer 8: Storage

Dietmar Köring
P[a]laste & Elaste

Dietmar Köring's project is a radical proposal for one of the most contested sites in Europe, the location of the old "Palace of the Republic" in Berlin, one of the most important buildings of the former East Germany. The building was demolished after it was found that it was contaminated with asbestos. The demolition caused a heated debate since many people thought that the building was an integral part of Berlin's history. A second wave of debates was aroused by the decision to rebuild on the site the old royal palace (Stadtschloss) which had been demolished in 1950 after having received significant damage during the war. The proposal is to rebuild an exact replica of the façades of the royal palace with a modern interior that will function as a museum. Dietmar Köring describes his alternative proposal as follows:

Once upon a time there was a kid, named "Palace of the Republic"; raised in the lap of his mother, but dwellers could not detach themselves from the shadow of the mother. First torn down and decoded to bring back the mother to the physical world - the child had to die. Why do they fear the new, why do they resurrect the dead?

Why do they try to reanimate the shine of a bygone era by rebuilding a long lost icon? The whole dispute is a farce, the creation of a zombie; the virtual flesh as P[a]laste and Elaste - all that remains in our polymeric world. The palace of the future is virtual and real at the same time, a physical cloud, an idea - visual cancer in the urban heart.

Recycling, from the leftovers of the eastern republic; at the same time building material of the future, symbolical as a dead bone; the flesh once so alive eaten by the nightingale; the only things left are the roots in the earth, that we call "home".

High and mighty in its urban environment, more like punk in its gesture; no regard for existing architectural treasures. Shining white, a shadow over the guild hall but also a shadow that will exist in our minds forever: The palace of the republic. Even if it lies in ruins, it will remain with us. We can bend, manipulate or change history, but never delete it.

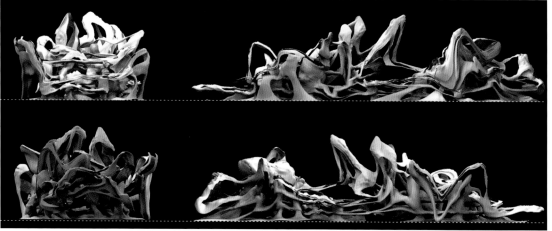

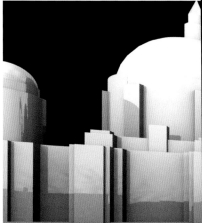

Top: Elevations.
Bottom: Site plan.

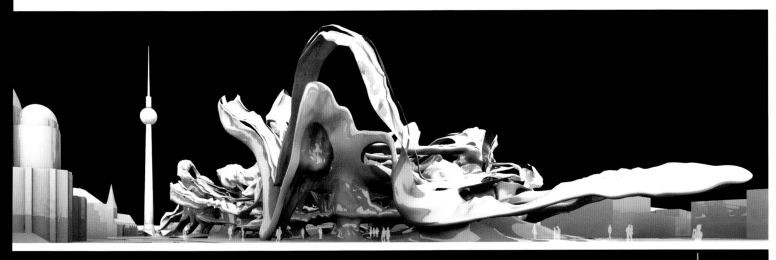

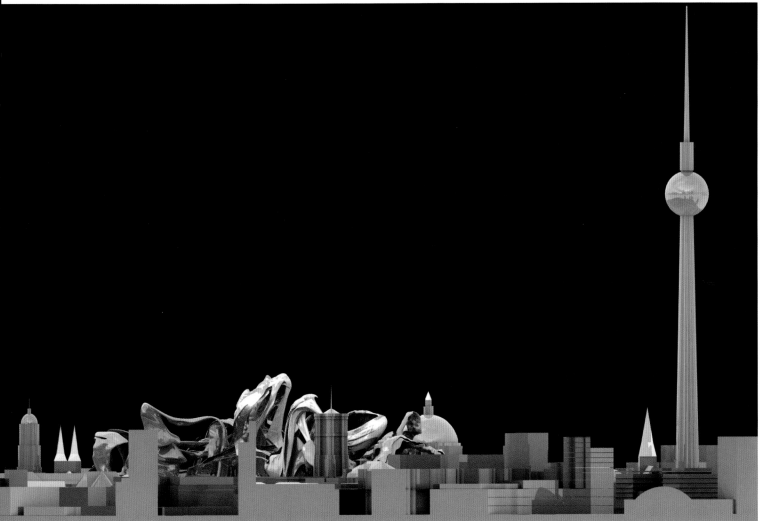

Florencia Pita
Alice

Alice is an installation that takes its form from a tale, its name comes from a narrative that creates multiple fictional landscapes. There is no literal relationship between the installation and the original story by Lewis Carroll, it is indeed an aim to capture the sensibility and atmosphere that is present in the story and therefore intends to embed the space with it. Much of the aesthetic of the piece is related to the images created by John Tenniel (1865) where the black and white engravings outline an incredible focus on the detail of overlapping patterns, which accentuate a very frontal two-dimensional graphic space with a shallow depth. Later iterations such as the illustrations by Arthur Rackham (1907) introduce color, which converts the patterns into moods.

Alice focuses on ideas of figuration and color. Figuration is developed as a way to exaggerate form, to capture very specific geometrical notations of given objects and manipulate them, a kind of exacerbated embellishment of curvaceous form. Color allows for the double manipulation of materiality and space; certain materials have a coded color condition that defines their character; this project intends to exacerbate materiality's character by exalting its pigmentation. In Alice the material is plastic and the color is orange, the idea was that the right sensibility for the object should be similar to that of a plastic toy, were you see how the parts lock, and you definitely have the urge to touch it. The work resides within an aesthetic of densely ornamented form that returns to a realm of embellishment and fantasy.

Team: Florencia Pita, Tanja Werner, Guillermina Chiu, McCall Holman, Ai Amano, Jerry Figurski, Zarmine N. Nigohossian, Clair Souki
Location: LA><ART gallery, 2007
Photographs: Monica Nouwens, Jin Tack

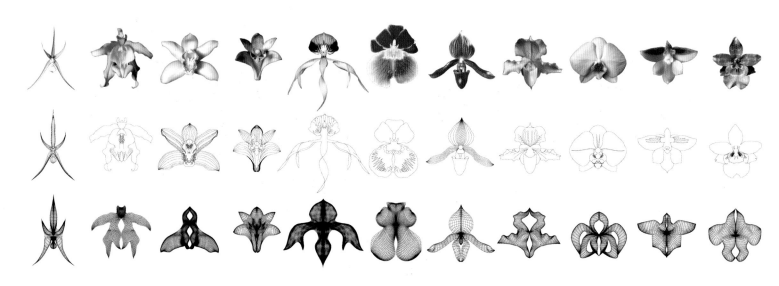

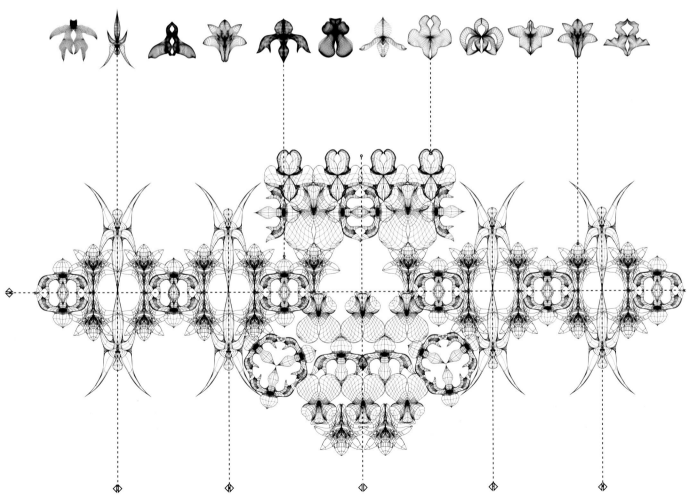

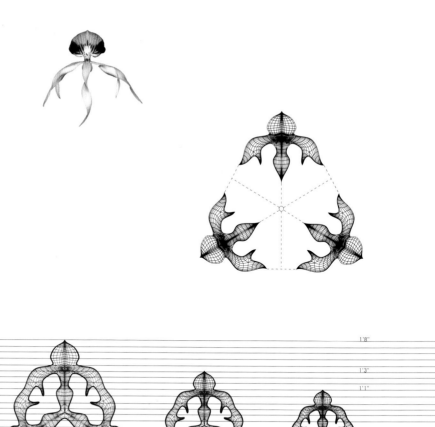

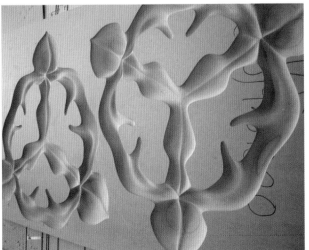
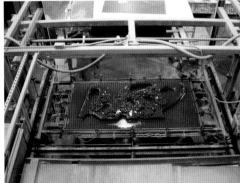

Terreform ONE
Homeway - The Great Suburban Exodus

How can our cities extend into the suburbs sustainably? This proposal puts future American dwellings on wheels. These retrofitted houses will flock towards downtown city cores and back. Existing highways between cities need to be reinforced with an intelligent renewable infrastructure. Therefore homes will be enabled to flow continuously from urban core to core.

The proposal envisions an immense and vital solution to a fundamental problem: American suburbs fail to work efficiently. In the next 25 years 56 million new homes will be built that will consume 18.8 million acres of virgin land and emit 7.3 billion tons of CO_2 per year. This framework of development needs to be rethought to meet our ecological carrying capacity. Why should we put more energy into outdated and inefficient models? America needs to deliver dwellings closer to the existing main infrastructural arteries, rather than over-extend thinly distributed resource lines.

America has always been a nation on the road. The architects propose moving the suburbs on smart networked wheels and affixing a diverse range of mobility mechanisms to home units that generate the novel Homeway system. In the future, the physical home will remain permanent but its location will be transient. The static suburbs will be transformed into a dynamic and deployable flow. Houses will have the option to switch from parked to low speed. Homes, big box retail, movie theaters, supermarkets, business hubs, food production, and power plants will depart from their existing sprawled communities and line up along highways to create a truly breathing interconnected metabolic urbanism. Dense ribbons of food, energy, waste and water will follow the direction of moving population clusters.

Design team: Mitchell Joachim, Maria Aiolova, Melanie Fessel, Philip Weller, Ian Slover, Landon Young, Cecil Howell, Andrea Michalski, Sofie Bamberg, Alex Colard, Zachary Aders

Networked housing flocks connected to smart renewable infrastructure system (top)

Central park farm with micro bioclimatic control for the seasons (right)

01. Wind farm
02. Solar updraft tower
03. Algae farm
04. Geothermal field
05. Hydrogen storage
06. Anaerobic reactors
07. Living machines

08. High speed meg lev
09. Homeway mobility
10. Solar field
11. Data and power
12. Gray water treatment
13. Black water treatment

01. Biofuel head from local vegetative materials
02. Summer cooling mist outlets
03. Winter radiant heaters
04. Wi-Fi hotspot and seeders
05. Steward with organic fertilizers

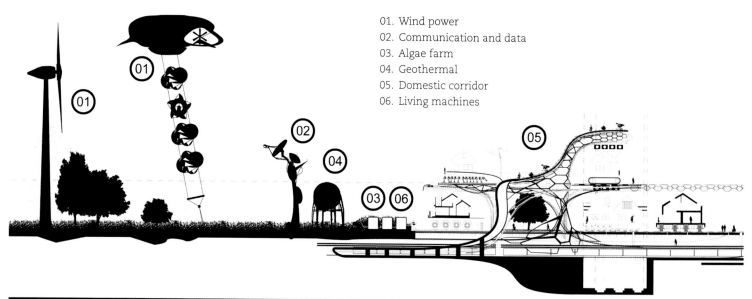

01. Wind power
02. Communication and data
03. Algae farm
04. Geothermal
05. Domestic corridor
06. Living machines

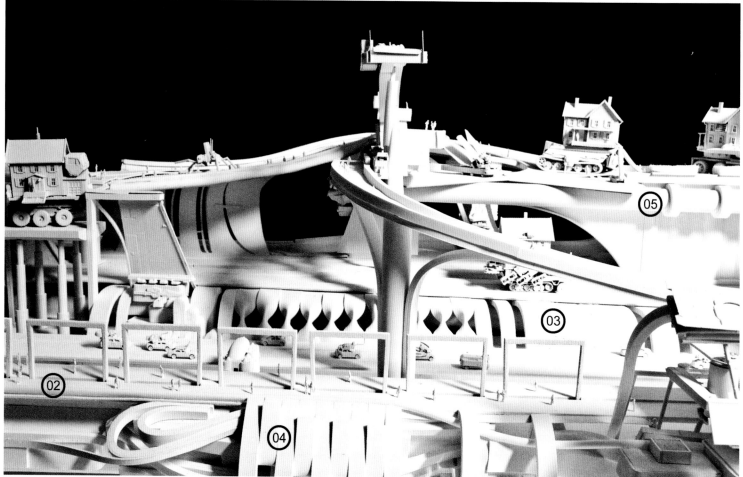

07. High speed meg lev
08. Slow-mo lanes
09. Hydrogen storage
10. Domestic travel
11. Passenger and freight lanes
12. Emergency lanes

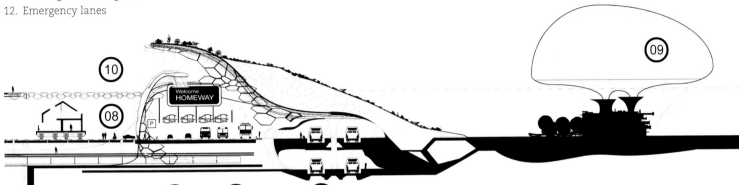

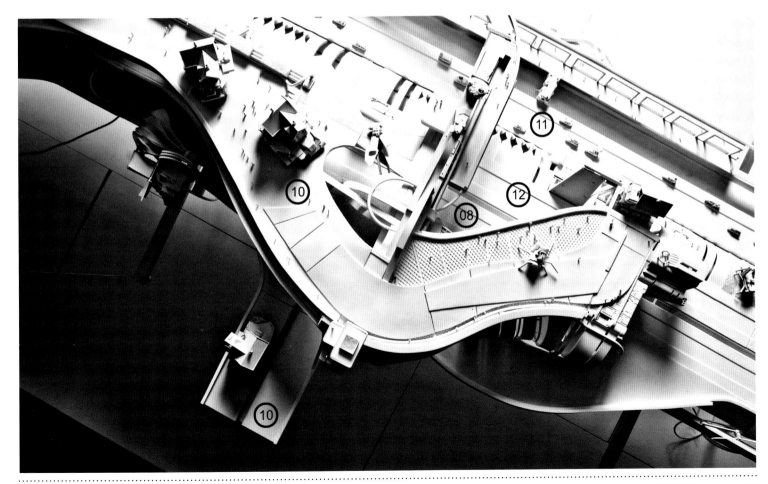

Terreform ONE
Rapid Re(f)use

New York City disposes of 38,000 tons of waste per day. Most of this discarded material ended up in Fresh Kills landfill before it closed. The Rapid Re(f)use project supposes an extended New York reconstituted from its own landfill material. The concept remakes the city by utilizing the trash at Fresh Kills. The method enables the creation of seven entirely new Manhattan islands at full scale. Automated robot 3D printers are modified to process trash and complete this task within decades. These robots are based on existing techniques commonly found in industrial waste compaction devices. Instead of machines that crush objects into cubes, these devices have jaws that make simple shape grammars for assembly. Different materials serve specified purposes; plastic for fenestration, organic compounds for temporary scaffolds, metals for primary structures, and etc. Eventually, the future city makes no distinction between waste and supply.

Design team: Mitchell Joachim, Emily Johnson, Maria Aiolova, Melanie Fessel, Zachary Aders, Webb Allen, Niloufar Karimzadegan, Lauren Sarafan, Philip Weller

Mine local landfill

Organic scafolds deacy after use

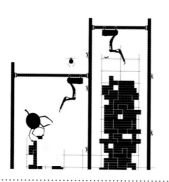

Modified crushers build compressive based structures

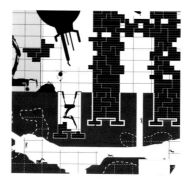

The new perpetual eco-urbanism: waste is resource

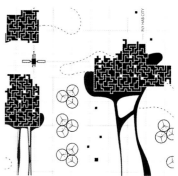

Automated robot 3d prototyping system

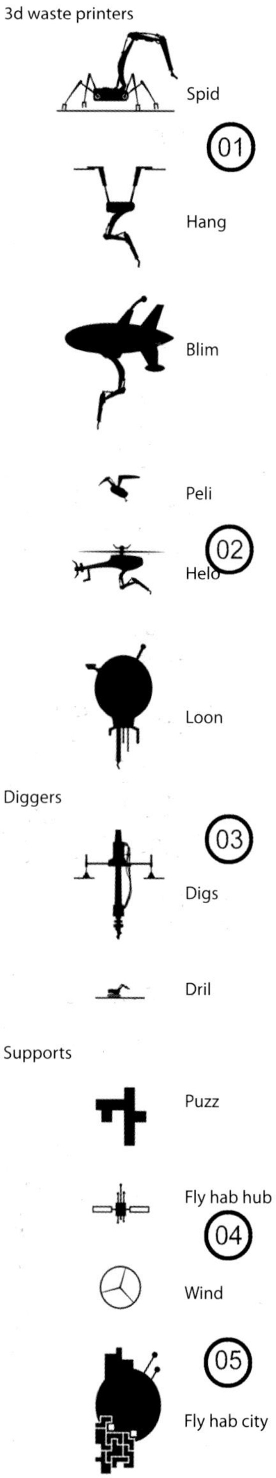

3d waste printers

Spid

① 01

Hang

Blim

Peli

Helo ② 02

Loon

Diggers

Digs ③ 03

Dril

Supports

Puzz

Fly hab hub ④ 04

Wind

Fly hab city ⑤ 05

01. Landboat assembly team
02. Skyboat supply drones
03. Waste harvest machines
04. Puzzle fit components
05. Urban hub float
06. Agro-chemical print bond
07. Low pressure exchange
08. Drum and grinder
09. Separate organics
10. Plastic and glass for façades

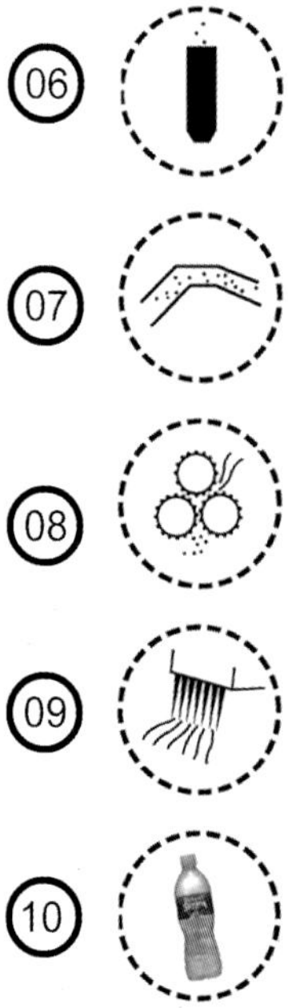

⑥ 06

⑦ 07

⑧ 08

⑨ 09

⑩ 10

Deployable smart brick transports

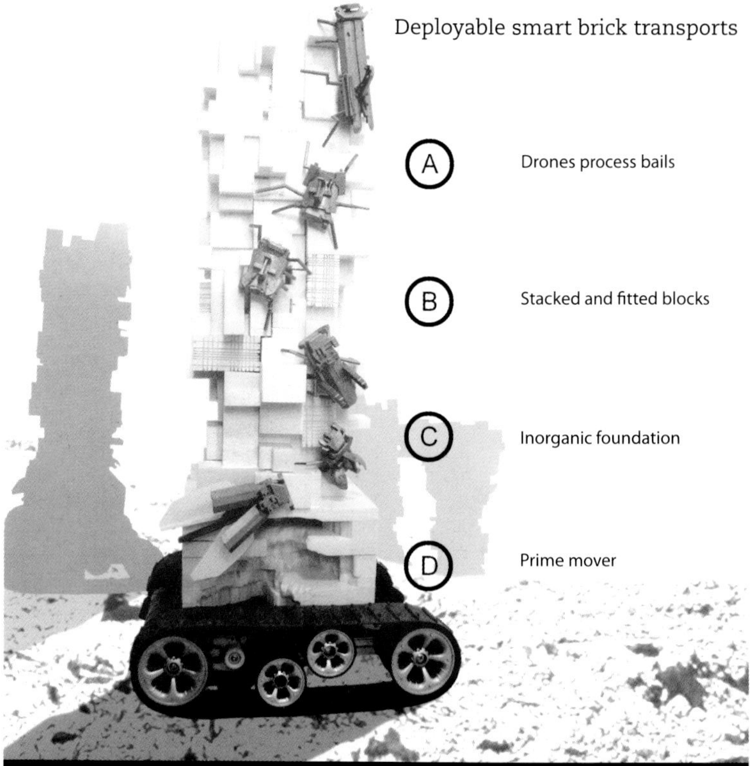

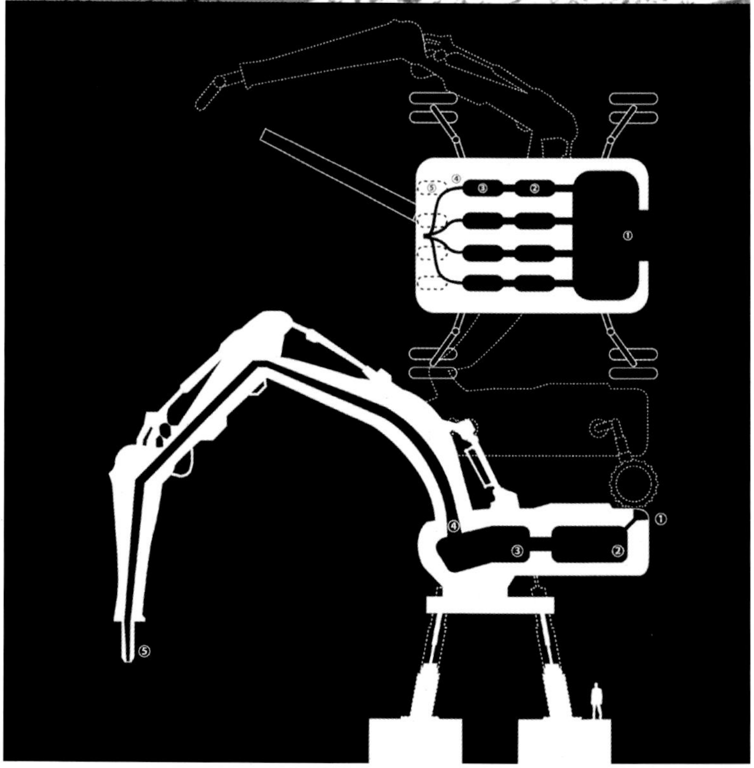

Ⓐ A   Drones process bails

Ⓑ B   Stacked and fitted blocks

Ⓒ C   Inorganic foundation

Ⓓ D   Prime mover

Squidirt: waste reconnaisance nano device

01. Scans surface
02. Penetrates sub layer
03. Embeds in landfill
04. Extends sensors
05. Releases R-feed roaches
    with micro cameras

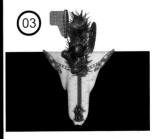

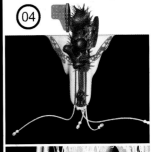

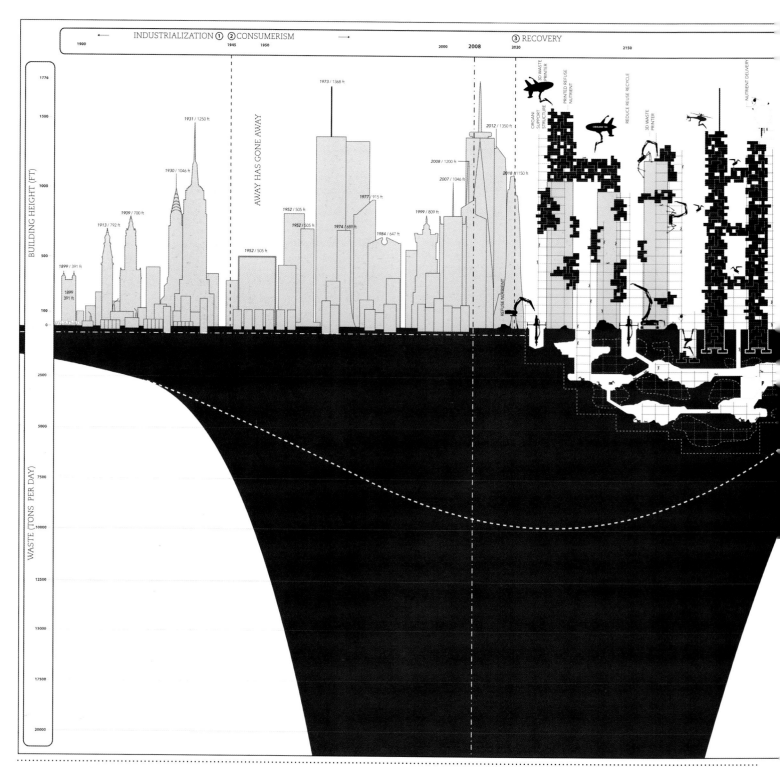

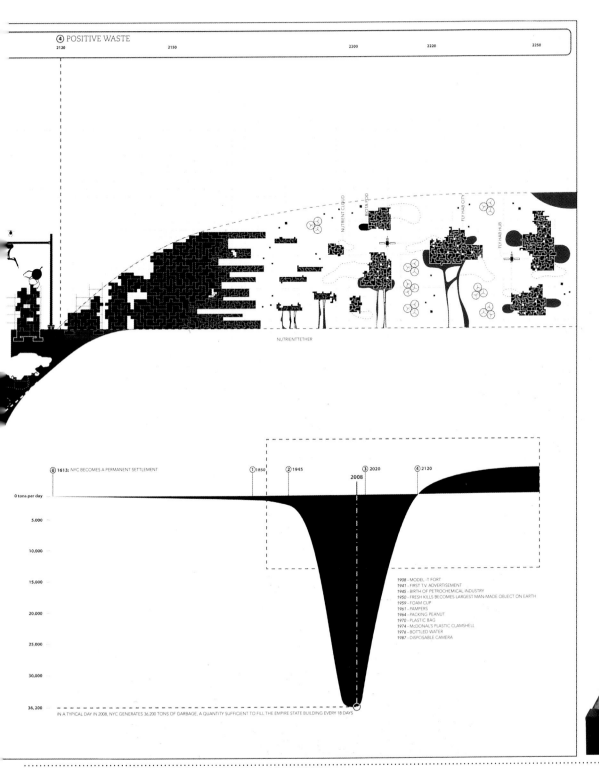

④ POSITIVE WASTE

| 2120 | 2150 | 2200 | 2220 | 2250 |

NUTRIENT CLOUD

BIOTA POD

FLY HAB CITY

FLY HAB HUB

NUTRIENTTETHER

⓪ 1613: NYC BECOMES A PERMANENT SETTLEMENT

① 1850
② 1945
③ 2020
④ 2120

2008

0 tons per day

5,000

10,000

15,000

20,000

25,000

30,000

36,200

1908 - MODEL-T FORT
1941 - FIRST T.V. ADVERTISEMENT
1945 - BIRTH OF PETROCHEMICAL INDUSTRY
1950 - FRESH KILLS BECOMES LARGEST MAN-MADE OBJECT ON EARTH
1959 - FOAM CUP
1961 - PAMPERS
1964 - PACKING PEANUT
1970 - PLASTIC BAG
1974 - McDONAL'S PLASTIC CLAMSHELL
1974 - BOTTLED WATER
1987 - DISPOSABLE CAMERA

IN A TYPICAL DAY IN 2008, NYC GENERATES 36,200 TONS OF GARBAGE, A QUANTITY SUFFICIENT TO FILL THE EMPIRE STATE BUILDING EVERY 18 DAYS.

Jorge Ayala
Ecotransitional Urbanism

Ecotransitional Urbanism started first with a research of new materials for the city with regards to performance and functionality. The project generated a rich base of indexes which translate environmental, topographical and geographical parameters into a material ready to be used for the design.

The usage of the graphic material and selection of processes help the project to move from a fundamentally constrained 2D drawing which outlines boundaries into a more propositional engagement with the context.

The proposition consists of a mesh as a model of density and diversity within an urban framework that seeks to understand, articulate, and visualize possibilities for the hyper dense, programmatically different, and radically optimized new urban agglomerations in China.

The structure of the site is guided by two principal facts: the existing landscape (topography and shoreline) and the existing rural village, Qi'Ao Village. These two parameters were paramount in order to establish the general overall strategy. It was on the available space pockets that the project was established. An urban model –a mesh- was developed, able to control simultaneously the entire site, and to shift from one scale to another: from landscape and urbanism scales, to the architectural one.

The site, located on Qi'Ao Dao, a 27 square kilometer island in the north of Zhuhai, has the potential to become a gateway for Hong Kong - Shenzhen due to its strategic location and the increasing passenger-flow through it. The island threatens to become another generic Chinese urbanization that spreads across the farmlands. Signs of scarcity of water resources, deforestation, fish farming and industrial pollution are already present.

The project seeks to develop a strategy of landscaping and urban planning that embraces the overall site, including its natural energy sources such as tidal variation, a local mangrove reserve and seasonal rainfall, to ensure the island's sustainability.

This mesh is used in order to control the territory but also, in order to test several factors: plot testing, irrigation and water canals configuration, slope analysis, etc. The work based on this mesh seeks to establish a way to operate, at a scale that today is very difficult to manage.

Once the mesh has been deployed upon the site, it allows different variables to be introduced and mixed with different uses. These digital skills help to carry out a major production in a brief amount of time, as well as gathering the maximum amount of information possible in a very flexible way that will facilitate the task of decision making.

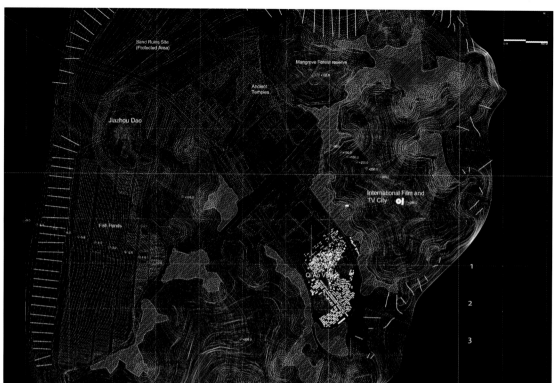

1. **Fields and wetlands:** Water pollution renders the existing wetlands unsuitable for irrigation, aquaculture or potential recreational uses and, by damaging fish breeding grounds, it harms the economy.

2. **Tidal variation:** Domestic and industrial wastewater discharges, urban storm water run-off and non point source pollution from agricultural and livestock farm run-off are the main stagned pollutants when it comes to tidal varation.

3. **Rainfall and water energy points:** In most of this region there is very little precipitation during the winter. Summer rainfall comes from the East Asian Monsoon and from frequent typhoons. Annual rainfall is frequently over 1000 mm.

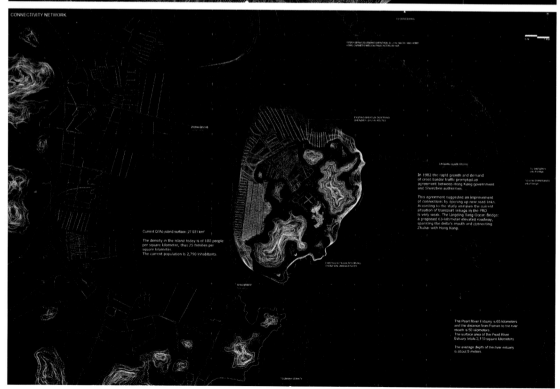

Current Qi'Ao island surface: 27.931 Km².

Population density: 100 people per square kilometer.

Population: 2790.

The Lingding Yang Ocean Bridge is a proposed 63-kilometer elevated roadway, spanning the Delta's mouth and connecting Zhuhai with Hong Kong.

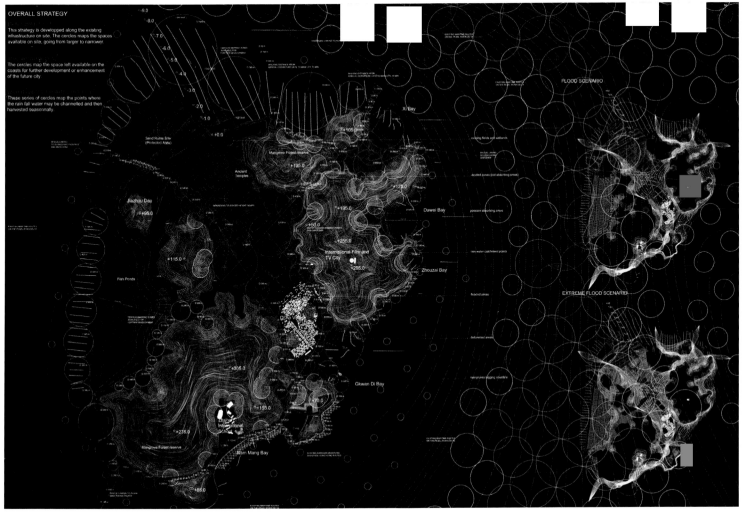

OVERALL STRATEGY

This strategy is developped along the existing
infrastructure on site. The circles maps the spaces
available on site, going from larger to narrower.

The circles map the space left available on the
coasts for further development or enhancement
of the future city.

These series of circles map the points where
the rain fall water may be channelled and then
harvested seasonally.

Main strategy: This strategy is developed along the existing
infrastructure on site. The red circles map the spaces availble
on site.

Auxiliary strategy: The blue circles map the space left available
on the coast for further development or enhancement of
the future city.

Water harvest points strategy: The white circles mark the
points where rain water may be channeled and gathered seasonally.

Right image: Circulation hierarchy

1. Existing road infrastructure
2. First layer
3. Second layer
4. Auxiliary layer

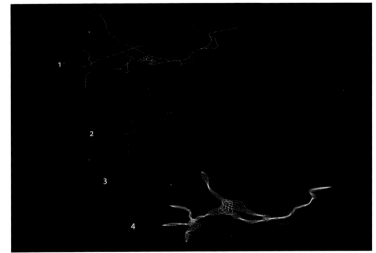

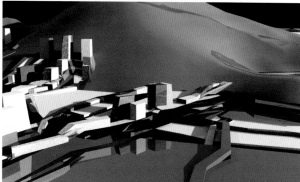

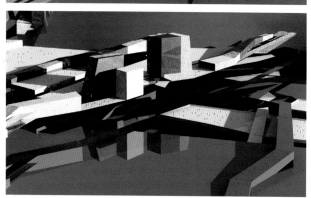

Models
1-2. Artifical topography
3-4. Density scenario 1
5-6. Density scenario 2

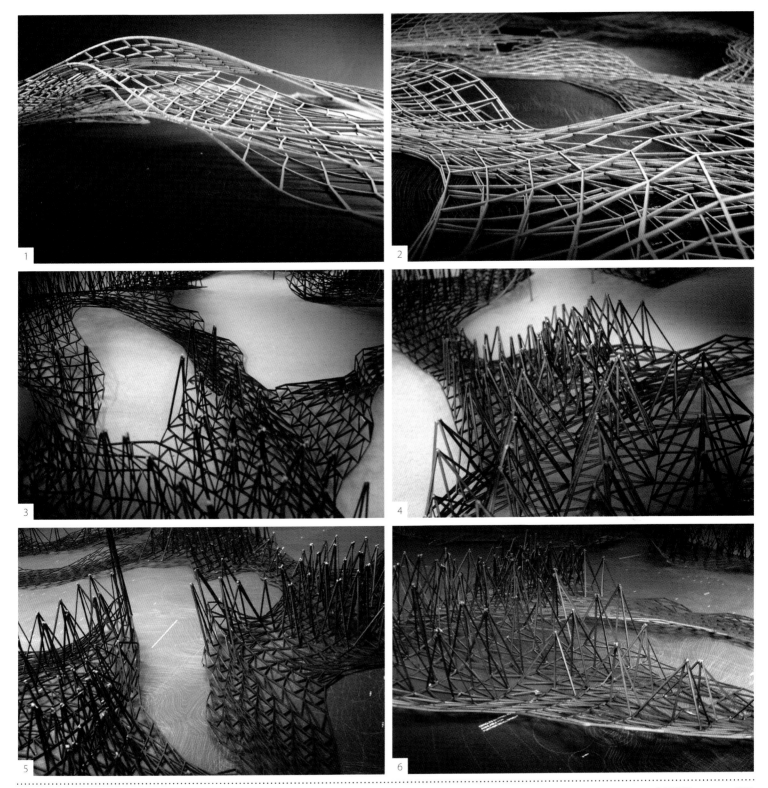

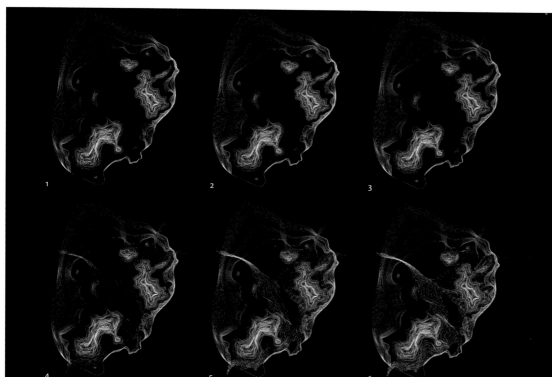

Mesh evolution
1. 0-25 meters length
2. 25-50 meters length
3. 50-75 meters length
4. 75-100 meters length
5. 100-125 meters length
6. 125-150 meters length

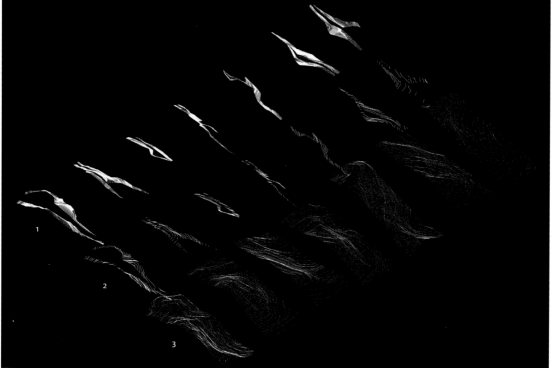

Form finding
1. Bands system
2. Artificial topography
3. Transportation / connections

Proposed structural grid

1. Structural grid
2. 50 meters distance offset perpendicular to the mountains
3. Floodable zones in flat areas
4. Site topography and coastline

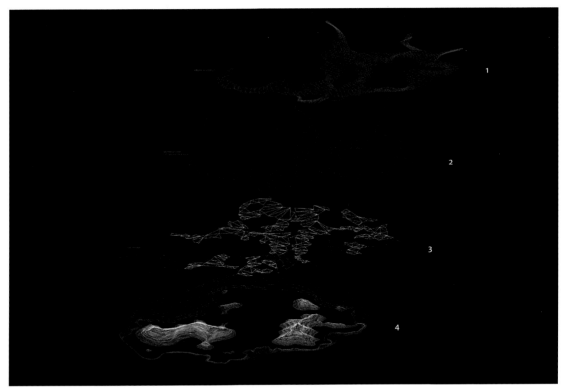

Architectural transition

1. Vistas directions
2. Topographical adaptation
3. Growth testing
4. Program distribution

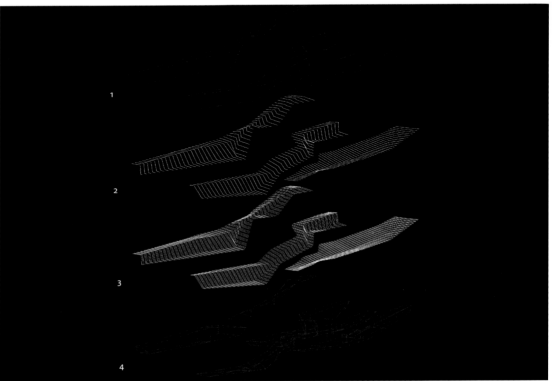

Jaenes Bong - Jonathan Alotto
Biometamorphic architecture -
Organ transplantation clinic and laboratory

The project serves as an important metaphor for the hybridized cultural and topographical qualities of Hong Kong, represented through a set of digital drawings and models.

The early studies and final design proposal controversially explored the actual and virtual conditions of the mysterious narrative landscapes in terms of complex systems: east and west cultural roots, natural and artificial tectonics, public and dangerously private circulations, the true and the disguised identities, stolen and not stolen kidney storage...

In the 21-century, Bio-medical development of organ transplantation has opened up the possibility for patients to replace their dysfunctional body parts from donated individuals. According to global statistic, due to the lack of organs supply, an increasing number of patients are waiting for life saving treatments as many are suffering from long term illness.

The project is sited in Hong Kong, a city known for its world class reputation on trading industry since the British Colonization. The architectural investigation explores the notion of trade in bio-medical transplantation. This controversial design speculates a new mode of activities and architectural model by bringing a place for private [organ] trading.

The design is based on two joint individual researches, "Fear of the Invisibility" and "Concealment and Disguise". The joint researches have generated a narrative design based on revealing the qualities of the invisible secret spaces. The public and the intimate have been made to interact with each other by introducing the atmospheric qualities created by the hidden secret spaces where the "dirty" activities take place.

Inspired by Hieronymus Bosch's painting '*The Garden of Earthly Delights*", hell's scenery abstracts the metamorphic relationship between human and nature, leading to a poetic narrative which led to the creation of a proposal that reflected Hong Kong's hidden natural beauty and its Chinese spiritual mythology.

The final proposal is a semi-living transplantation clinic surgically nestled in the topographical conditions of the mid-level hill gardens and grows behind a modernistic old hospital façade. The boundaries are blurred between the metaphoric and the static. The architecture is disguised with vegetation that hides the project into its site and yet acts as a responsive skin. There also lies the public realm and roof-garden which blend with the green quality as an ornament yet an organic materiality. As time passes, seasonal changes affect the atmosphere through density and natural reactions. The biological design approach allows sophisticated control over the morphing of natural and artificial architectural elements, encoding hidden agendas within its volumes and circulations. Its technological green building envelope farms pharmaceutical ingredients, blending and disguising private programs, but also providing a public garden within the ecology of the hilly city.

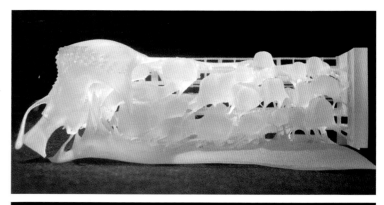

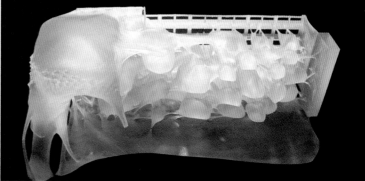

Top: View of pods hidden behind main façade.
Left: Organ storage room.
Right: Cross sections.

Top: Longitudinal section.
Left: Detail of mother skin opening.
Bottom: Research studies: network connections formed by mutation.
Right: Secret entrance disguised as vegetation hidden behind bush.

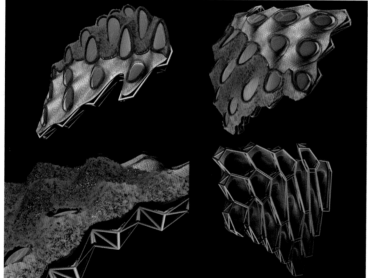

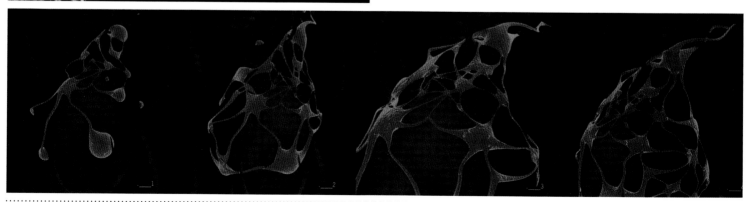

Kenny Kinugasa-Tsui
Plantmorphic Void

Plantmorphic Void is a research title conducted by Kenny Kinugasa-Tsui affiliated with the experimental network of Horhizon. The research investigates the lost terms of 'void' in the vocabulary of digital architecture. Through the technological explorations of complex organic plant forms where cellular systems undergo bio-metamorphosis, the notions of mass and void seemingly slip, flip, oscillate and pulsate. Such organic notions of the void are infused with contemporary parallels in terms of excessive social and economic values, to redefine the spatial and poetic definitions of emptiness in the current digital exploration.

The Basilica of St' Clemente in Rome is an archaeological site of mystic edifices. Evidence suggests a blissful mosaic depiction of the Bible, the Holy Tree of Life that once sanctified the underground spaces of the basilica. The symbolical foliage has been poetically interpreted as 'digital veils', of which their inherent particles contain pre-established information that could spark a projective construction system of divine architectural tectonics.

The veils would continue to project, duplicate, repeat, and multiply into layers of interstitial boundaries to divide and create voids from mass. The projective system is composed with nodes of voids, which generate expansion and compression fields. The voids are inhabited for public circulation and confessional uses. Similar to the behavior of mass and voids as seen in the anatomy of plant cells, these inhabitable voids are concealed and formed by layers of skins that would define their corporeal volumes. The directional forces of the veils' surface morphology generate an intuitive guidance route for circulation and exploration, allowing one to discover the voids on a choreographic journey.

The poetic experience of the voids is created by the illusionistic qualities of excessiveness, lavishness, extravagance, exuberance, and lushness. The proposed Pilgrimage hotel reinvigorates the original basilicas by acting as a vertical intervention into the historical archaeological strata, of which the morphological tectonics intertwine the old and the new voids for confessional activities.

plan 1:150

07
08
09
01
11
12

1330 sun axis

section 1:150

2007 A.D.

1200 A.D.

800 A.D.

100 A.D.

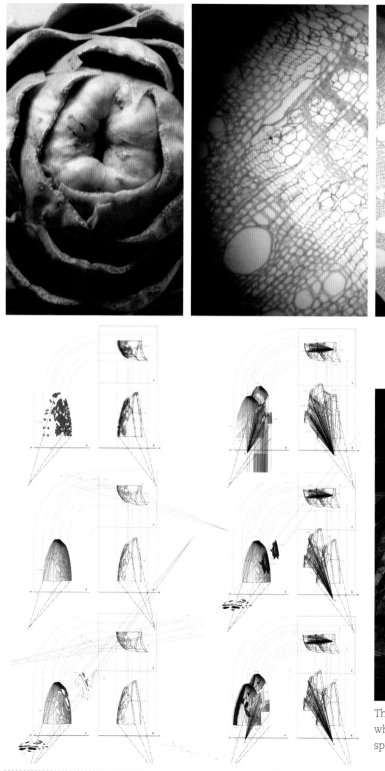

Anatomy of plant cells showing anomalous activity of interior and exterior cells transformation. It is, however, nature's pre-established system for bio-metamorphosis where voids and mass are able to mediate.
Left: Clipped Artichoke, by joyosity (flickr user)
Middle and right: Pyrostegia venusta, transversal section of the stem of Pyrostegia venusta, by _dé (flickr user)

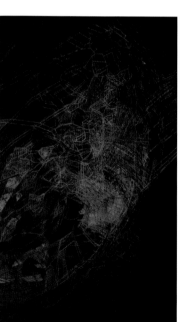

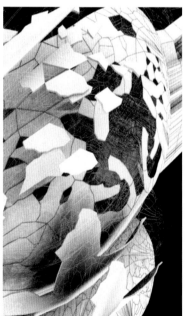

The symbolical foliage has been poetically interpreted as 'digital veils', of which their inherent particles contain pre-established information that could spark a projective construction system of divine architectural tectonics.

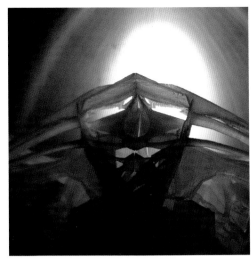

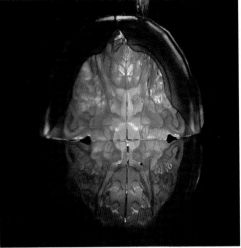

A set of photographic analysis showing the tectonics of the veils undergoing bio-metaphoric projection, duplication, repetition, surface creation, and multiplication into layers of flesh skins to conceal three-dimensional interstitial volumes and voids.

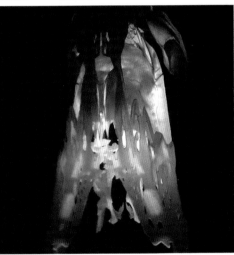

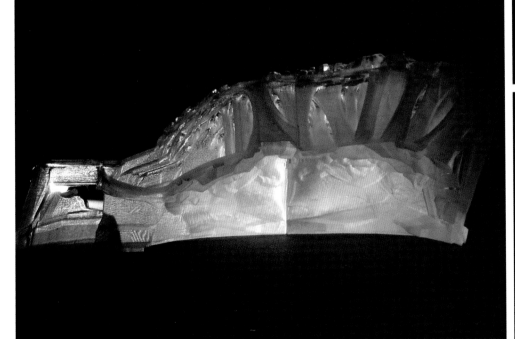

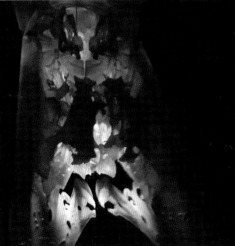

b

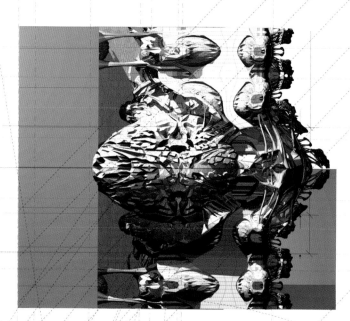

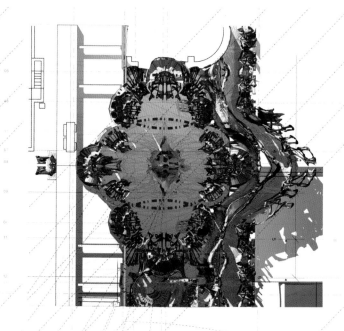

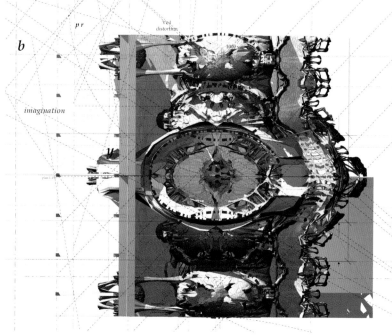

b

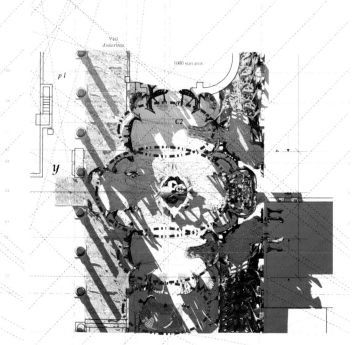

The pilgrimage hotel is an extension of the basilica. The main void can be used as a hotel lobby and for confessional activities.

The curious exploration is enabled by the morphological foliage, which creates surface deformations from the external orthogonal basilica grid to the internal fluid dynamics.

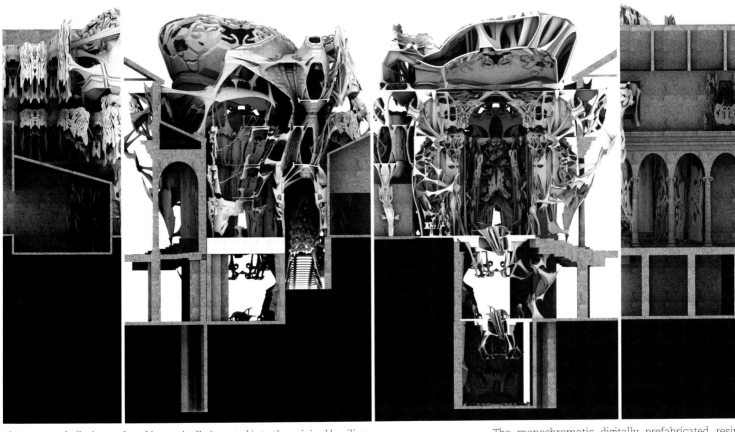

The proposed Pilgrimage hotel is surgically inserted into the original basilica, and acts as a vertical intervention into the historical and archaeological strata. Hence, old and new voids entwine, to host the confessional activities.

The monochromatic digitally prefabricated resin prototypes mimic natural charcoal, allowed to decay and deform, creating non-machine-like qualities.

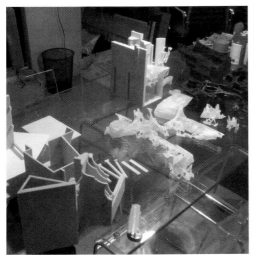

Yaojen Chuang
Opium - Studies of the Ephemeral

A project which explores the ephemeral, poly-sensorial experiences of the body, based on Jean Cocteau's 1952 book "Opium". Through an ongoing research into digital algorithms and simulations, environments were derived through a series of exploratory 'spatial collages' that correspond and capture these transient notions such as; a sense of sacredness, weightlessness, the disintegration of the boundaries between the body and its surroundings along with the spaces that engage these saturated emotions and the heightened senses.

The study suggests how the mythical sense of illusions, dreams can be spatially reconstructed: by careful manipulation of water, vapour, light and shadow. It represents the idea of emotional spaces – the concept of mood architecture.

The project begins with exploring the idea of smoke – its intangible and fluid quality, and the spatial exploration which brings a closeness between the body and its surroundings; a tactile and intimate sense of space.

Top and left: Spatial Morphology Study
The image reverses the norm of solid environments but instead the space becomes intangible and morphs around the rigid body. The study expresses a sense of motion and suggests a four-dimensional space.

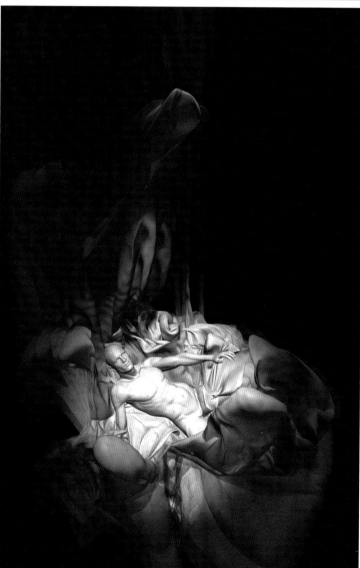

Top: The Euphoric Field. Right: The Zone

"The Euphoric Field" expresses the notion of ecstatic architecture, the sense of a delirious, dreamy but extremely intimate space where it begins and ends in nowhere. The figures were added through studies of rituals and social interactions that are involved in the culture of smoking.

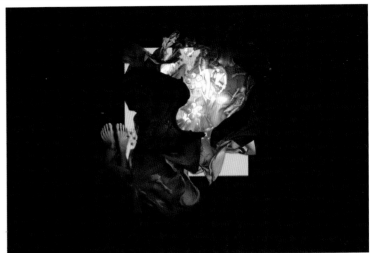

Yaojen Chuang
Chronicles of a Cure

Following the initial research which takes inspirations from Cocteau's writing. This concept led to the architectural proposal of Miami Transitorium - a transitory retreat situated along the canal side of South Beach Miami. The design plays with the theatrical experience of the sacredness, the elasticity of spaces, and the spatial manipulation of perceptions and senses. The dramatic scale and purposely manipulated experiences of the building aim to engage the emotions of the viewer by appealing to all the senses, with an underlying objective of promoting a coherence of physical and spiritual wellbeing.

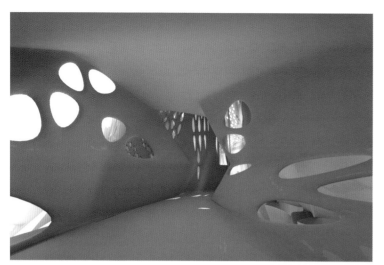

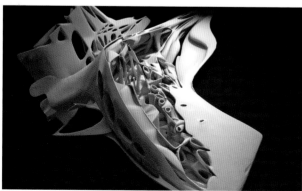

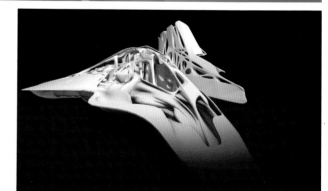

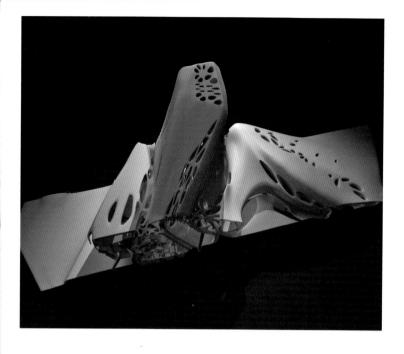

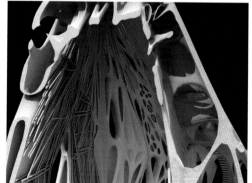

Yaojen's project seeks to derive spatial representations from the concept of architecture of moods. It posits a series of environments that correspond and capture a sense of sacredness and weightlessness, of the senses and of well-being. But also of sexuality and corporality: an elusive conversation in contemporary architecture.

A phenomenological introspection of personal, subjective, intellectual and cognitive processes has not much in common with the 'geeky' and 'techy' talk of doctrinaire technocrats. On the contrary, projects like these tend towards what I call 'POrnamentation'. POrnamentation is to do with the visual consumption of the unequivocal athleticism and ergonomics of shapes and forms; the purely sensual neural experiences of folded and distorted figures/shapes; a digital, extrinsic corporeal impression of the isolated, deformed and dissipated forces of bodies. Ornament becomes intrinsic to the exuberant dynamic form, to the [baroque] deformation of convoluted lines and bodies; of Gestalten. Ornamentation here is not intellectual; in this instance, the values of ornament do not address aesthetics and applications, but esthesis and performance.

A voyage through the uncanny and the sublime.

Marjan Colletti, 2009

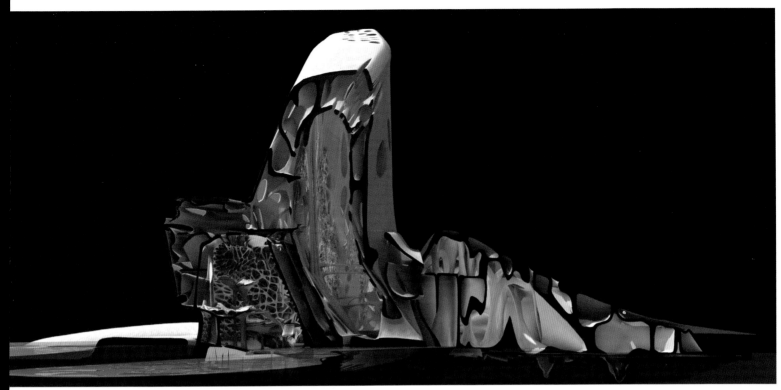

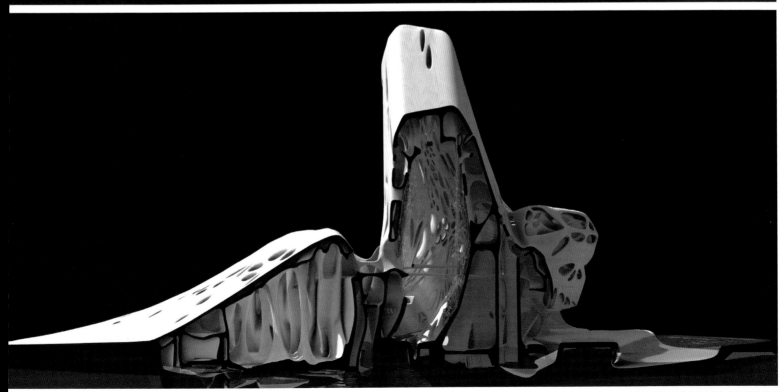

Bibliography

Bullivant, Lucy. *Responsive Environments: Architecture, Art and Design (V&A Contemporaries).*
Victoria and Albert Museum, 2006

Flachbart, Georg & Peter Weibel. *Disappearing Architecture _From Real to Virtual to Quantum.*
2005, Basel.

Flake, Gary William. *The Computational Beauty of Nature: Computer Explorations of Fractals, Chaos, Complex Systems, and Adaptation.*
MIT Press, 2000

Fox, Michael, Miles Kemp. *Interactive Architecture.*
Princeton Architectural Press, 2009

Frazer, John. *An Evolutionary Architecture.*
Architectural Association Publications, 1995

Hensel, Michael , Achim Menges, Michael Weinstock (eds). *Emergence: Morphogenetic Design Strategies (Architectural Design).*
Academy Press, 2004

Hensel, Michael , Achim Menges, Michael Weinstock (eds). *Techniques and Technologies in Morphogenetic Design (Architectural Design).*
Academy Press, 2006

Iwamoto,Lisa. *Digital Fabrications: Architectural and Material Techniques.*
Princeton Architectural Press, 2009

Kalay, Yehuda E. *Architecture's New Media: Principles, Theories, and Methods of Computer-Aided Design.*
MIT Press, 2004

Kolarevic, Branko (ed). *Architecture in the Digital Age: Design and Manufacturing.*
Taylor & Francis, 2005

Kolarevic, Branko, Ali Malkawi (eds). *Performative Architecture: Beyond Instrumentality.*
Routledge, 2005

Meredith, Michael, Aranda-Lasch, Mutsuro Sasaki (eds). *From Control to Design: Parametric/Algorithmic Architecture.*
Actar, 2008

Pérez-Gómez, Alberto, Louise Pelletier. *Architectural Representation and the Perspective Hinge.*
MIT Press, 2000

Pottmann, Helmut, Andreas Asperl, Michael Hofer, Axel Kilian, Daril Bentley. *Architectural Geometry.*
Bentley Institute Press. 2007

Rahim, Ali. *Catalytic Formations: Architecture and Digital Design.*
Taylor & Francis, 2006

Reas, Casey, Ben Fry. *Processing: A Programming Handbook for Visual Designers and Artists.*
MIT Press, 2007

Schodek, Daniel, Martin Bechthold, James Kimo Griggs, Kenneth Kao, Marco Steinberg. *Digital Design and Manufacturing:*
CAD/CAM Applications in Architecture and Design.
Wiley, 2004

Spiller, Neil. *Digital Architecture Now: A Global Survey of Emerging Talent.*
Thames & Hudson, 2009

Terzidis, Kostas. *Expressive Form: A Conceptual Approach to Computational Design.*
Routledge, 2003

Terzidis, Kostas. *Algorithmic Architecture.*
Architectural Press, 2006

Tierney, Therese. *Abstract Space: Beneath the Media Surface.*
Taylor & Francis, 2007